Holt Multicultural Reader

- **Respond to and Analyze Texts**
- **Apply Reading Skills**
- **Develop Vocabulary and Practice Fluency**

HOLT, RINEHART AND WINSTON

A Harcourt Education Company

Orlando • **Austin** • New York • San Diego • London

Contents

To the Student xii

A Walk Through the Book xiv

• PART ONE •

READING LITERATURE 1

COLLECTION 1 Plot and Setting 2

Academic Vocabulary for Collection 1 3

Before You Read: My Horse 4

Literary Focus: Plot and Conflict 4

Reading Skills: Making Predictions 4

Vocabulary Development 5

Devon A. Mihesuah **My Horse** .... SHORT STORY 6

Skills Practice: Plot Diagram 12

Skills Review: Vocabulary and Comprehension 13

Before You Read: Music Lady 14

Literary Focus: Setting and Mood 14

Reading Skills: Visualize the Story 14

Vocabulary Development 15

Vickie Sears **Music Lady** .... SHORT STORY ... 16

Skills Practice: Mood Chart 22

Skills Review: Vocabulary and Comprehension 23

Before You Read: Trees 24

Literary Focus: Plot 24

Reading Skills: Making Predictions 24

Jennifer Tseng **Trees** .... POEM ... 25

Skills Practice: Plot Chart: Past and Present 29

COLLECTION 2 Character 30

Academic Vocabulary for Collection 2 31

Before You Read: My Delicate Heart Condition 32

Literary Focus: Character 32

Reading Skills: Drawing Conclusions 32

Vocabulary Development 33

Toni Cade Bambara **My Delicate Heart Condition** . . . . SHORT STORY . . . **34**

Skills Practice: Character Profile 44

Skills Review: Vocabulary and Comprehension 45

Before You Read: The One Who Watches **46**

Literary Focus: Dialogue 46

Reading Skills: Making Inferences 46

Vocabulary Development 47

Judith Ortiz Cofer **The One Who Watches** . . . . SHORT STORY . . . **48**

Skills Practice: Character Traits Chart 60

Skills Review: Vocabulary and Comprehension 61

COLLECTION 3 **Narrator and Voice** **62**

Academic Vocabulary for Collection 3 63

Before You Read: The Lesson **64**

Literary Focus: Narrator and Voice 64

Reading Skills: Comparing and Contrasting 64

Vocabulary Development 65

Dianne E. Dixon **The Lesson** . . . . SHORT STORY . . . **66**

Skills Practice: Narrator Questionnaire 79

Skills Review: Vocabulary and Comprehension 80

Before You Read: Mr. Shaabi **81**

Literary Focus: Narrator's Point of View 81

Reading Skills: Read for Details 81

Vocabulary Development 82

Pnina Kass **Mr. Shaabi** . . . . SHORT STORY . . . **83**

Skills Practice: Narrator: Point of View 88

Skills Review: Vocabulary and Comprehension 89

COLLECTION 4 **Comparing Themes** **90**

Academic Vocabulary for Collection 4 91

Before You Read: *from* Hunger of Memory **92**

Literary Focus: Theme and Conflict 92

Reading Skills: Finding Theme 92

Vocabulary Development 93

Richard Rodriguez   *from* **Hunger of Memory** . . . . AUTOBIOGRAPHY . . . **94**

Skills Practice: Theme Chart 100

Skills Review: Vocabulary and Comprehension 101

Before You Read: All-American Girl **102**

Literary Focus: Theme and Genre 102

Julia Alvarez   **All-American Girl** . . . . AUTOBIOGRAPHY . . **103**

Skills Practice: Genre Chart 105

Before You Read: Kipling and I **106**

Literary Focus: Theme and Character 106

Reading Skills: Making Inferences 106

Vocabulary Development 107

Jesús Colón   **Kipling and I** . . . . ESSAY . . **108**

Skills Practice: Universal Themes Chart 114

Skills Review: Vocabulary and Comprehension 115

COLLECTION 5   **Irony and Ambiguity** **116**

Academic Vocabulary for Collection 5 117

Before You Read: The New Girl **118**

Literary Focus: Situational Irony 118

Reading Skills: Making Inferences 118

Vocabulary Development 119

Nicole Keeter   **The New Girl** . . . . SHORT STORY . . **120**

Skills Practice: Ambiguity Chart 124

Skills Review: Vocabulary and Comprehension 125

Before You Read: Three Wise Guys **126**

Literary Focus: Situational Irony 126

Reading Skills: Making Predictions 126

Vocabulary Development 127

Sandra Cisneros   **Three Wise Guys** . . . . SHORT STORY . . **128**

Skills Practice: Irony Chart 136

Skills Review: Vocabulary Development 137

Before You Read: Hurdles **138**

Literary Focus: Verbal and Situational Irony 138

Reading Skills: Cause and Effect 138

Derek Kirk Kim   **Hurdles** . . . . GRAPHIC STORY . . **139**

Skills Practice: Cause-and-Effect Chart 142

Skills Review: Reading Comprehension 143

COLLECTION 6   **Symbolism and Allegory** **144**

Academic Vocabulary for Collection 6 145

Before You Read: Prologue *from* Walking with the Wind . . . **146**

Literary Focus: Symbols and Allegory 146

Reading Skills: Making Inferences 146

Vocabulary Development 147

John Lewis   **Prologue *from* Walking with the Wind** . . . . . . MEMOIR . . **148**

Skills Practice: Allegory Chart 154

Skills Review: Vocabulary and Comprehension 155

Before You Read: March **156**

Literary Focus: Symbolism and Allegory 156

Reading Skills: Making Inferences 156

Vocabulary Development 157

Clay Goss   **March** . . . . MONOLOGUE . . **158**

Skills Practice: Allegory Chart 162

Skills Review: Vocabulary and Comprehension 163

COLLECTION 7   **Poetry** **164**

Academic Vocabulary for Collection 7 165

Before You Read: Slam, Dunk, & Hook **166**

Literary Focus: Imagery 166

Reading Skills: Reading a Poem 166

Yusef Komunyakaa   **Slam, Dunk, & Hook** . . . . POEM . . **167**

Skills Practice: Imagery Chart 170

Before You Read: Dream Deferred **171**

Literary Focus: Figures of Speech 171

Reading Skills: Reading for Meaning 171

Langston Hughes   **Dream Deferred** . . . . POEM . . **172**

Skills Practice: Figure of Speech Chart 174

Before You Read: "jump mama" 175

Literary Focus: The Sounds of Poetry 175

Reading Skills: Finding the Rhythm in Free Verse 175

Kurtis Lamkin   **"jump mama"** . . . . POEM . . **176**

Skills Practice: Sounds of Poetry Diagram 179

COLLECTION 8   **Literary Criticism: Evaluating Style** **180**

Academic Vocabulary for Collection 8 181

Before You Read: The Pocketbook Game 182

Literary Focus: Style—Diction and Tone 182

Reading Skills: Monitoring Your Comprehension 182

Vocabulary Development 183

Alice Childress   **The Pocketbook Game** . . . . MONOLOGUE . . **184**

Skills Practice: Style Chart 187

Skills Review: Vocabulary and Comprehension 188

Before You Read: Codes of Conduct 189

Literary Focus: Style and Humor 189

Reading Skills: Visualizing 189

Vocabulary Development 190

Adrienne Su   **Codes of Conduct** . . . . AUTOBIOGRAPHY . . **191**

Skills Practice: Style Analysis Chart 195

Skills Review: Vocabulary and Comprehension 196

Before You Read: Transformation 197

Literary Focus: Comparing Style 197

Reading Skills: Understanding Cause and Effect 197

Vocabulary Development 198

Lydia Minatoya   **Transformation** . . . . AUTOBIOGRAPHY . . **199**

Skills Practice: Style Analysis Chart 206

Skills Review: Vocabulary and Comprehension 207

COLLECTION 9   **Literary Criticism: Biographical and Historical Approach** **208**

Academic Vocabulary for Collection 9 209

Before You Read: Ellis Island 210

Literary Focus: Biographical and Historical Approach 210

Reading Skills: Recognizing Historical and
Biographical Details 210

Joseph Bruchac   **Ellis Island** . . . . POEM   **211**

Skills Practice: Historical and Biographical Analysis Chart 213

Before You Read: The Habit of Movement **214**

Literary Focus: Biographical Approach 214

Reading Skills: Monitor Your Reading 214

Judith Ortiz Cofer   **The Habit of Movement** . . . . POEM   **215**

Skills Practice: Literary Criticism—Biographical Approach 217

Before You Read: The Memory Stone **218**

Literary Focus: Historical Approach 218

Reading Skills: Making Inferences 218

Vocabulary Development 219

Paul Yee   **The Memory Stone** . . . . FOLK TALE   **220**

Skills Practice: Motivation Chart 228

Skills Review: Vocabulary Development 229

COLLECTION 10   **Epic and Myth** **230**

Academic Vocabulary for Collection 10 231

Before You Read: The Story of the Eagle **232**

Literary Focus: Myths 232

Reading Skills: Analyzing Myth 232

Vocabulary Development 233

Joseph M. Marshall III   **The Story of the Eagle** . . . . MYTH   **234**

Skills Practice: Character Traits Chart 245

Skills Review: Vocabulary and Comprehension 246

Before You Read: The Spirit Wife **247**

Literary Focus: Myth and Archetypes 247

Reading Skills: Identifying Cause and Effect 247

Vocabulary Development 248

**Richard Erdoes /
Alfonso Ortiz**   **The Spirit Wife** . . . . MYTH   **249**

Skills Practice: Cause-and-Effect Chart 258

Skills Review: Vocabulary and Comprehension 259

Before You Read: Orpheus and Eurydice 260

Literary Focus: Hero Myths 260

Reading Skills: Summarizing 260

Vocabulary Development 261

William F. Russell **Orpheus and Eurydice** . . . . MYTH . . 262

Skills Practice: Hero Chart 268

Skills Review: Vocabulary and Comprehension 269

COLLECTION 11 Drama 270

Academic Vocabulary for Collection 11 271

Before You Read: *from* Now Let Me Fly 272

Literary Focus: Drama 272

Reading Skills: Paraphrasing 272

Vocabulary Development 273

Flo Ota De Lange **Barbara Johns: Carrying on the Speaking** . . . . . ESSAY . . 274

Marcia Cebulska *from* Now Let Me Fly . . . . DRAMA . . 282

Skills Practice: Drama Chart 288

Skills Review: Vocabulary and Comprehension 289

• PART TWO •

READING INFORMATIONAL TEXTS 290

Academic Vocabulary: Informational Articles 291

Before You Read: Interview with Mae 292

Informational Focus: How to Generate Research Questions . . 292

Reading Skills: Make a KWL Chart 292

Vocabulary Development 293

Mae Jemison   **Interview with Mae** .... INTERVIEW . . 294

Skills Practice: *5W-How?* 298

Skills Review: Vocabulary and Comprehension 299

Before You Read: Homecoming / Ishi Apparently Wasn't the Last Yahi / The Repatriation of Ishi, the Last Yahi Indian 300

Informational Focus: Synthesizing Sources 300

Reading Skills: Author's Purpose 300

Vocabulary Development 301

Richard Rodriguez   **Homecoming** .... ESSAY . . 302

Gretchen Kell   **Ishi Apparently Wasn't the Last Yahi** .... PRESS RELEASE . 306

Smithsonian National Museum of Natural History   **The Repatriation of Ishi, the Last Yahi Indian** .... PRESS RELEASE . . 310

Skills Practice: Synthesizing Sources 312

Skills Review: Vocabulary and Comprehension 313

Before You Read: Free Minds and Hearts at Work / Jackie Changed the Face of Sports 314

Informational Focus: Primary and Secondary Sources 314

Reading Skills: Identifying and Elaborating on Main Ideas . . 314

Vocabulary Development 315

Jackie Robinson   **Free Minds and Hearts at Work** .... ARTICLE . . 316

Larry Schwartz   **Jackie Changed the Face of Sports** .... ARTICLE . . 319

Skills Practice: Analysis, Evaluation, and Elaboration Grid . . . 322

Skills Review: Vocabulary and Comprehension 323

Before You Read: Be an Everyday Freedom Hero! 324

Informational Focus: Argument 324

Reading Skills: Paraphrasing 324

Vocabulary Development 325

Be an Everyday Freedom Hero! .... ARTICLE . . 326

Skills Practice: Argument Evaluation Chart 331

Skills Review: Vocabulary and Comprehension 332

Academic Vocabulary: Consumer, Workplace, and Public Documents 333

Before You Read: Equal Employment Opportunity
Is the Law **334**

Informational Focus: Workplace Documents 334

Equal Employment Opportunity
Is the Law . . . . WORKPLACE DOCUMENT . . **335**

Skills Practice: Workplace Documents Organizer 338

Skills Review: Reading Comprehension 339

Before You Read: Documenting Invention /
Victor Ochoa's Biographical Sketch **340**

Informational Focus: Technical Documents 340

Alison Oswald   **Documenting Invention** . . . . TECHNICAL DOCUMENT . . **341**

Victor Ochoa's Biographical Sketch TECHNICAL DOCUMENT . . **344**

Skills Practice: Key Information Chart 347

Skills Review: Reading Comprehension 348

Before You Read: *from* Recycling Guide for Native
American Nations / U.S. Recycling Symbols **349**

Informational Focus: Functional Documents 349

***from* Recycling Guide for Native**
American Nations . . . . FUNCTIONAL DOCUMENT . . **350**

U.S. Recycling Symbols . . . . FUNCTIONAL DOCUMENT . . **352**

Skills Practice: Sequence Chart 353

Skills Review: Reading Comprehension 354

Before You Read: Works Cited List: Recycling **355**

Informational Focus: Documentation 355

Works Cited List: Recycling . . . . DOCUMENTS . . **356**

Skills Review: Reading Comprehension 358

Index of Authors and Titles **359**

Vocabulary Development **360**

To the Student

A Book for You

Teachers open the door, but you must enter by yourself.
—Chinese Proverb

Reading is an interactive process. The more you put into it, the more you get out of it. This book is designed to do just that—help you interact with the selections you read by marking them up, asking your own questions, taking notes, recording your own ideas, and responding to the questions of others.

A Book Designed for Your Success

The *Holt Multicultural Reader* goes hand-in-hand with *Elements of Literature*. It is designed to help you interact with the selections and master the language arts skills.

To do this, the book has two parts that each follow a simple format:

Part 1 Reading Literature

To help you master how to respond to, analyze, evaluate, and interpret literature, the *Holt Multicultural Reader* provides—

For each collection:
- The academic vocabulary you need to know to master literature skills for the collection, defined for ready reference and use.
- Selections printed in an interactive format to support and guide your reading. As you read and respond to these selections, you will apply and extend your skills and build toward independence.

For each selection:
- A Before You Read page that preteaches the literary focus and provides a reading skill to help you comprehend the selection.
- A Vocabulary Development page that preteaches selection vocabulary and provides a vocabulary skill to use while reading the prose selections.
- Literature printed in an interactive format to guide your reading and help you respond to text.
- A Skills Practice graphic organizer that helps you understand the literary focus of the selection.
- A Skills Review page that helps you practice vocabulary and assess your understanding of the selection you've read.

To help you master how to read informational texts, this book contains—

For Informational Articles:
- The academic vocabulary you need to know to master informational skills, defined for ready reference and use.
- A Before You Read page that preteaches the informational focus and provides a reading skill to help you comprehend the selection.
- A Vocabulary Development page that preteaches selection vocabulary and provides a vocabulary skill to use while reading the selection.
- Informational selections in an interactive format to guide your reading and help you respond to the text.
- A Skills Practice graphic organizer that helps you understand the informational focus of the selection.
- A Skills Review page that helps you practice vocabulary and assess your understanding of the selection you've read.

For Consumer, Workplace, and Public Documents:
- The academic vocabulary you need to know to master the skills, defined for ready reference and use.
- A Before You Read page that preteaches the document focus and defines specialized terms.
- New documents in an interactive format to guide your reading and help you respond to the text.
- A Skills Practice page that helps you understand the focus of the selection.
- A Skills Review page that helps you practice test-taking skills.

A Book for Your Own Thoughts and Feelings

Reading is about *you*. It is about connecting your thoughts and feelings to the thoughts and feelings of the writer. Make this book your own. The more you give of yourself to your reading, the more you will get out of it. We encourage you to write in it. Jot down how you feel about the selection. Question the text. Note details you think need to be cleared up or topics you would like to learn more about.

A Walk Through the Book

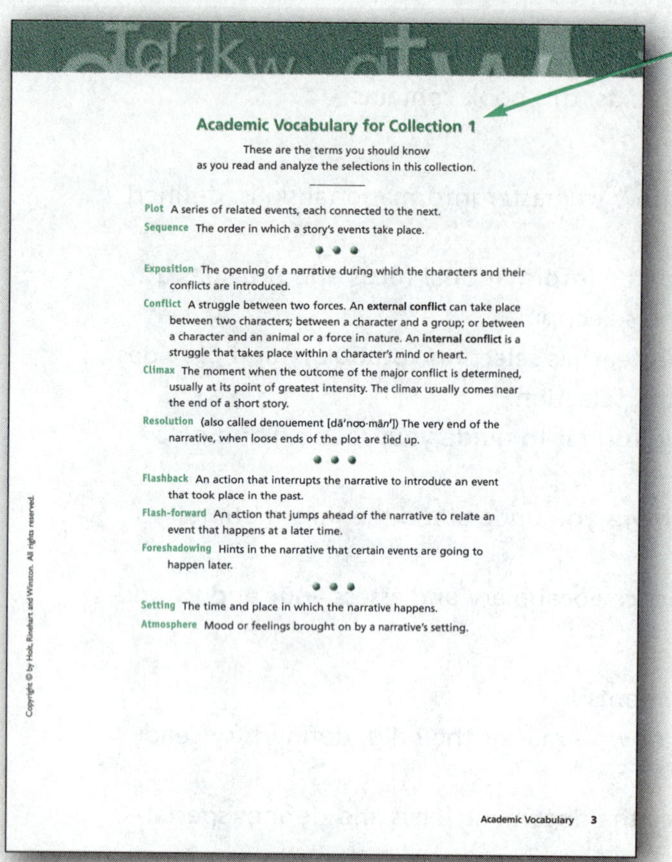

Academic Vocabulary

Academic vocabulary refers to the language of books, tests, and formal writing. Each collection begins with the terms, or academic language, you need to know to master the skills for that collection.

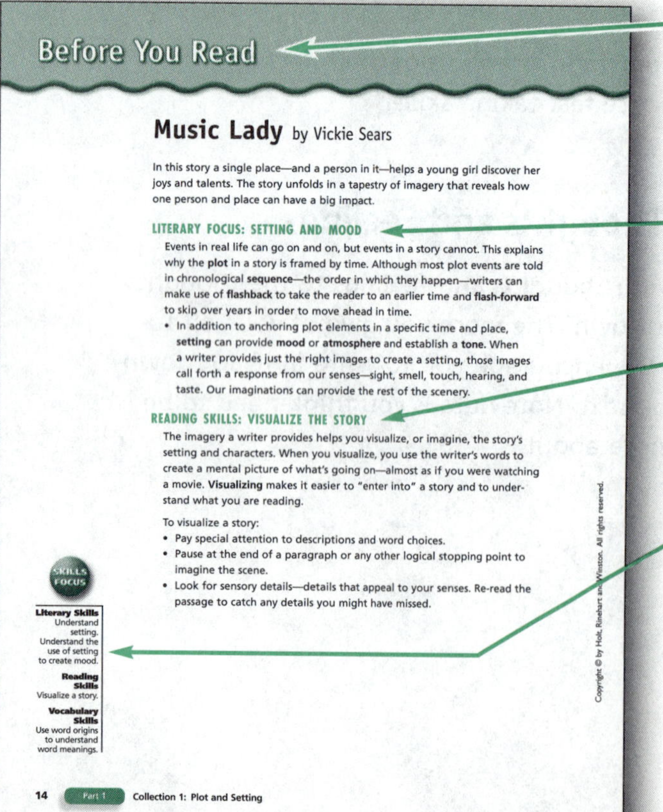

Before You Read

Previewing what you will learn builds success. This page tells you what the selection is about and prepares you to read it.

Literary Focus

This feature introduces the literary focus for the selection.

Reading Skills

This feature provides a reading skill for you to apply to the selection. It ties into and supports the literary focus.

Language Arts Skills

The skills covered with the selection are listed here.

Vocabulary Development

Vocabulary words for the selection are pretaught. Each entry gives the pronunciation and definition of the word as well as a context sentence.

Vocabulary Skills

When you read, you have to not only recognize words but also decode them and determine meaning. This feature introduces a vocabulary skill to use to understand words in the selection.

Side-Column Notes

Each selection is accompanied by notes in the side column that guide your interaction with the selection. Many notes ask you to underline or circle in the text itself. Others provide lines on which you can write your responses to questions.

Types of Notes

The different types of notes throughout the selection help you—

- Focus on literary elements
- Apply the reading skill
- Apply the vocabulary skill
- Think critically about the selection
- Develop word knowledge
- Build vocabulary
- Build fluency

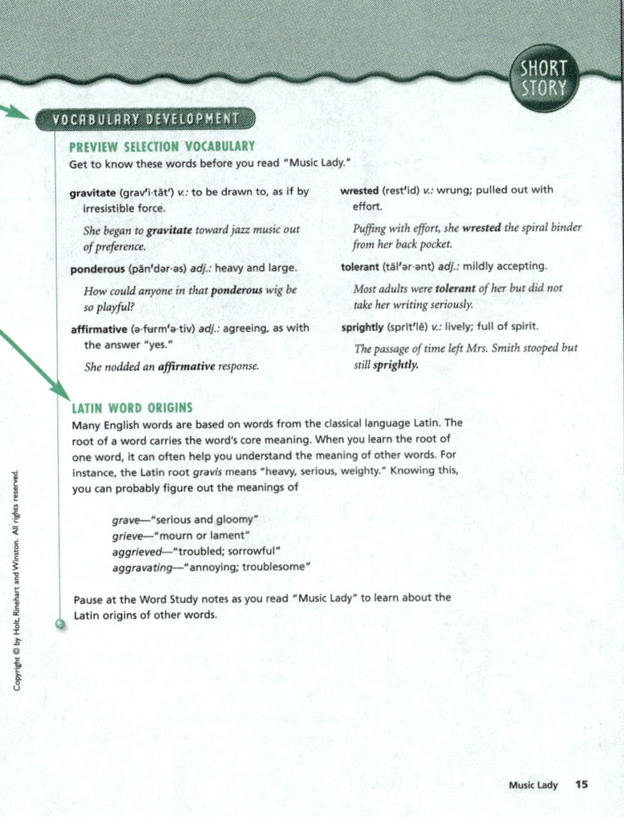

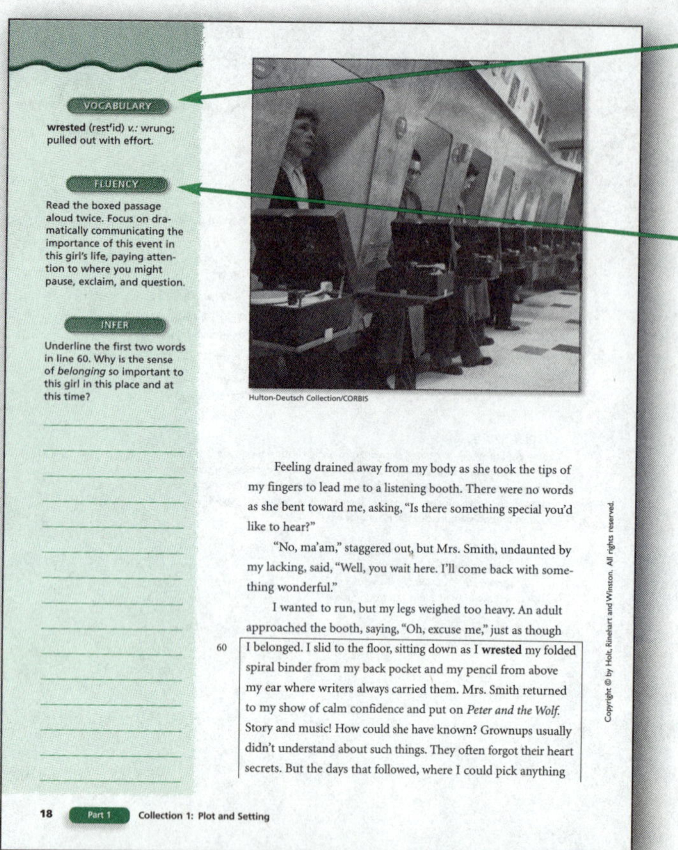

Vocabulary

The vocabulary words that were pretaught are defined in the side column and set in boldface in the selection, allowing you to see them in context.

Fluency

Successful readers are able to read fluently—clearly, easily, quickly, and without word identification problems. In most selections, youll be given an opportunity to practice and improve your fluency.

Meet the Writer

A short biography of the writer appears after each literature selection.

Skills Practice

Graphic organizers help reinforce your understanding of the literary focus in a highly visual and creative way.

Skills Review: Vocabulary

Test your knowledge of the selection vocabulary and the vocabulary skill by completing this short activity.

Reading Comprehension

This feature allows you to see how well youve un derstood the selection you have just read.

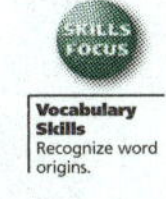

Part One

Reading Literature

Collection 1 Plot and Setting

Collection 2 Character

Collection 3 Narrator and Voice

Collection 4 Comparing Themes

Collection 5 Irony and Ambiguity

Collection 6 Symbolism and Allegory

Collection 7 Poetry

Collection 8 Literary Criticism: Evaluating Style

Collection 9 Literary Criticism: Biographical and Historical Approach

Collection 10 Epic and Myth

Collection 11 Drama

Plot and Setting

MedioImages/Getty Images

Academic Vocabulary for Collection 1

These are the terms you should know
as you read and analyze the selections in this collection.

———————

Plot A series of related events, each connected to the next.

Sequence The order in which a story's events take place.

Exposition The opening of a narrative during which the characters and their conflicts are introduced.

Conflict A struggle between two forces. An **external conflict** can take place between two characters; between a character and a group; or between a character and an animal or a force in nature. An **internal conflict** is a struggle that takes place within a character's mind or heart.

Climax The moment when the outcome of the major conflict is determined, usually at its point of greatest intensity. The climax usually comes near the end of a short story.

Resolution (also called denouement [dā′nōō·mä*n*′]) The very end of the narrative, when loose ends of the plot are tied up.

Flashback An action that interrupts the narrative to introduce an event that took place in the past.

Flash-forward An action that jumps ahead of the narrative to relate an event that happens at a later time.

Foreshadowing Hints in the narrative that certain events are going to happen later.

Setting The time and place in which the narrative happens.

Atmosphere Mood or feelings brought on by a narrative's setting.

My Horse by Devon A. Mihesuah

Imagine chasing a herd of wild horses and catching one to tame and make your own. "My Horse" is the story of Ralph, who did just that.

LITERARY FOCUS: PLOT AND CONFLICT

The **plot** of a story is a series of related events. These events take place as one or more characters take steps to resolve a **conflict,** or problem of some kind. Some events are hinted at through the use of **foreshadowing.**

The **setting** in this story plays an important role in establishing the narrator's **internal** and **external conflicts.** Although the setting in *place* is the same throughout the story, the setting in *time* changes. As you read, note how the setting affects the characters, the conflicts, and the plot.

READING SKILLS: MAKING PREDICTIONS

Before you read "My Horse," take a few minutes to make predictions using a "plot impression." Plot impressions work like this: You are given details from the story. Then you weave the details together to create an impression of the plot as you predict it might be. Here are the details for your plot impression of "My Horse." The narrator describes three settings. Predict which is the setting that matters the most to him and why.

Key Details	
Ralph, 16 years old (beginning)	the Marines and a war, 1941
Skeeter, his horse	marriage and two kids
the home place	crowded, noisy California, 1950
nature and wildlife	
Plot Impression	

SKILLS FOCUS

Literary Skills
Understand plot and conflict. Identify setting.

Reading Skills
Make predictions.

Vocabulary Skills
Recognize word derivations.

VOCABULARY DEVELOPMENT

PREVIEW SELECTION VOCABULARY

Preview the following words from the story before you begin reading.

mustangs (mus′taŋz′) *n.:* wild horses.

> *Mustangs ran freely across Aunt Tish's land.*

suspicious (sə·spish′əs) *adj.:* state of being mistrustful; suspecting harm or bad motives.

> *Ralph was **suspicious** of the man who cared for his horse, so he called frequently to check on things.*

deteriorating (dē·tir′ē·ə·rāt′iŋ) *v.* used as *adj.:* decaying; falling apart.

> *The **deteriorating** house needed work before anyone could move back into it.*

parcel (pär′səl) *n.:* here, piece or section.

> *Ralph inherited a **parcel** of land when his aunt Tish passed away.*

adjoining (ə·join′iŋ) *adj.:* next to or touching.

> *A fence separated Ralph's land from the **adjoining** property.*

WORD DERIVATIONS

The history, or origin, of a word—where it comes from—is called its **derivation.** English contains words whose early origins may be found in Old English, Latin, Greek, Norse, and other ancient languages. English continues to gain words through these languages' modern descendants, such as Spanish or Portuguese, as well as through other sources, such as African and Native American languages. *Coyote,* for example, comes from the Nahuatl (Aztec) word *coyōtl,* and *Oklahoma* comes from the Choctaw words *okla* ("people") and *homma* ("red").

Word derivations are handy to know because the original meanings often contain clues to the modern meanings. You may want to keep a Word Derivation chart to list the word origins you have learned. Here is a sample chart:

Word	Origin and Meaning	Modern Definition
deteriorate	Latin *deteriorare*: "to make worse"	"decaying; falling apart"

Pause at the Word Study notes as you read "My Horse" to learn about the origins of other words.

My Horse

Devon A. Mihesuah

> **BACKGROUND: Literature and Social Studies**
> Part of this story takes place during a time when the U.S. government implemented a policy called "relocation" to encourage Native Americans to move from reservations to urban areas so that they might better assimilate into American society. Some Native Americans had no desire to move, and many of those who left returned to the reservations after a period of time.

VOCABULARY

mustangs (mus′taŋz′) *n.:* wild horses.

SETTING

Circle the words and phrases in lines 3–8 that show how Ralph feels about the **setting** of his aunt Tish's house. What mood, or feeling, do these words create in you?

____

____

____

____

____

____

____

____

"You can have the horse you catch," Aunt Tish said.

"Catch? How?"

I was sixteen years old and had wanted one of my great-aunt's **mustangs** since I was nine. I loved to watch the herd run across Tish's creek-crossed allotment[1] that nourished cotton-woods, oaks, and tall grasses hiding deer, antelope, turkeys, and coyotes. I imagined myself riding the lead horse, a dark brown mustang stallion with his mane in his face.

"How you catch one's up to you, Ralph," said my aunt.

10 "They come when I have the bucket of sweet feed,[2] but they're hard to rope."

Then she patted me on the back and said she was going to town. I walked to the garden fence and watched the horses graze.

---

1. **allotment:** Under the Dawes Act of 1887, also called the General Allotment Act, Congress divided up Native American tribal lands into small units, or allotments. These allotments were distributed among individual members of the tribes.
2. **sweet feed:** mixture of food for animals, typically made from grains and molasses.

"My Horse" from *The Roads of My Relations* by Devon A. Mihesuah. Copyright © 2000 by Devon A. Mihesuah. Reproduced by permission of **The University of Arizona Press**.

Eastcott Momatiuk/Getty Images

The next day I followed the twenty horses. They ran from me morning till afternoon, surely wondering what I was doing. I was tired and hungry; and came back to the house. But I did have a plan.

20   The next morning I chased the horses through a low spot in the creek that was bounded by a steep bank in hopes they'd slow down enough for me to rope one. All the horses ran through the bottleneck except one, a young brown mare with black spots on the left side of her rib cage. She tripped and fell in the mud at the edge of the creek. As she struggled to her feet I dropped the rope around her neck.

    She stood and looked at me, then over her shoulder at the herd. With a panicked whinny she turned and ran through the creek, dragging me over the rocks. She finally stopped and faced me with wide eyes. Although she was scrawny, not exactly the

30 horse I wanted to ride across the plains on, a bigger horse would have kept pulling me. "I'm not lettin' go," I said. I decided she would do.

Horse derives from the Middle English *hors,* a word that has remained virtually unchanged for centuries.

Read the boxed passage aloud two times. Try to improve the speed and smoothness of your delivery on your second reading.

Pause at line 32 to imagine how Ralph looks at this point. Now, imagine how the horse looks. Predict who will win this **conflict.**

INFER

Underline details in lines 38–46 that describe how Ralph and Skeeter get along. How would you describe the bond between the two?

____

____

____

PLOT

Pause at line 63. The **plot** moves quickly from 1941 to 1950. Circle some of the key events.

IDENTIFY

Re-read lines 47–63. Why does Ralph have to leave Skeeter in 1941 and again in 1950?

____

____

____

____

____

VOCABULARY

suspicious (sə·spish′əs) *adj.:* state of being mistrustful; suspecting harm or bad motives.

deteriorating (dē·tir′ē·ə·rāt′iŋ) *v.* used as *adj.:* decaying; falling apart.

I had to think of a name for my horse. Mosquito bites covered me by the time we got back to the barn so I named her Skeeter. I didn't know a thing about breaking a horse so for days I led her around by a rope with a blanket on her back. After a week I put Tish's old saddle on her, then slowly tightened the cinch.[3]

A few days later I stepped into the saddle and after a few jumps and a run across the field Skeeter understood what I wanted. I rode her every day before and after school, down the roads, into town, across unfenced land. She ran with the other horses, but she came to me when I called her. My favorite picture is of me standing on Skeeter's back without my shirt, hands on hips. She wasn't moving, of course, but the way her front feet were placed made her look like she was. That's what I told everybody.

After my last year of high school my father died and his allotment outside of Tuskahoma became mine. When I entered the Marines in 1941, I moved Skeeter from Tish's land to ours. Tish sold her herd to an outfit that made me **suspicious.** I've always wondered what they did with those horses.

I leased my allotment to Orville Johnston, a cattleman who agreed to watch Skeeter. Six months after I left, Johnston wrote to say that Skeeter learned how to open the gate and to come get her. I told him to forget about renewing his lease unless he latched the gate better and took care of my horse. He agreed.

I returned home after the war and worked on Daddy's **deteriorating** house and found a job as a diesel mechanic for three years. I still rode Skeeter even though she was older and I was heavier. I married a girl named Ange, had two kids in four years, and under the relocation program moved my family to California in 1950. I had to leave Skeeter behind once again. She was sixteen and I called Johnston twice a month to check on her.

In June of 1954, we returned for Tish's funeral. She was ninety-four and never seemed to age except for those last weeks of her full life.

---

3. **cinch** (sinch) *n.:* band put around the belly of a horse to tighten a saddle.

It had been four years since I had seen my horse. She was twenty years old and walked slowly. I let my son and daughter ride her but I was afraid my weight would hurt her back. For a week I walked around the home place with my children, fishing and watching for deer and turkeys. Skeeter followed me like a puppy.

Skeeter, my old horse, was a measure of my life. I was a boy when I captured and tamed her. Yet I watched her grow old at a distance and I felt guilt at not being with her. Tish had told me that the problem with pets is that we always outlive them.

Skeeter was older and so was I. The house I was born in looked smaller than I remembered. It creaked and groaned with each step across the floor. Wind found the open spaces to run through, bringing dirt and insects inside. The house was dying.

When we drove out the road back to California I saw Skeeter in the rearview mirror, standing at the fence, ears pricked. That was the last time I saw her.

Richard T. Nowitz/CORBIS

Pause at line 91. Why does Ralph move his family back to the reservation? Underline the sentences that tell you.

Pause at line 102. Ralph allows his allotment to return to its natural state, but not as a form of neglect. Explain why this choice makes sense to Ralph.

____

____

____

Underline the words in lines 109–115 that show how Ralph feels when he discovers the bones. What do you feel? Why is there no sense of **resolution** to Ralph's relationship with Skeeter?

____

____

____

____

parcel (pär′səl) *n.:* here, piece or section.

adjoining (ə·join′iŋ) *adj.:* next to or touching.

That week Johnston called to say Skeeter was probably dead. At least he thought she was. He looked for five days and couldn't find her. I cried until I was sick.

We didn't like the noise and crowds of California, so a year later I moved my family back to Oklahoma. I had longed for the quiet of home and the activity of our tribe. We didn't live on the

90 allotment as the house and barn were falling apart, and I let them go. We moved just a mile from the home place.

Johnston quit the cattle business and my allotment grew back to the way it looked before I was born. Now, seventy-five years after my father built his home, all that is left is rotting wood, with oaks and bushes growing up through the splintered beams. The fence lay where it fell, a rectangle of broken posts.

A few years later I received yet another **parcel** of land **adjoining** my land from my widowed, childless sister. Sitting on it is an old, solid house that once belonged to Ruel Battiest. Now I use the

100 home place for hunting. I strung another set of barbed wire to keep out poachers, but sometimes they cut the fence and hunt my animals. Lots of Indians with allotments have the same problem.

Once while scouting on the home place, I stopped to rest and to eat juicy plums in the fruit orchard. It didn't take long to realize chiggers[4] covered the thick green grass, so I sat on what appeared to be the leg bone of a deer. The rest of the decayed and odorless carcass was still attached to the bone, held together by tough hide and tendons.

I moved the grass apart to look closer. The bones were

110 bigger than a deer's. I turned the hide over and saw brown with black spots. My horse. I sat on the grass, knowing my backside would start to itch, but I cried for Skeeter anyway.

I buried the bones in the plum orchard. I thought of making a small cross but didn't know what good that would do so I did nothing except tell Skeeter good-bye.

---

4. **chiggers** (chig′ərz) *n.:* tiny red larvae of mites.

Two weeks later I got a phone call from Johnston. He sounded a bit hesitant to tell me what he needed to. "I never found your horse."

"I did. Under the plum trees."

120 "Well, I'd been over there a few times but didn't see nothin'. Hey, listen. I know I was just supposed to graze cattle, but I also ran a few horses over there."

"Yeah. And?"

"Two were stallions, and, well, your horse had a few colts. One every other year, actually. Do you want a couple? They look like Skeeter. One's pregnant."

I stood with the receiver to my ear, staring at the framed picture of me standing on Skeeter. It sat on the phone table next to the pictures of my children.

130 "I'll be there in five minutes," I said.

MEET THE WRITER

Devon A. Mihesuah is a professor of history at North American University and a member of the Choctaw Nation of Oklahoma. In her teaching and writing, Mihesuah strives to increase people's understanding of Native American history. Mihesuah is also the award-winning editor of the journal *American Indian Quarterly.* Her story "My Horse" comes from her first novel, *The Roads of My Relations.* Based on her family's stories, it chronicles eleven generations of a Choctaw family.

PLOT

Why is Johnston's offer a second chance for Ralph? Do you think he will do anything differently this time? Explain.

My Horse

SKILLS FOCUS

Literary Skills
Analyze plot.

Plot Diagram   Review the plot structure of "My Horse." Then, fill in the plot diagram below with key story events.

Climax:

6.

5.

Resolution:

4.

3.

**Main events
(Complications):**

2.

1.

Basic situation:

Setting:

Skills Review

My Horse

VOCABULARY AND COMPREHENSION

A. Word Derivations   Match the following words from the story with their derivations. You will not use all the words from the Word Box.

Word	Origin and meaning
1. _______________	Latin *pars* (meaning "part")
2. _______________	Wolof (African) *jiga* (meaning "insect")
3. _______________	Latin *cingere* (meaning "to surround")
4. _______________	Latin *jungere* (meaning "to join")
5. _______________	Latin *deterior* (meaning "worse")

Word Box

mustangs

suspicious

chiggers

deteriorating

parcel

adjoining

cinch

B. Reading Comprehension   Answer each question below.

1. Describe the setting of "My Horse."

____

____

2. How does Skeeter come to be Ralph's horse?

____

____

3. What happens to Ralph after he leaves the reservation? Why does he leave Skeeter behind?

____

____

____

4. How does Ralph find out what has become of Skeeter?

____

____

5. What does Ralph learn about Skeeter at the end of the story?

____

SKILLS FOCUS

Vocabulary Skills
Recognize word derivations.

Music Lady by Vickie Sears

In this story a single place—and a person in it—helps a young girl discover her joys and talents. The story unfolds in a tapestry of imagery that reveals how one person and place can have a big impact.

LITERARY FOCUS: SETTING AND MOOD

Events in real life can go on and on, but events in a story cannot. This explains why the **plot** in a story is framed by time. Although most plot events are told in chronological **sequence**—the order in which they happen—writers can make use of **flashback** to take the reader to an earlier time and **flash-forward** to skip over years in order to move ahead in time.

- In addition to anchoring plot elements in a specific time and place, **setting** can provide **mood** or **atmosphere** and establish a **tone.** When a writer provides just the right images to create a setting, those images call forth a response from our senses—sight, smell, touch, hearing, and taste. Our imaginations can provide the rest of the scenery.

READING SKILLS: VISUALIZE THE STORY

The imagery a writer provides helps you visualize, or imagine, the story's setting and characters. When you visualize, you use the writer's words to create a mental picture of what's going on—almost as if you were watching a movie. **Visualizing** makes it easier to "enter into" a story and to understand what you are reading.

To visualize a story:
- Pay special attention to descriptions and word choices.
- Pause at the end of a paragraph or any other logical stopping point to imagine the scene.
- Look for sensory details—details that appeal to your senses. Re-read the passage to catch any details you might have missed.

Literary Skills
Understand setting. Understand the use of setting to create mood.

Reading Skills
Visualize a story.

Vocabulary Skills
Use word origins to understand word meanings.

VOCABULARY DEVELOPMENT

PREVIEW SELECTION VOCABULARY

Get to know these words before you read "Music Lady."

gravitate (grav′i·tāt′) *v.:* be drawn to, as if by irresistible force.

*She began to **gravitate** toward jazz music out of preference.*

ponderous (pän′dər·əs) *adj.:* heavy and large.

*How could anyone in that **ponderous** wig be so playful?*

affirmative (ə·fʉrm′ə·tiv) *adj.:* agreeing, as with the answer "yes."

*She nodded an **affirmative** response.*

wrested (rest′id) *v.:* wrung; pulled out with effort.

*Puffing with effort, she **wrested** the spiral binder from her back pocket.*

tolerant (täl′ər·ənt) *adj.:* mildly accepting.

*Most adults were **tolerant** of her but did not take her writing seriously.*

sprightly (sprīt′lē) *v.:* lively; full of spirit.

*The passage of time left Mrs. Smith stooped but still **sprightly**.*

LATIN WORD ORIGINS

Many English words are based on words from the classical language Latin. The root of a word carries the word's core meaning. When you learn the root of one word, it can often help you understand the meaning of other words. For instance, the Latin root *gravis* means "heavy, serious, weighty." Knowing this, you can probably figure out the meanings of

> *grave*—"serious and gloomy"
> *grieve*—"mourn or lament"
> *aggrieved*—"troubled; sorrowful"
> *aggravating*—"annoying; troublesome"

Pause at the Word Study notes as you read "Music Lady" to learn about the Latin origins of other words.

Music Lady

Vickie Sears

On days of rain, when poetry often came to paper, I'd sneak away from the orphanage, running to leg tautness and chest burn all the way to 15th and 65th streets to the record store. That's where the music lady lived. Where there were sounds that made my poetry seem brighter. Where the music lady smiled under high cheekbones, patted my head, and whispered words of encouragement.

It wasn't an ordinary record store, then or now. It had listening booths and rows of deep, wooden, forest-green troughs filled with the faces of musicians and instruments. These were the instruments of the big band music[1] my mother liked. Different from the flutes, bells, and drums of my father's family. Different, too, from the silence of the orphanage, except for the dinner bell. Here trumpets and cellos blared in silence from cardboard covers. Grownups strolled the aisles and flicked through the records, like playing cards, choosing their hand of music before taking it to one of the narrow rectangles, each equipped with turntable and speakers, to listen. The sound-proofed booths created individual worlds of monophonic[2] magic seeping through the glass doors.

---

1. **big band music:** jazz music from the 1930s and 1940s.
2. **monophonic** (män′ō·fän′ik) *adj:* relating to a sound reproduction with a single channel to carry and reproduce sounds. (*Monophonic* is the opposite of *stereophonic*.)

"Music Lady" from *Simple Songs* by Vickie Sears. Copyright © 1990 by Vickie Sears. Reproduced by permission of **Firebrand Books**.

IDENTIFY

Circle the words in lines 1–7 that give important information about the **narrator**. Then, in the lines below, jot down your first impressions. What do you know about her?

VISUALIZE

Pause at line 20. Imagine this scene at the record store. Underline the narrator's uses of **imagery**. (Imagery is language that appeals to the senses.) What senses are combined in surprising ways?

It never really mattered much what was playing, although I began to **gravitate** to jazz and playful Bach.[3] Bach sounded of creek-skipping water and duck laughs. It was hard for me to understand how a man who dressed with lace edging his jacket and pants, and wearing such a **ponderous** wig, could have so much fun. Still, I'd walk beside the booths, spiral binder and pencil in hand, searching for just the right music to write near. As casually as a walnut-colored nine-year-old among tall, mostly white adults could, I'd position myself against a booth's door-

30 jamb and lean an ear to sound. I'd close my eyes for filling, follow the strings of music, and slip down into its colors. All other sounds faded. My body, rainrhythm, and the music became all. After awhile I could make a poem and slide back into the downpour, happy in its beat. I felt special in the rain-song and slow walk home.

One afternoon as I wandered the aisles, the slim creamed-skinned lady with rouge-circled cheeks motioned to me. As she crooked her finger my first thought was to apologize for enter-ing this world supposed to be for adults. Yet she didn't seem

40 really threatening. Cautiously, I went toward the woman, noting the gray day through the window framing her pale hazel hair and the openness of her arms held still at either side of herself. She smelled of softness as she asked, "Would you like to have a booth for yourself?"

Magic!

The only thing I could say was, "I can't buy no music."

A smile spread as she slowly shook her head asking, "No? Well, can you listen anyway?"

I jiggled an **affirmative** head. She said, "I'm Mrs. Smith and

50 this is my store so you're welcome here anytime."

---

3. **Bach:** Johann Sebastian Bach (1685–1750) was a German composer and organist who is regarded as one of the geniuses of classical music.

wrested (rest′id) *v.:* wrung; pulled out with effort.

Read the boxed passage aloud twice. Focus on dramatically communicating the importance of this event in this girl's life, paying attention to where you might pause, exclaim, and question.

Underline the first two words in line 60. Why is the sense of *belonging* so important to this girl in this place and at this time?

Hulton-Deutsch Collection/CORBIS

Feeling drained away from my body as she took the tips of my fingers to lead me to a listening booth. There were no words as she bent toward me, asking, "Is there something special you'd like to hear?"

"No, ma'am," staggered out, but Mrs. Smith, undaunted by my lacking, said, "Well, you wait here. I'll come back with something wonderful."

I wanted to run, but my legs weighed too heavy. An adult approached the booth, saying, "Oh, excuse me," just as though

60　I belonged. I slid to the floor, sitting down as I **wrested** my folded spiral binder from my back pocket and my pencil from above my ear where writers always carried them. Mrs. Smith returned to my show of calm confidence and put on *Peter and the Wolf.* Story and music! How could she have known? Grownups usually didn't understand about such things. They often forgot their heart secrets. But the days that followed, where I could pick anything

I wanted to listen to, proved me wrong. Billie Holiday[4] sang sadness after I'd listen to tribal music and wonder where my father was. Big band sounds signaled tears of missing Mother, but
70 Scott Joplin[5] had a "Maple Leaf Rag" that warmed. Beethoven got mad and made thunderous rain. Haydn[6] knew the calm of a sunny Lake Washington.

Mrs. Smith asked me what I was writing as though it were really important and not merely an adult being **tolerant.** She let me read her poem after poem without laughing or correcting the English or telling me not to dream. She'd say, "You keep doing that," and patted my head. I'd leave the music store with the feeling of being cuddled in sunlight, even in the rain. It was really quite all right to be a cross-eyed funny Indian kid who

---

4. **Billie Holiday** (1915–1959): famous jazz singer.
5. **Scott Joplin:** famous ragtime pianist and composer.
6. **Haydn:** Joseph Haydn (1732–1809) was an Austrian composer of classical music.

Leo Vals/Getty Images

Underline the narrator's uses of **imagery** in lines 65–72. What moods are created by her use of imagery?

____

____

____

____

The word *important* comes from the Latin root *port,* meaning "to carry"—as do *portfolio, sport,* and *report.* What other words can you think of with the Latin root *port*?

____

____

Lines 73–82 describe a series of repeated events. **Paraphrase** these events, and explain their effect on the narrator.

____

____

____

____

tolerant (tăl′ər·ənt) *adj.:* mildly accepting.

80   secretly scribbled poetry. Mrs. Smith said it was good. And all those different people of all those colors and looks on all those records knew it was too.

    Many years later, when I was forty-five and in a cold early-spring-drizzle mood, I went into Standard Records and Hi-Fi feeling the need for some new music to match the time I wanted to spend writing. In one of the floorworn aisles still narrow with record bins, I stopped for the passage of an Elder. Her thin body, shoulder-stooped and year-wrinkled, slipped **sprightly** past me. She smiled at my having bowed with hand gesturing for her to

90   have the right of way. A warm rush flooded over me; I watched her bending toward a customer, her slight hands softly bridging the width of a record as she placed it on a turntable. She had not been in the store the other times I had come since growing up. I waited until she was behind the counter again, then stood before her, feeling shy.

    Mrs. Smith asked me if there was anything else I wanted other than the Billie Holiday I'd chosen. I took in deep air and said, "I want to thank you for all the times you listened to my poetry as a kid, and for your patting my head."

100   A puzzled face turned up toward me, a broad smile cresting her mouth. I told her about her gift. She grinned more widely and said, "How nice that I could be there for you to help you save some beauty. The world needs people like you in it. Well, I'll pat your head again."

MEET THE WRITER

Vickie Sears (1941–1999) was a writer, therapist, and teacher of Cherokee, Spanish, and English ancestry. Born in California, Sears spent much of her childhood in the foster care system. Her father, who was Cherokee, taught Sears traditional Cherokee beliefs; at the same time, Sears learned about Catholicism from her mother. Sears went on to explore many world religions but remained most devoted to her Native American roots and spiritual practices. Sears spent most of her life living and working in the Seattle, Washington, area.

Music Lady

Literary Skills
Analyze mood.

Mood Chart   Fill in the chart below to analyze the **mood** of this story. In the top of the first column, write words or phrases from the story used to describe the **setting.** Then, in the second column, describe the mood created by these phrases. Next, in the bottom of the first column, write **imagery** from the story. Then, describe the mood that imagery creates. The first row of each has been filled in as an example. Finally, make a statement about the overall mood of the story.

Setting—Words and Phrases	Mood Created
"listening booths and rows of deep, wooden, forest-green troughs"	peaceful
Imagery—Words and Phrases	**Mood Created**
"creek-skipping water and duck laughs"	playful

Overall Mood: ____________________________________

____

____

Skills Review

Music Lady

VOCABULARY AND COMPREHENSION

A. Word Origins   Match the following words from the story with their origins.

Latin Origin and Meaning	Word
1. *pendere,* "heavy; large"	_________________
2. *affirmare,* "to strengthen"	_________________
3. *tolerare,* "to bear"	_________________
4. *spiritus,* "breath; spirit"	_________________
5. *gravis,* "heavy; weighty"	_________________

Word Box

tolerant

ponderous

sprightly

gravitate

affirmative

The words below also came from the Latin origins above. See if you can identify
the Latin root. If you don't know the meaning of the word, take an educated
guess based on the meaning of the root word before going to a dictionary to
check your accuracy. Write your guess in the third column.

Word	Latin Root	Meaning
6. inspire	_________________	_________________
7. engraved	_________________	_________________

B. Reading Comprehension   Answer each question below.

1. Describe the narrator of "Music Lady."

____

____

2. Why does the narrator like going to the music store? What does she enjoy
   doing there?

____

____

3. What does the narrator, as an adult, tell the music store owner when she
   sees her again?

____

____

Vocabulary Skills
Recognize word origins.

Trees by Jennifer Tseng

If you had a choice, what kind of tree would you be? Why?

LITERARY FOCUS: PLOT

Plot is the series of related events that make up a story. This is true whether that story is told in prose, as in "My Horse" and "Music Lady," or in poetry, as in "Trees," the poem you are about to read.

- Much of the story in "Trees" is told in the past tense. Be on the lookout for the point at which the **setting** comes forward to the present.

READING SKILLS: MAKING PREDICTIONS

What do you predict will be the **plot** of "Trees"? You may not be able to anticipate the specific events but might be able to guess what the author's **setting** or **subject** will be. Use the following key details from "Trees" to anticipate some elements of this poem:

Key Details	
two parents	a young pear tree
their children	a single pear
Setting	
Subject	

SKILLS FOCUS

Literary Skills
Understand plot and flash-forward.

Reading Skills
Make predictions.

 Trees

Jennifer Tseng

One summer he planted a tree
it was young, just a few branches
no bigger than a rosebush.
We were intent on watching it
5   we were young
we wanted the fruit to come.

Father brought the coffee can outside
paced between the tree and the backyard spigot.°
We liked to watch him fill the can
10   feed water to the little tree.
We liked to see the brown soil
blacken beneath his fingers.

Young trees keep their fruit inside
for so long.
15   You have to stay with them
for years before
they'll bear it.

When the first pear came
we forgot about the water
20   and the soil and the man
with the coffee can.
We could already taste
its sweetness through the hard, green skin.

---

8.   **spigot:** faucet.

"Trees" by Jennifer Tseng from *Ploughshares: The Literary Journal at Emerson College,* Poetry, Winter 1999–00. Copyright © 2000 by **Jennifer Tseng.** Reproduced by permission of the author.

IDENTIFY

Underline the words in the first stanza that establish a strong **mood.** What mood do these words suggest?

____

____

____

____

INTERPRET

How could lines 13–17 be a metaphor for children as they grow? Explain.

____

____

____

____

CAUSE & EFFECT

Re-read lines 18–23. Now, re-read lines 9–10. What is the **cause-and-effect** relationship between these two parts of the poem?

____

____

____

____

____

____

____

____

____

____

PREDICT

In lines 26–28, Father gives a command. What does he fear will happen if the children touch the fruit? **Predict** what happens next.

____

____

____

____

____

____

ANALYZE

Pause at line 38. Were Father's fears warranted? Explain.

____

____

____

____

____

____

Design Pics Inc./Alamy

It hung there new,
25   like so many curves we recognized.
Don't touch
he said
don't touch.
We listened at first, we obeyed
30   because it was small then
easier to resist
but later we could see
its size would fill up our hands
and at night when he went away
35   we held it.
Finally, the yellow ink took over
the flesh was soft
we became gentle.

Father decided it was time

40   to pluck it

he decided it was

time to eat.

Mother brought out the special plate

the red one mottled with Chinese birds.

45   He placed the yellow pear on the red plate

divided the fruit with a knife.

It lay there open like a flower

a pale tropical thing with four

petals, keen with the smell of sugar

50   each one dripping juice, almost tears

each one, riven° from the others,

so yellow against the red birds.

Choose one

he said

55   and we knew he would watch

to see which one we chose.

The old story was thickly printed in the air

he did not have to speak

to tell it

60   the story of the child with the most honor

the one who saves the best

for her mother.

All of us fight

for the smallest piece.

65   Soon the fruit is gone

eaten under his watchful eye.

Time to wait for the next one.

Mother rinses the plate

shines the birds with her swift cloth.

---

51. riven: divided; split.

Re-read lines 70–78. Circle the words that signal a jumping forward in time, or a **flash-forward**. Make some notes about what seems to have changed.

Pause at line 78. The title of this poem is plural, although the tree in the story is singular. What else might the **title** signify?

70   Now he has cut the tree down.

He says it interferes with the plumbing

too many roots.

Mother is a bird flying.

Sister sends me fruit in the mail:

75   dried apricots, cranberries, apples, plums.

We are young, small

hungry as squirrels,

hiding our fruit in the cupboards.

MEET THE WRITER

In high school, **Jennifer Tseng** had an English teacher who submitted one of Tseng's poems to a competition. The poem won Tseng one hundred dollars, and the author knew she had found her calling. Tseng has since published a book of poems and written a novel. Her work has also appeared in many literary journals. Although she writes both fiction and poetry, Tseng says her first love is poetry. She believes that poetry has a quality of intimacy that is like the feeling of someone whispering in your ear.

Trees

Plot Chart: Past and Present   Most of "Trees" is told in the past tense. However, the end of the poem takes place in the present. Fill out the Plot Chart below with the major events of the poem that take place in the past. Then, try to fill out the right side for the present narrative in the poem. Fill in only what can be inferred through the poem.

Literary Skills
Analyze plot.

PLOT CHART	
Past	**Present**
Exposition Lines 1–17		
Conflict Lines 18–25		
Complications Lines 26–38		
Climax Lines 39–64		
Resolution Lines 65–69		

Character

Paul Chesley/Getty Images.

Academic Vocabulary for Collection 2

These are the terms you should know
as you read and analyze the selections in this collection.

Characterization The way writers create characters in a story. In **direct characterization,** writers tell us directly what a character is like ("good" or "evil" or "lazy"). In **indirect characterization** the reader uses clues in the story to decide what kind of person a character is. Clues may be descriptions of how the character acts, speaks, and thinks and how other people respond to the character.

● ● ●

Protagonist The main character in a story.

Antagonist The character that the main character (protagonist) struggles against.

Subordinate characters Minor characters in the story.

● ● ●

Motivations The reasons behind a character's actions and feelings.

Flat character A character who is not fully developed in the story. A flat character is almost never the main character.

Round character A character who is fully developed, just as a person in actual life is.

Dynamic character A character who changes during the story. The change might involve recognition of some truth about life.

Static character A character who does not change during the story.

● ● ●

Dialogue The conversations characters have with other characters.

First-person narration A story told by an "I" narrator. An "I" narrator is a character in the story.

My Delicate Heart Condition

by Toni Cade Bambara

Harriet Watkins loves excitement as much as she loves scaring other kids with her spooky stories. She also loves watching the Fly family perform death-defying feats on the high wire at the circus. Nothing scares Harriet. Or does it?

LITERARY FOCUS: CHARACTER

"My Delicate Heart Condition" has a **first-person narrator,** who refers to herself as "I" or "me." This narrator is also the story's main **character** (or protagonist). The **protagonist** is the character in the story whose actions set the plot in motion and whose choices typically bring it to resolution. The protagonist is the "main actor" in the story.

- In the course of this story, the main character says and does some curious things. Look for clues that help you understand her **motivations**—the reasons for her actions.

READING SKILLS: DRAWING CONCLUSIONS

A **conclusion** is a judgment you make based on evidence, or important details. You probably draw conclusions about the world around you every day. For example, one rainy morning your friend arrives unexpectedly at your house, dripping wet and out of breath. You might conclude that he forgot his umbrella and that he has run to your house in an attempt to stay dry.

You also make judgments based on evidence as you read a story. You think about what the narrator tells you and what the story's characters say and do. Then you put those details together—along with what you know from your own life experiences—to form a conclusion. As you read, you check to see if your conclusions are correct.

Literary Skills
Understand first-person narration. Understand character motivation.

Reading Skills
Draw conclusions.

Vocabulary Skills
Understand literal and figurative word meanings.

PREVIEW SELECTION VOCABULARY

The following words appear in "My Delicate Heart Condition." Look them over before you begin the story.

withstand (with·stand′) *v.:* endure; not give in.

> *Harriet's courage and inner strength help her* **withstand** *fear.*

vacant (vā′kənt) *adj.:* empty; suggesting lack of attention.

> *His* **vacant** *look made me think he wasn't paying attention.*

suspended (sə·spen′did) *v.* used as *adj.:* hung by a support from above.

> *The acrobat hung in the air,* **suspended** *by only a thin rope.*

proportions (prə·pôr′shənz) *n.:* size; dimensions.

> *His hands were small, but his feet had the* **proportions** *of a giant.*

CLARIFYING WORD MEANINGS: LITERAL AND FIGURATIVE MEANING

The **literal** meaning of a word is its dictionary definition. For example, if you say, "The computer is broken," you are using the word *broken* in a literal sense: The computer doesn't work. However, if you say, "My heart is broken," you are using the word *broken* in a **figurative,** or imaginative, sense. Your heart is still pumping blood—it is "working," in the literal sense. What you really mean by "My heart is broken" is that you are feeling deep sorrow or hurt. You feel as if your heart is broken into pieces.

Figurative language is based on a comparison between two unlike things. We use it all the time. Writers use figurative language to create vivid pictures and striking comparisons. As you read a story, be alert to the writer's use of figurative language.

My Delicate Heart Condition

Toni Cade Bambara

My cousin Joanne has not been allowed to hang out with me for some time because she went and told Aunt Hazel that I scare her to death whenever she sleeps over at our house or I spend the weekend at hers. The truth is I sometimes like to tell stories about bloodthirsty vampires or ugly monsters that lurk in clothes closets or giant beetles that eat their way through the shower curtain, like I used to do at camp to entertain the kids in my bunk. But Joanne always cries and that makes the stories even weirder, like background music her crying. And too—I'm

10   not going to lie about it—I get spookier on purpose until all the little crybabies are stuffing themselves under their pillows and throwing their sneakers at me and making such a racket that Mary the counselor has to come in and shine her flashlight around the bunkhouse. I play like I'm asleep. The rest of them are too busy blubbering and finding their way out from under the blankets to tell Mary that it's me. Besides, once they get a load of her standing against the moonlight in that long white robe of hers looking like a ghost, they just start up again and pretty soon the whole camp is awake. Anyway, that's what I do

20   for fun. So Joanne hasn't been around. And this year I'll have to go to the circus by myself and to camp without her. My mother said on the phone to Aunt Hazel—"Good, keep Jo over there and maybe Harriet'll behave herself if she's got no one to show off to." For all the years my mother's known me, she still doesn't understand that my behaving has got nothing to do with who I hang out with. A private thing between me and me or maybe between me and the Fly family since they were the ones that first got me to sit through monster movies and **withstand** all the terror I could take.

30   For four summers now, me and the Fly family have had this thing going. A battle of nerves, you might say. Each year they raise the rope closer and closer to the very top of the tent—I hear they're going to perform outdoors this year and be even higher—and they stretch the rope further across the rings where the clowns and the pony riders perform. Each year they get bolder and more daring with their rope dancing and the swinging by the legs and flinging themselves into empty space making everyone throw up their hands and gasp for air until Mr. Fly at the very last possible second swings out on his bar to catch them

40   up by the tips of their heels. Everyone just dies and clutches at their hearts. Everybody but me. I sit there calmly. I've trained myself. Joanne used to die and duck her head under the benches and stay there till it was all over.

      Last summer they really got bold. On the final performance just before the fair closed, and some revival-type tent show comes in and all the kids go off to camp, the Fly family performed without a net. I figured they'd be up to something so I made sure my stomach was like steel. I did ten push-ups before breakfast, twenty sit-ups before lunch, skipped dinner altogether. My

50   brother Teddy kidded me all day—"Harriet's trying out for the Olympics." I passed up the icie man on the corner and the pizza and sausage stand by the schoolyard and the cotton candy and jelly-apple lady and the pickle and penny-candy boy, in fact I passed up all the stands that lead from the street down the little roadway to the fair grounds that used to be a swamp when we first moved from Baltimore to Jamaica, Long Island. It wasn't easy, I'm not going to lie, but I was taking no chances. Between the balloon man and the wheel of fortune was the usual clump of ladies from church who came night after night to try to win

60   the giant punch bowl set on the top shelf above the wheel, but had to settle night after night for a jar of gumdrops or salt-and-pepper shakers or some other little thing from the bottom shelf. And from the wheel of fortune to the tent was at least a million stands selling B.B. bats and jawbreakers and gingerbread and

---

DRAW CONCLUSIONS

Pause and re-read lines 30–35. Who is the Fly family? What does the family do?

____

____

____

____

IDENTIFY

Underline the words in lines 40–41 that tell what "everyone" does while watching the Flys. Then, circle what Harriet does.

INTERPRET

In lines 48–49, Harriet works on making sure her "stomach was like steel." Is she using this phrase in a **literal** or a **figurative** sense? Explain.

____

____

CHARACTER

Pause at line 57. What do you think motivates Harriet to pass up all the delicious food? What does she want to accomplish?

____

____

____

____

sweet potato pie and frozen custard and—like I said it wasn't easy. A million ways to tempt you, to unsettle your stomach, and make you lose the battle to the Fly family.

I sat there almost enjoying the silly clowns who came tumbling out of a steamer trunk no bigger than the one we have in the basement where my mother keeps my old report cards and photographs and letters and things. And I almost enjoyed the fire-eater and the knife-thrower, but I was so close up I could see how there wasn't any real thrill. I almost enjoyed the fat-leg girls who rode the ponies two at a time and standing up, but their costumes weren't very pretty—just an ordinary polo shirt like you get if you run in the PAL[1] meets and short skirts you can wear on either side like the big girls wear at the roller rink. And I almost enjoyed the jugglers except that my Uncle Bubba can juggle the dinner plates better any day of the week so long as Aunt Hazel isn't there to stop him. I was impatient and started yawning. Finally all the clowns hitched up their baggy pants and tumbled over each other out of the ring and into the dark, the jugglers caught all the things that were up in the air and yawning just like me went off to the side. The pony girls brought their horses to a sudden stop that raised a lot of dust, then jumped down into the dirt and bowed. Then the ring-master stepped into the circle of light and tipped his hat which was a little raggedy from where I was sitting and said—"And now, Ladieeez and Gentlemen, what you've alll been waiting forrr, the Main aTTRACtion, the FLY FAMILEEE." And everyone jumped up to shout like crazy as they came running out on their toes to stand in the light and then climb the ropes. I took a deep breath and folded my arms over my chest and a kid next to me went into hiding, acting like she was going to tie her shoelaces.

There used to be four of them—the father, a big guy with a bald head and bushy mustache and shoulders and arms like King Kong; a tall lanky mother whom you'd never guess could

____

1. **PAL:** Police Athletic League, an organization sponsored by police departments that provides after-school activities for children.

Enigma/Alamy.

INTERPRET

Re-read lines 102–107. Why do you think Harriet identifies with the younger son?

even climb into a high chair or catch anything heavier than a Ping-Pong ball to look at her; the oldest son who looked like his father except he had hair on his head but none on his face and a big face it was, so that no matter how high up he got you could always tell whether he was smiling or frowning or counting; the younger boy about thirteen, maybe, had a **vacant** stare like he was a million miles away feeding his turtles or something, anything but walking along a tightrope or flying through the air with his family. I had always liked to watch him because he was as cool as I was. But last summer the little girl got into the act. My grandmother says she's probably a midget cause no self-respecting mother would allow her child to be up there acting like a bird. "Just a baby," she'd say, "Can't be more than six years old. Should be home in bed. Must be a midget." My grandfather

VOCABULARY

vacant (vā′kənt) *adj.:* empty; suggesting lack of attention.

Vacant comes from the Latin word *vacare,* meaning "to be empty."

suspended (sə·spen′did) *v.*
used as *adj.:* hung by a
support from above.

The verb *suspend* is from the
Latin *sub–,* meaning "under,"
and *pendere,* meaning "to
hang." *Suspend* has the same
word origin as *suspense,*
which means leaving the
reader "hanging," or waiting
to learn what happens next.

What does Harriet mean
when she says, "I almost
thought I too had to tie my
shoelaces" (line 128)?

____

____

____

____

____

Re-read lines 131–145. As you
read, circle the verbs that the
author uses to describe this
tense scene. How does her
choice of verbs contribute to
the effect of this scene?

____

____

____

____

____

____

would give me a look when she started in and we'd smile at her together.

They almost got to me that last performance, dodging around with new routines and two at a time so that you didn't know which one Mr. Fly was going to save at the last minute. But he'd fly out and catch the little boy and swing over to the opposite stand where the big boy was flying out to catch them both by the wrists and the poor woman would be left kind of dangling there, **suspended,** then she'd do this double flip which would kill off everyone in the tent except me, of course, and swing out on the very bar she was on in the first place. And then they'd mess around two or three flying at once just to confuse you until the big drum roll started and out steps the little girl in a party dress and huge blindfold wrapped around her little head and a pink umbrella like they sell down in Chinatown. And I almost—I won't lie about it—I almost let my heart thump me off the bench. I almost thought I too had to tie my shoelaces. But I sat there. Stubborn. And the kid starts bouncing up and down on the rope like she was about to take off and tear through the canvas roof. Then out swings her little brother and before you know it, Fly Jr. like a great eagle with his arms flapping grabs up the kid, her eyeband in his teeth and swoops her off to the bar that's already got Mrs. Mr. and Big Bro on it and surely there's no room for him. And everyone's standing on their feet clutching at their faces. Everyone but me. Cause I know from the getgo that Mr. and Mrs. are going to leave the bar to give Jr. room and fly over to the other side. Which is exactly what they do. The lady in front of me, Mrs. Perez, who does all the sewing in our neighborhood, gets up and starts shaking her hands like ladies do to get the fingernail polish dry and she says to me with her eyes jammed shut "I must go finish the wedding gowns. Tell me later who died." And she scoots through the aisle, falling all over everybody with her eyes still shut and never looks up. And Mrs. Caine taps me on the back and leans over and says,

"Some people just can't take it." And I smile at her and at her twins who're sitting there with their mouths open. I fold my arms over my chest and just dare the Fly family to do their very worst.

The minute I got to camp, I ran up to the main house where all
150   the counselors gather to say hello to the parents and talk with the directors. I had to tell Mary the latest doings with the Fly family. But she put a finger to her mouth like she sometimes does to shush me. "Let's not have any scary stuff this summer, Harriet," she said, looking over my shoulder at a new kid. This new kid, Willie, was from my old neighborhood in Baltimore so we got friendly right off. Then he told me that he had a romantic heart so I quite naturally took him under my wing and decided not to give him a heart attack with any ghost tales. Mary said he meant "rheumatic" heart,[2] but I don't see any difference.
160   So I told Mary to move him out of George's tent and give him a nicer counselor who'd respect his romantic heart. George used to be my play boyfriend when I first came to camp as a little kid and didn't know any better. But he's not a nice person. He makes up funny nicknames for people which aren't funny at all. Like calling Eddie Michaels the Watermelon Kid or David Farmer Charcoal Plenty which I really do not appreciate and especially from a counselor. And once he asked Joanne, who was the table monitor, to go fetch a pail of milk from the kitchen. And the minute she got up, he started hatching a plot, trying to get the
170   kids to hide her peanut butter sandwich and put spiders in her soup. I had to remind everyone at the table that Joanne was my first cousin by blood, and I would be forced to waste the first bum that laid a hand on her plate. And ole George says, "Oh don't be a dumbhead, Harriet. Jo's so stupid she won't even notice." And I told him right then and there that I was not his play girlfriend anymore and would rather marry the wolfman than grow up and be his wife. And just in case he didn't get the message, that night around campfire when we were all playing

---

2. **rheumatic** (ro͞o·mat′ik) **heart:** heart with damaged valves, caused by rheumatic fever in childhood.

DRAW CONCLUSIONS

Re-read lines 177–183. From her actions, how old do you think Harriet is?

____

____

VOCABULARY

proportions (prə·pôr′shənz) *n.:* size; dimensions.

Circle a familiar word inside the larger word. What does the smaller word mean?

____

____

____

CHARACTER

Underline the sentence in lines 194–196 where the **narrator** describes what she did about the kids who laughed at Willie. Is she being honest or is she exaggerating? Explain.

____

____

____

____

____

____

____

Nancy Ney/Getty Images.

Little Sally Walker sittin' in a saucer and it was my turn to shake
it to the east and to shake it to the west and to shake it to the
very one that I loved the best—I shook straight for Mr. Nelson
the lifeguard, who was not only the ugliest person in camp but
the arch enemy of ole George.

And that very first day of camp last summer when Willie
came running up to me to get in line for lunch, here comes
George talking some simple stuff about "What a beautiful head
you have, Willie. A long, smooth, streamlined head. A sure sign
of superior gifts. Definitely genius **proportions.**" And poor Willie
went for it, grinning and carrying on and touching his head,
which if you want to know the truth is a bullet head and that's
all there is to it. And he's turning to me every which way, like
he's modeling his head in a fashion show. And the minute his
back is turned, ole George makes a face about Willie's head and
all the kids in the line bust out laughing. So I had to beat up a few
right then and there and finish off the rest later in the shower
for being so stupid, laughing at a kid with a romantic heart.

One night in the last week of August when the big campfire
party is held, it was very dark and the moon was all smoky, and
I just couldn't help myself and started in with a story about the

200   great caterpillar who was going to prowl through the tents and
nibble off everybody's toes. And Willie started this whimpering
in the back of his throat so I had to switch the story real quick
to something cheerful. But before I could do that, ole George
picked up my story and added a wicked witch who put spells
on city kids who come to camp, and a hunchback dwarf that
chopped up tents and bunk beds, and a one-eyed phantom giant
who gobbled up the hearts of underprivileged kids. And every
time he got to the part where the phantom ripped out a heart,
poor Willie would get louder and louder until finally he started
210   rolling around in the grass and screaming and all the kids went
crazy and scattered behind the rocks almost kicking the fire
completely out as they dashed off into the darkness yelling
bloody murder. And the counselors could hardly round us all
up—me, too, I'm not going to lie about it. Their little circles of
flashlight bobbing in and out of the bushes along the patches
of pine, bumping into each other as they scrambled for us kids.
And poor Willie rolling around something awful, so they took
him to the infirmary.

I was sneaking some gingersnaps in to him later that night when
220   I heard Mary and another senior counselor fussing at ole George
in the hallway.

"You've been picking on that kid ever since he got here,
George. But tonight was the limit—"

"I wasn't picking on him, I was just trying to tell a story—"

"All that talk about hearts, gobblin' up hearts, and
underpriv—"

"Yeh, you were directing it all at the little kid. You should
be—"

"I wasn't talking about him. They're all underprivileged
230   kids, after all. I mean all the kids are underprivileged."

I huddled back into the shadows and almost banged into
Willie's iron bed. I was hoping he'd open his eyes and wink at

CONNECT

Pause at line 230. In line
207 and in lines 225–230,
George uses the word
underprivileged to refer to
groups who have suffered
from poverty and discrimination. Do you think the children in the story understand
what George means? Why or
why not?

____

____

____

____

____

____

____

____

____

____

____

me and tell me he was just fooling. That it wasn't so bad to have an underprivileged heart. But he just slept. "I'm an underprivileged kid too," I thought to myself. I knew it was a special camp, but I'd never realized. No wonder Aunt Hazel screamed so about my scary stories and my mother flicked off the TV when the monsters came on and Mary was always shushing me. We all had bad hearts. I crawled into the supply cabinet to wait for

240 Willie to wake up so I could ask him about it all. I ate all the gingersnaps but I didn't feel any better. You have a romantic heart, I whispered to myself settling down among the bandages. You will have to be very careful.

It didn't make any difference to Aunt Hazel that I had changed, that I no longer told scary stories or dragged my schoolmates to the latest creature movie, or raced my friends to the edge of the roof, or held my breath, or ran under the train rail when the train was already in sight. As far as she was concerned, I was still the same ole spooky kid I'd always been. So Joanne was kept at

250 home. My mother noticed the difference, but she said over the phone to my grandmother, "She's acting very ladylike these days, growing up." I didn't tell her about my secret, that I knew about my heart. And I was kind of glad Joanne wasn't around 'cause I would have blabbed it all to her and scared her to death. When school starts again, I decided, I'll ask my teacher how to outgrow my underprivileged heart. I'll train myself, just like I did with the Fly family.

"Well, I guess you'll want some change to go to the fair again, hunh?" my mother said coming into my room dumping

260 things in her pocketbook.

"No," I said. "I'm too grown up for circuses." She put the money on the dresser anyway. I was lying, of course. I was thinking what a terrible strain it would be for Mrs. Perez and everybody else if while sitting there, with the Fly family zooming around in the open air a million miles above the ground, little

Harriet Watkins should drop dead with a fatal heart attack behind them.

"I lost," I said out loud.

"Lost what?"

270   "The battle with the Fly family."

She just stood there a long time looking at me, trying to figure me out, the way mothers are always doing but should know better. Then she kissed me goodbye and left for work.

MEET THE WRITER

Toni Cade Bambara (1939–1995) grew up in several New York City neighborhoods, including Harlem. Bambara's writing drew on the voices of her childhood: street-corner speechmakers, barbershop storytellers, and performers at Harlem's legendary Apollo Theater. The writer was deeply affected by her Harlem upbringing and spent much of her later life extolling the virtues of a strong community. Toni Cade adopted the name Bambara from a signature on a sketchbook she found in her great-grandmother's trunk. The Bambara are a people of northwestern Africa known for their skill in woodcarving.

INTERPRET

Pause at line 270. What does Harriet mean when she says she has lost her battle with the Fly family?

DRAW CONCLUSIONS

Think again about the story's title. Do you agree that Harriet's heart is delicate or "underprivileged"? If you disagree, then what words would you choose to describe Harriet's heart?

My Delicate Heart Condition

SKILLS FOCUS

Literary Skills
Analyze character.

Character Profile   To fully understand characters in a story, you take note of what they say and what they do, and you draw conclusions about them. Fill in the following chart with the conclusions you draw about Harriet, this story's narrator. Base your conclusions on her words and actions, which are cited in the left-hand column.

Harriet's Words and Actions	My Conclusions
"The truth is I sometimes like to tell stories about bloodthirsty vampires or ugly monsters that lurk in clothes closets or giant beetles that eat their way through the shower curtain. . . ."	
"And from the wheel of fortune to the tent was at least a million stands selling B.B. bats and jawbreakers and gingerbread and sweet potato pie and frozen custard. . . ."	
"I had to remind everyone at the table that Joanne was my first cousin by blood, and I would be forced to waste the first bum that laid a hand on her plate."	
"So I had to beat up a few right then and there and finish off the rest later in the shower for being so stupid, laughing at a kid with a romantic heart."	
"'I'm an underprivileged kid too.' . . . No wonder Aunt Hazel screamed so about my scary stories and my mother flicked off the TV when the monsters came on and Mary was always shushing me."	

Skills Review

My Delicate Heart Condition

VOCABULARY AND COMPREHENSION

A. Literal and Figurative Meaning   Circle the letter of each correct response.

1. The phrase "a battle of nerves"—

   A means that nerve cells are fighting

   B has nothing to do with nerves

   C suggests a mental and not a physical conflict

   D means that people are scared

2. When Harriet says she hopes to out-grow her "underprivileged heart," she is using **figurative language** to suggest that—

   A her heart is too small for her body

   B she wants to be brave again

   C she needs money for an operation

   D she may need a heart transplant

B. Vocabulary in Context   Fill in the blanks in the paragraph below with words from the Word Box, using context clues to help you.

Daniel's mouth watered when he saw the huge (1) ___________________ of the ice cream sundaes on the posters that were (2) ___________________ from each beam of the restaurant ceiling. It was hard to (3) ___________________ the misery of dieting. His (4) ___________________ place mat, empty of delights, was too much to bear.

<table>
<tr><td>Word Box</td></tr>
<tr><td>withstand</td></tr>
<tr><td>vacant</td></tr>
<tr><td>suspended</td></tr>
<tr><td>proportions</td></tr>
</table>

C. Reading Comprehension   Answer each question below.

1. What does Harriet do to scare the other children at camp?

   ____

   ____

2. What is Harriet's "battle" with the Fly family?

   ____

   ____

3. How has Harriet changed by the end of the story? Do you think she has really changed, or has just her behavior changed?

   ____

   ____

SKILLS FOCUS

Vocabulary Skills
Identify and interpret figurative language.

The One Who Watches

by Judith Ortiz Cofer

Do you know someone "larger than life"? In the short story "The One Who Watches," a young girl's best friend fits that description. But what happens when her friend's appetites grow larger than either of them can really afford?

LITERARY FOCUS: DIALOGUE

In "The One Who Watches," three characters—Yolanda, Doris, and Doris's mother—interact in revealing ways. The characters show themselves to one another and to the reader through **dialogue,** or conversation. As you read, notice what these characters say to each other—and what they don't say.

As you read, look for other details that bring the characters to life. For example, what do the characters' actions and appearances tell you about them? What does the setting tell you about them?

READING SKILLS: MAKING INFERENCES

An **inference** is an educated guess—a guess based on good evidence. When you make an inference, you use details in the text and your own experience to guess about something you don't know for sure.

For example, the writer may say, "My mother's voice sounded really sweet, like she was really singing the song for once." The writer doesn't tell you directly that the mother sometimes sings songs without passion, but based on what the writer has told you, you can infer that that has happened.

To make an inference:
- Look for details in the text.
- Relate the details to what you know about life.
- Make a careful guess.

Make inferences as you read "The One Who Watches." Look for clues that reveal important information about the characters. Then, read on to see how the characters develop.

Literary Skills
Understand how character traits are revealed through dialogue.

Reading Skills
Make inferences.

Vocabulary Skills
Understand synonyms and shades of meaning.

VOCABULARY DEVELOPMENT

PREVIEW SELECTION VOCABULARY

Review the following words from the story before you begin reading.

monstrous (män′strəs) *adj.:* horrible.

> *How can the guy in the purple skintight bodysuit have the nerve to call Yolanda's earrings* **monstrous**?

offended (ə·fend′id) *v.* used as *adj.:* displeased.

> *She could act annoyed—even outright* **offended**—*better than anybody I know.*

sautéing (sô·tā′iŋ) *v.* used as *adj.:* quick pan-frying.

> *She overcooked the fish,* **sautéing** *it too long.*

sentimental (sen′tə·ment″l) *adj.:* showing emotions such as love, pity, or sadness too strongly.

> *I don't like Yolanda to think I'm a* **sentimental** *pushover.*

CLARIFYING WORD MEANINGS: SYNONYMS

A **synonym** is a word that has the same or almost the same meaning as another word. Although synonyms sometimes share an exact meaning, often they have different shades of meaning. When writers are dissatisfied with a word, they may replace it with a synonym that expresses the meaning more exactly. When writers feel they have repeated a word too often, they may replace one of its uses with a synonym.

Synonyms/Shades of Meaning

Original Sentence	Synonyms for *surprised*
Doris was **surprised** by all the attention.	**shocked**—"extremely surprised" **amazed**—"filled with wonder" **astounded**—"bewildered with sudden surprise" **dumbfounded**—"speechless with amazement" **overwhelmed**—"overcome with emotion"

Replace *surprised* with each of the synonyms to see how the meaning and impact of the original sentence change.

Doris was _________________________ by all the attention.

The One Who Watches

Judith Ortiz Cofer

"Mira! Mira!"[1] my friend Yolanda yells out. She's always telling me to look at something. And I always do. I look, she does. That's the way it's always been. Yolanda just turned sixteen, I'm six months younger. I was born to follow the leader, that's what my mother says when she sees us together, and it's true.

It's like the world is a deli full of pricey treats to Yolanda, and she wants the most expensive ones in fancy boxes, the ones she can't afford. We spend hours shopping downtown. Sometimes when Yolanda gets excited about an outfit, we go

10 into the store and she tries it on. But the salespeople are getting to know us. They know we don't have any money. So we get chased out of places a lot. Yolanda always yells at the security man, "I've been thrown out of better places than this!" And we have.

One time Yolanda and I skipped school and took a bus into the city—just because Yolanda wanted to look around the big store on Thirty-fourth Street. They were having a teen fashion show that day, for all the rich girls in New York and their over-dressed mothers. And guess what? Yolanda sneaked into one of

20 the dressing rooms, with me following her, and she actually got

---

1. **mira:** Spanish for "look."

in line for one of the dresses being handed out by all these busy-looking women with tape measures around their necks who called all the girls "honey" and measured their chest, waist, and hips in about thirty seconds flat. Then this guy in a purple skintight body suit screeches out, "Hey, you!" and I nearly pass out, thinking we had gotten caught.

"Those earrings are **monstrous**!" he screams at Yolanda, who's wearing pink rubber fish earrings to match her pink-and-black-striped minidress.

30 "Here, try these!" He hands her a set of gold hoops in a very fancy black velvet box; then he screams at another model. I go into a dressing stall to hide and Yolanda runs in and sits on my lap, laughing her head off.

"Mira, Doris, mira." She shows me the earrings, which look like real gold. I hug Yolanda—I just love this girl. She's crazy and will try anything for fun.

I help Yolanda put on the dress she says she's going to model. The price tag inside says $350.00. It's my turn to say "Mira" to Yolanda. She shrugs.

40 "I ain't gonna steal it, Doris," she says. "I'm just gonna walk down that runway, like this." She walks out of the dressing room with one hand on a hip, looking like a real model in a green velvet dress, gold earrings, and her white sneakers. The man in the body suit runs up to her, screaming, "No, no! What do you think you're doing? Those shoes are monstrous!" He waves over one of the women with measuring tapes around their necks and has her take down Yolanda's shoe size. Soon I'm helping her try on shoes from a stack as tall as I am. She decides on black patent leather pumps.

50 There's such confusion back there that Yolanda doesn't get caught until the girls are lined up for the show to begin. Then nobody can find Yolanda on the list. She really does a good job of acting **offended** at all the trouble. I think it's her New Jersey Puerto Rican accent that gives her away. The others talk with

Stockbyte Photography/Veer.

Rubberball/Getty Images.

their noses way up in the air, sounding like they have a little congestion.

"Whaddaya mean my name ain't there?" Yolanda demands, sticking her nose up there in orbit too.

60   I just stand to the side and watch everything, pretending that it's a play and Yolanda is the star. I promise myself that if it gets too dangerous, I'll just slip out. See, I'm not flashy like Yolanda. I'm practically invisible. My hair is kinky, so I keep it greased down, and I'm short and plain. Not ugly, not beautiful. Just a nothing. If it wasn't for Yolanda, nobody would know I'm around. She's great, but she scares me, like the modeling thing at the store. I have enough problems without getting arrested. So I

tell myself that if the police come, I'll just make myself invisible and walk away. Then I'd be really alone. If Yolanda knew how scared I really am, she'd leave me anyway. Yolanda always says that nothing scares her except scared people. She says she hates a snitch worse than anything, and that's what scared people do, she tells me. They blame others for their troubles. That's why she dumped her last best friend, Connie Colón. Connie got scared when her mother found out she'd been skipping school with Yolanda, and told. Yolanda gets a cold look in her eyes when she talks about Connie, like she wants her dead. I don't want Yolanda to ever look at me that way.

Anyway, a big bossy woman came to lead us to her office on the top floor. It was bigger than my bedroom and her desk was at least the size of my bed. There was a rug under our feet that was as thick as a fur coat. From her window you could see most of New York. She looked at Yolanda with an expression on her face like I see on people walking by street people. It's like they want to ask them, "What are you doing on *my* sidewalk?" The lady didn't even look at me, so I glued myself to the gray wall.

"Young lady, do you realize that what you did today could be considered a crime?" She spoke very slowly, sounding out each word. I guess she knew by now that we were Puerto Rican and wanted to make sure we understood.

Yolanda didn't answer. They had made her take off the velvet dress, the shoes, and the earrings. The woman who carried them out with her fingertips put them in a plastic bag before handing them to this woman in front of us now.

Holding up the plastic bag in front of Yolanda, she asked another question: "Do you know how much money the things you took are worth?"

I watched Yolanda get up slowly from tying her shoestrings. She put on her pink fish earrings next without any hurry. Then she straightened out her tight skirt. She still looked offended. And maybe like she wanted a fight.

CHARACTER

In lines 69–72, we learn that Yolanda hates snitches because they are scared and they "blame others for their troubles." Are there any other reasons that Yolanda might hate snitches? Explain.

CHARACTER

Re-read lines 75–77, in which Doris describes Yolanda's "cold look." In your own words, describe what this "look" might be like. What does Doris's reaction to Yolanda's look tell you about Doris?

INFER

Re-read lines 90–93. What **inferences** can you make based on how the "bossy" woman handles Yolanda's things?

"I wasn't stealing your *theengs*," she said, imitating the woman's uptown accent.

"Then what were you doing in our dressing room, trying to disrupt the fashion show?"

"No. I was going to model the dress." Yolanda put her hands on her hips as if daring the woman to argue with her.

"Model? You wanted to model clothes *here*?" The woman laughed. "Young lady—"

"My name is Yolanda." Yolanda was getting angry, I could 110 tell by the way she made her eyes flash at the woman, like a cat getting ready to pounce. It was strange to watch Yolanda, who is barely five feet tall, facing off with this big woman in a gray suit and high heels.

"All right, Yolanda. Let me tell you something. You can't just decide to be a model, sneak into a dressing room, and go on a runway. These girls have been to modeling school. They have been practicing for weeks. Did you really think you could get away with this?" She was sounding angry now. I edged toward the door. "I'll tell you what. I'm not going to turn you 120 in. I'm going to have our security guard escort you outside. And I never want to see you in this store again. Look." She pointed to a camera practically invisible on the ceiling.

"We have pictures of you now, Yolanda." She finally looked over at me. "And of your partner there. If you come back, all I have to do is show them to the judge."

We were shown the way out to Thirty-fourth Street by the security guard, who looked just like any rich shopper in his wool sweater and expensive jeans. You never know who's watching you.

So Yolanda is telling the truth when she tells the store 130 people that we've been thrown out of better places. She's always looking for a better place to get thrown out of. But the Thirty-fourth Street store may be hard to beat.

That same day we went up to the eighty-sixth floor of the Empire State Building—it's just down the street from the store. Yolanda went all around the viewing deck like a child, yelling out, "Mira! Mira!" from every corner. She was feeling good.

At home there is always salsa music playing, but it's not because anyone is happy or feels like dancing. To my parents music is a job. They're both in a Latino music band called ¡Caliente![2] He plays the drums and she sings, so they're always listening to tapes. They play at the same barrio[3] club every night, the Caribbean Moon, and the regular customers want to hear new songs every week. So Mami sings along with the tapes, but she looks bored while she's doing it. Most of my life she stopped

---

2. **caliente:** Spanish for "hot."
3. **barrio:** neighborhood.

G.K. and Vikki Hart/Jupiter Images.

Re-read lines 143–153. What are the sounds in Doris's apartment? Underline the words and phrases that tell you. Based on these details, what statements could you make about Doris's life at home?

Colita/CORBIS.

sautéing (sô·tā′iŋ) *v.* used as *adj.:* quick pan-frying.

singing only to tell me to do something or to yell at me. My father doesn't say much. He's hardly ever around during the day; either he sleeps until the afternoon, since they play sets until three in the morning, or he goes down to the basement to practice his drums. The super of our building, Tito, is his

150 best friend and lets Papi keep his drums in a storage room near the washers and dryers. Our apartment has walls thin and crumbly as old cardboard, and if he tried to play drums in it they'd probably crash around our heads.

My mother is singing along with Celia Cruz, the old Cuban *salsera*,[4] when I come in. She's at the stove, **sautéing** some codfish. I can smell the olive oil simmering, but I'm not hungry.

---

4. *salsera:* Spanish for "salsa dancer."

Yolanda and I ate a whole bagful of butterscotch candy. She wouldn't tell me where she got it and I never saw her buy it, although I spent the whole day with her.

160   "*Hola,*[5] Doris, how's school?" my mother asks. But she doesn't look at me and she doesn't wait for me to answer. She just keeps on singing something about leaving the cold American city and going home to a lover in the sun. I stand there watching her; I'm feeling invisible again. The tape ends and she asks me where I've been, since school let out hours ago.

"New York."

She finally looks at me and smiles as if she doesn't believe me. "I bet you've been following that Yolanda around again. Niña, I'm telling you that señorita is trouble. She's trying to
170   grow up too fast, sabes?[6] Mira . . ." Mami takes my chin into her hand that smells like oregano and garlic and other Island spices. She looks really tired. She's short like me and we look a lot alike, but I don't think she's noticed. "Doris, tonight is not a school night, why don't you come to the club with us and listen to some music?" She's asked me to do that once a week for years, but I'm not interested in hanging out at a cheap nightclub with a bunch of drunks. Besides, I'd have to sit in the back the whole time because I'm a minor. In case the police do a check—I can slip out the kitchen door. When I was little, I had to go with
180   them a lot, and it wasn't fun. I'd rather stay home by myself.

I shake my head and go into my room. I put a pillow over my face so I won't hear the music and my mother singing about people in love and islands with beaches and sun.

I spend all day Saturday at Yolanda's. We have the place to ourselves because her mother works weekends. She believes in spiritism, so there are candles everywhere with things written on the glass jars like "For money and luck," and "For protection against your enemies," and "To bring your loved one home."

---

5. *hola:* Spanish for "hello."
6. **sabes:** Spanish for "you know."

INFER

Pause at line 159. What **inference** can you make about how Yolanda got the butterscotch candy? Underline the clues that support your inference.

INTERPRET

In lines 160–165, circle the words that identify how Doris is feeling. What words would *you* use to describe her feelings at this moment?

INFER

Pause at line 183. Doris doesn't want to hear her mother singing about love, islands, and sunny beaches. What can you infer about Doris and her mother's relationship based on this information?

In lines 194–217, there are clues regarding the **character** differences between Doris and Yolanda. These are evident in what each of them longs for. How would you describe Doris's needs and wants? How are they different from Yolanda's?

____

____

____

____

____

____

sentimental (sen′tə·ment″l) *adj.:* showing emotions such as love, pity, or sadness too strongly.

Doris is afraid Yolanda will think her a "sentimental baby." In its different shades of meaning, the word *sentimental* can indicate sweetness or foolishness. What shade of meaning does *sentimental* have in line 209? Explain.

____

____

____

____

190 She's got a little table set up as an altar with statues of *santos*[7] and the Virgin Mary, and a picture of her dead husband, Yolanda's father, who was killed during a robbery. Yolanda says she doesn't remember him that well anymore, even though it's only a couple of years since he died.

The place is stuffy with incense smells, and Yolanda tells me we are going shopping today.

"You got money?" I notice that she's wearing a big raincoat of her mother's. It's made of shiny bright green plastic and it has huge pockets. I start feeling a little sick to my stomach and almost tell her I'm going home to bed.

200 "I got what it takes, honey." Yolanda models the ugly raincoat for me by turning around and around in the small room.

We have to pass my apartment on our way out, and I can hear my mother singing an old song without the usual music tape accompanying her in the background. I stop to listen. It's "Cielito Lindo"[8]—a sort of lullaby that she used to sing to me when I was little. Her voice sounds sweet, like she is really into the song for once. Yolanda is standing in front of me with her hands on her hips, giving me a funny look like she thinks I'm a **sentimental** baby. Before she says something sarcastic, I run

210 down the stairs.

Yolanda is not just window-shopping today. She tells me that she's seen something she really wants. When we get to the store—one of the most expensive ones downtown—she shows me. It's a black beaded evening bag with a long strap. She puts it on over her shoulder.

"It's cute," I tell her, feeling sicker by the minute. I want to get out of the store fast, but I'm too weak to move.

"You really like it, Doris?" Yolanda unlatches the flap on the purse and takes out the crumpled paper in it. She reaches into

220 her pocket for a fistful of candy. "Want some?" In one motion she has stuffed the little bag into her coat pocket.

---

7.   *santos:* Spanish for "saints." Statues of santos are representations of a blend of traditions from Catholicism and African religions.
8.   **"Cielito Lindo":** informal Spanish for "sweetheart"; literally, "pretty little angel."

"Yolanda . . ." I finally begin to feel my legs under me. I am moving back, away from the scene that starts happening really fast in front of me, as if someone had yelled "Action!" on a movie set. Yolanda is standing there eating candy. I am moving backward even as she tries to hand me some. A man in a gray suit is moving toward her. I am now behind a rack of purses. I smell the leather. It reminds me of my father's drums that he used to let me play when I was little. Yolanda looks around, but she can't see me. I'm still moving back toward the light of the door. I know that I can't act scared, that I shouldn't run. People look at me. I know they can see me. I know where my arms are, where my legs are, where my head is. I am out on the street in the sun. A woman with a baby carriage bumps into me and says, "Excuse me!" She can see me! I hear a police car siren getting louder as I hurry across the street. I walk faster and faster until I am running and the world is going by so fast that I can't tell what anyone else is doing. I only hear my heart pounding in my chest.

When I crash through the door at home, Mami comes out of the bedroom looking like she just woke up from a deep sleep. I lie down on the sofa. I am sweating and shaking; a sick feeling in my stomach makes me want to curl up. Mami takes my head into her hands. Her fingers are warm and soft. "Are you sick, hija?"[9] I nod my head. Yes. I am sick. I am sick of following Yolanda into trouble. She has problems that make her act crazy. Maybe someday she'll work them out, but I have to start trying to figure out who I am and where I want to go before I can help anybody else. I don't tell my mother any of this. It's better if I just let her take care of me for a little while.

Even as she feels my forehead for fever, my mother can't help humming a tune. It's one I used to know. It's a song about being lonely, even in a crowd, and how that's the way life is for most people. But you have to keep watching out for love because it's out there waiting for you. That's the chorus, I mean. I keep

---

9. **hija:** Spanish for "daughter."

CHARACTER

Re-read lines 245–258. Doris has had realizations about her own **character** and about Yolanda's **character**. What are these realizations? How do you think these realizations will change Doris's attitude toward her friend— and toward herself?

Pause at the end of the story. Consider the story's title. One who is *watching* is often one who is *waiting.* What do you think Doris has been waiting for? Has it come to her by the end of this story? Explain.

my eyes closed until the words come back to me, until I know it by heart. And I know that I will keep watching but not just watching. Sometimes you have to run fast to catch love because it's hard to see, even when it's right in front of you. I say this

260   to Mami, who laughs and starts really singing. She is really into it now, singing like she was standing in front of hundreds of people in Carnegie Hall, even though I'm the only one here to hear her. The song is for me.

Judith Ortiz Cofer (1952–   ) moved with her family to New Jersey from Hormingueros, Puerto Rico, in 1956. Her father was in the United States Navy, and whenever he was out at sea, the family would travel back to Puerto Rico. Living in two cultures gave Cofer a unique childhood that would inspire her later writings. Cofer went on to receive her graduate degree in English and to teach literature and creative writing. Her novel, *The Line of the Sun,* nominated for a Pulitzer Prize, is based on her life growing up Puerto Rican in the United States. *The Latin Deli,* a collection of her fiction, poetry, and essays, also portrays Cofer's experience navigating two cultures. She is currently the Franklin Professor of English and Creative Writing at the University of Georgia.

Notes

The One Who Watches

Literary Skills
Analyze
character traits.

Character Traits Chart   In this story, much of what you learn about the **characters** is revealed through their actions and their words. Read the box of **character traits** below. Which traits apply to Doris? Which apply to Yolanda? List the traits in the correct columns in the chart below, and find details in the story to support your answers.

Character Traits				
nervous	doer	watchful	loud	flashy
plain	sarcastic	timid	aggressive	sensitive

Doris	Yolanda

Story Details	Story Details

Skills Review

The One Who Watches

VOCABULARY AND COMPREHENSION

A. Clarifying Word Meanings: Synonyms   Match the following words from the story with their synonyms—words that have the same or almost the same meaning.

Word Box

monstrous

offended

sautéing

sentimental

1. monstrous
2. offended
3. sautéing
4. sentimental

a. stir-frying
b. horrible
c. foolish
d. displeased

B. Reading Comprehension   Answer each question below.

1. What activities do Doris and Yolanda enjoy doing together?

   ____

   ____

2. Why did Yolanda stop being friends with her last best friend, Connie Colón?

   ____

   ____

3. Describe Doris's parents.

   ____

   ____

4. Why do Doris and Yolanda get evicted from the store on 34th Street?

   ____

   ____

5. Toward the end of the story, Doris says, "Sometimes you have to run fast to catch love because it's hard to see. . . . " What does she mean?

   ____

   ____

   ____

SKILLS FOCUS

Vocabulary Skills
Analyze shades of meaning of synonyms.

Narrator and Voice

Colin McPherson/CORBIS.

Academic Vocabulary for Collection 3

These are the terms you should know
as you read and analyze the selections in this collection.

———

Narrator The voice telling a story. A narrator tells a story from one of three points of view.

- In a story told from the **omniscient** (äm·nish′ənt) **point of view,** the narrator can tell us everything about the characters, including how they think and feel. This narrator is not a character in the story.
- A **first-person** narrator is a character who participates directly in the story's action and refers to himself or herself as "I" or "me." In a story told from the first-person point of view, the reader knows only what this narrator knows and chooses to reveal. Some first-person narrators are **credible,** or trustworthy. Others are **unreliable;** they may not always tell the truth about characters or events in the story.
- Like an omniscient narrator, a **third-person-limited narrator** is not a character in the story. This narrator, however, focuses on a single character's actions and feelings.

Diction The writer's choice of words.

Tone The writer's attitude toward the subject of the story, toward a character, or toward the audience (the readers). A story's tone can be described with words such as *humorous, serious, sad, sarcastic,* and *sympathetic.*

Voice The writer's use of language and overall style, created by tone and choice of words.

The Lesson by Dianne E. Dixon

Can you remember a teacher who taught you something important, something you will never forget? The lesson Dianne Dixon learns in sixth grade isn't one you might expect.

LITERARY FOCUS: NARRATOR AND VOICE

This **essay** is told by a **first-person narrator.** Dianne Dixon, the author, is the "I" in the story. She relates an experience that had a major impact on her life and, in the process, tells us about herself.

A narrator's **voice** is created by the combination of his or her **diction** (word choice) and **tone** (the author's attitude toward characters, the subject, and the events that make up the plot). As you read this selection, note Dianne's attitude, which ranges between lighthearted, direct, angry, and musing. Look to see what word choices she makes to communicate her attitude.

READING SKILLS: COMPARING AND CONTRASTING

When you make comparisons, you are looking for similarities. When you note contrasts, you are looking for differences.
- When authors **compare** subjects, characters, or ideas, the authors draw attention to an aspect or quality the subjects, characters, or ideas share.
- When authors **contrast** subjects, characters, or ideas, the authors draw attention to an aspect or quality only one possesses or to the distance between them.

As you read "The Lesson," look for instances of comparison and of contrast, and then note the tone they set and the message they communicate.

Literary Skills
Understand
first-person
narrator.
Understand
voice.

**Reading
Skills**
Understand
comparison and
contrast.

**Vocabulary
Skills**
Understand
connotation and
denotation.

VOCABULARY DEVELOPMENT

PREVIEW SELECTION VOCABULARY

Before you read "The Lesson," get to know these words from the essay.

transported (trans·pôrt′id) *v.:* taken; carried.

> *The writer is **transported** into the past by her memories.*

audacity (ô·das′ə·tē) *n.:* insolence; excessive boldness.

> *Mr. Perlman is infuriated by what he sees as Dianne's **audacity**.*

predominantly (prē·däm′ə·nənt·lē) *adv.:* mainly.

> *The student population in Dianne's new school is **predominantly** white.*

agitated (aj′i·tāt′id) *adj.:* excited; upset; disturbed.

> *Mr. Perlman becomes **agitated** when Dianne defends herself.*

pathetic (pə·thet′ik) *adj.:* deserving of scornful pity.

> *Mr. Perlman declares Nat's grammar **pathetic**.*

atrocious (ə·trō′shəs) *adj.:* exceptionally bad.

> *He also considers Nat's spelling **atrocious**.*

CONNOTATION AND DENOTATION

The **connotations** of a word are the meanings, associations, or emotions attached to the word beyond its literal meaning. The connotations of a word are different from its **denotation,** or dictionary definition.

Connotation is an important part of word choice, or diction. Writers use different types of words depending on their audience, their subject, and the effect they are trying to produce. For example, someone who is *upset* may frown; someone who is *agitated* may pace, fidget, or shout. Even though both *upset* and *agitated* have the same denotation, *agitated* conveys greater emotional intensity.

Writers choose words carefully for connotations that create a specific tone. As you read "The Lesson," notice how Dianne Dixon's diction helps her create a precise and powerful narrative.

The Lesson

Dianne E. Dixon

Often when I sit down to write, I am **transported** momentarily back to the sixth grade. It was 1969. One year earlier, Dr. Martin Luther King, Jr., had been murdered, and fifteen years before that, the United States Supreme Court had delivered the landmark *Brown v. Board of Education of Topeka* decision. Throughout the country, people were protesting against racism while black children were being attacked on school buses for having the **audacity** to attend white schools.

In Bedford-Stuyvesant, Brooklyn, where I lived, racism was something that I had only seen on TV or heard about in my parents' stories of growing up in the South. I had graduated from an all-black elementary school two blocks from my home, where the majority of my teachers were black and their expectations that I and my classmates would succeed had been both obvious and uplifting. In the school where I attended sixth grade, everything changed.

It seemed like my mother had called every school official in the city to make sure I got into that school. I overheard her explain to my aunt, "Dianne is a bright girl. That school is the nearest one to us with a program for gifted kids. I know it's a long ride on the bus, and I know she will have to get up real early to get there on time. But they have smaller classes and newer equipment—and why shouldn't our kids get the best that's out there?" So, with little fanfare, I boarded the city bus alone every day and rode for fifty minutes to a **predominantly** white school, in an all-white neighborhood, with all-white teachers. Mr. Perlman was one of those teachers, and I still remember the lessons he taught me.

Cone 6 Productions/Jupiter Images.

"Well, Miss Dixon, I had hoped that you would do better
than this," Mr. Perlman sneered as he handed me back my writing assignment. The bright red F on the first page of my paper
was so large that I was sure everyone in the class had seen it. An
F. An F! I had never gotten an F before. I shoved my paper inside
my notebook and tried not to look around to see who was
watching me. I knew, of course, that Nancy Cicero had seen the
F. How could she miss it? She was sitting right next to me.

"Good job, Nancy!" Mr. Perlman made a point of saying as
he handed Nancy back her paper with a normal-sized B+ on it.

"Thank you, Mr. Perlman," she said. And then, turning to
me, she said, "I didn't think I was going to do well on this paper
at all. I didn't write it until the night before we had to hand it in.
What did you get, Dianne?"

INFER

Circle the word in line 30 that describes Mr. Perlman's tone. From this single word, how would you describe Mr. Perlman? Underline other details that support your inference.

Pause at line 62. Dianne and Nat have several things in common. What draws them together?

____

____

____

INFER

Lines 55–62 give important information about Dianne's experience at this school. Underline the words that give this information. Does Mr. Perlman create her only difficulty? Are her feelings portrayed through direct (telling) or indirect (showing) writing strategies? Explain.

____

____

____

____

____

VOCABULARY

agitated (aj′i·tāt′id) *adj.:* excited; upset; disturbed.

How would the **tone** of the sentence in line 73 change if *agitated* were replaced with *concerned*?

____

____

____

"A headache," I answered, turning my head to look out the window.

"Those of you who received a D or lower, please see me after the bell rings," Mr. Perlman announced, looking directly at me.

"Well, I guess you'll have to stick around, won't you, Dianne?" Nancy laughed.

50   "Drop dead, Nancy," I shot back.

I waited to see who the other kids with bad grades would be, gathering around Mr. Perlman's desk. But only one kid remained with me. It was Nat, the only other black kid in my class. I didn't know what I would have done had I not had him to talk to. The kids in the other classes—even the few black ones—hated us for being in the gifted program. And the kids in our gifted class acted like we didn't exist. It was because of Nat that I tried to ignore my Sunday night headaches and the nosebleeds that I so often got on Monday mornings. And it

60   was because of him that I tried never to be absent from school. I couldn't do that to Nat, and I knew he wouldn't do it to me. We both had perfect attendance records.

After class I asked Mr. Perlman what I had done wrong on the assignment.

"Well, for one thing, you didn't write on the topic I assigned the class. Do you remember what it was supposed to be?"

"Yeah, I remember," I said. "You told us to write an essay about an event in our lives that changed the way others viewed us."

"And what did you write about?"

70   I told him what he already knew, that I had written about the double-Dutch contest between me and my friend Charlene the preceding summer.

He became **agitated.** "You see? You see what I mean? Now what has *that* got to do with the assignment I gave? You write about a rope jumping contest which, I might add, you didn't even win."

"No, I didn't win it," I agreed, "but I was new on the block and when I stood up to Charlene's rope-jumping challenge, everybody stopped thinking of me as an outsider."

80   My explanation had not moved Mr. Perlman. He just sucked his teeth and rolled his tiny blue eyes at me. "Listen, Dianne, if you intend to pass this class, you are going to have to do the assignments properly. And that goes for you, too, Nathaniel. Your grammar is **pathetic,** surpassed only by your **atrocious** spelling."

    Nat said nothing. He just stared at Mr. Perlman, but I could see he was mad.

    "I want the two of you to read chapters seven through nine in your writing textbooks and answer the questions at the end

90 of each chapter. Maybe by reading some information on essay writing, you'll get it. Now, tomorrow I'm going to ask a few of the students to read their essays to the class to illustrate the proper way the assignment should have been done. Be sure to listen carefully. In fact, I'll be doing this for the rest of the school year, so you'll get to hear lots of good writing."

    Nat and I tried to ignore the fact that Mr. Perlman was really telling us that he thought we could never write anything good enough to read to the class, and that all we could ever hope to do well was listen. In the hall, as we walked to our lockers,

100 Nat exploded. He hated Mr. Perlman for always picking on us. He seemed to enjoy telling people on the sly how Nat and I didn't belong in the gifted program. The fact that both of us had been in gifted classes our entire school lives and that we performed well above average on every test put in front of us seemed to escape him.

    The next day, instead of waiting until the end of class, Mr. Perlman asked for the homework assignment he had given Nat and me as soon as everybody had taken their seats. With every-one watching, we had to walk up to Mr. Perlman's desk and

110 hand in our work. We both knew that Mr. Perlman wanted to

---

VOCABULARY

pathetic (pə·thet′ik) *adj.:* deserving of scornful pity.

atrocious (ə·trō′shəs) *adj.:* exceptionally bad.

COMPARE & CONTRAST

Pause here, and re-read lines 91–99. What is the expectation Mr. Perlman communicates? Does it stand in comparison with or in contrast with the expectations of Dianne's previous teachers?

____

____

____

____

____

CHARACTER

What is Mr. Perlman's motivation for telling others that Nat and Dianne don't belong in the gifted program? Explain.

____

____

____

____

____

____

____

embarrass us, but I refused to give him the satisfaction. I held my head up high, put a smile on my face, and handed him the homework, saying, "Here, Mr. Perlman. It really helped. Thanks." Watching his face turn red made my smile genuine.

Before Nat and I could return to our seats, Mr. Perlman told the class that he was giving another writing assignment. "I want to see those creative juices flowing," he said. "There is no particular topic on which you must write, which should make the assignment easier for some of you," he said, looking directly at me. All papers are due on Monday, so you have the entire weekend to create your masterpiece. Are there any questions?"

When no hands went up, Mr. Perlman began the day's exercise. But I didn't listen to anything he was saying. I was excited about the opportunity to show Mr. Perlman how I could write. Since no specific topic was required, nothing I wrote could be wrong. Here was my chance, and Nat's too, to prove to Mr. Perlman and the class that we belonged there. Maybe then Mr. Perlman would treat us like the other kids.

After school I asked Nat what he was going to write about. He wrinkled his face and shrugged his shoulders like he was trying really hard to come up with an answer. Then he smiled. "I don't know, Dianne, but maybe I'll write a murder mystery with Mr. Perlman as the corpse."

I shook my head. I really wanted to come up with a good topic. Nat was somewhat less enthusiastic. "You know, whatever we do, Mr. Perlman is going to hate it."

But I insisted that this time had to be different. "This time we can write anything. If we just double-check our grammar and spelling—"

"—Why do *we* have to dot every I and cross every T?" Nat interrupted me.

He had a point, but I was certain that if we did a good job on the paper Mr. Perlman would not have any excuse to treat us differently from the rest of the class.

Nat just looked at me and said nothing.

By the time I reached home I had my topic. I had seen twin girls on the bus. They made me wonder what it would be like to have a twin, and so I decided to write about twin sisters. I shouted a hello to my mother and ran to my room to change
150 my clothes and begin writing. At first, all I could do was stare at the paper and chew my pencil eraser. I knew I wanted to write something about twin sisters, but what exactly? At dinner that night I stared at my plate, mad at myself for not having come up with an adventure for my twins.

I barely heard my father speaking to me. "Dianne, that food on your plate did not do a thing to you, so why are you giving it such a dirty look?"

"I'm not that hungry, Dad."

He looked at my mother for explanation, but she offered
160 none. "Are you feeling okay, Dianne?"

"Yeah, I'm okay. I'm just thinking about something," I said.

"Uh-huh. Well, try eating some of those black-eyed peas on your plate. Don't you know that black-eyed peas are good for thinking?" He teased me further. "Yeah, black-eyed peas—not fish—is the real brain food."

"Black-eyed peas, huh, Daddy?"

"That's right. I heard tell that George Washington Carver himself used to eat a bowl of black-eyed peas every day. That's how come he was able to make his discoveries about the peanut
170 and the sweet potato. A lot of people don't know that."

"I bet they don't," I said, laughing and scooping up a forkful of the new brain food. Then it hit me. Why not make my twins geniuses like George Washington Carver? Why not have them discover something, as he did? I quickly finished my dinner, making sure to eat my black-eyed peas, and rushed back to my room. This time, when I sat down to write, the words began to flow. I wrote for hours, until I was so sleepy I had to go to bed.

I spent Sunday, after church, cleaning up my grammar and spelling. I wasn't going to let Mr. Perlman use that excuse to
180 keep from giving me an A.

Imagine for a moment that you are an **omniscient narrator** and can let the reader into the mind of Dianne's father. What is he thinking during the scene in lines 155–177? Connect his thoughts and his motivation to tell the story about the black-eyed peas.

Notes

Monday morning, Nat was waiting for me in front of the school building when I got off the bus. We exchanged stories, sitting on the steps. His story was good, and what impressed me even more was that Nat said it was true. He had written about his grandparents, who were threatened by the Ku Klux Klan after refusing to sell their land in South Carolina to a white farmer who wanted it, but they were able to defend themselves and keep their land.

I asked Nat what he thought of my story. When he told 190 me that he really liked it, I thought we both had Mr. Perlman this time.

We hurried into the building to beat the late bell. That was probably the first time that I had actually looked forward to Mr. Perlman's class. But by the time the bell rang, I began to have some doubts. I kept thinking of different ways I could have written my story. We barely had a chance to take our seats before Mr. Perlman demanded our assignments. He announced that he would return them that Friday. Great! All I had to do was make it to Friday.

200 The week just dragged. Nat kept telling me not to worry, that we were sure to do well. But nothing he said could make the sickly feeling in my stomach go away. The more I tried to put the story out of my mind, the more I thought about nothing else. Every day I tried to read the expression on Mr. Perlman's face for some clue about whether he had read and liked my story. Was he smiling at me or was that a sneer? It was hard to tell with his thin lips. Finally, Friday came.

Nat made a point of telling me that we were going to get our papers back that day. I rolled my eyes at him. Like I needed 210 him to remind me about Friday. I asked him what grade he thought we would get on our papers. He frowned for a moment and then laughed. "Knowing Mr. Perlman, I bet he didn't like me putting down the Ku Klux Klan. And in your story the black girls are smart, which he probably didn't like either, so we'll both only get C's. But, hey, a C is better than an F."

I didn't laugh.

When the bell rang, my heart jumped. This was it. I stared at Mr. Perlman's face as I entered the classroom. Was he happy, upset, aggravated, excited? I couldn't tell. I took my seat next to Nancy Cicero and waited for the verdict.

"Settle down, please, everyone." I have your papers to return, and I must say there were some interesting stories from some of you. Of course, others showed no improvement at all."

Was he looking at me when he said that?

He walked around the classroom handing back the papers and making his usual comments. "Well done, Rebecca. George, watch your spelling. Nice job, Nancy."

Nancy smiled and laid her story on her desk to make sure I saw her B.

Mr. Perlman gave Nat back his story without saying a word. Nat looked at his paper and shrugged. Then he looked at me, holding up the title page to show me the C+ scribbled across the top. We both knew that Nat deserved better. There was not one red mark for grammar or spelling corrections, so why the C+? I shook my head and frowned. Things didn't look good for me, and I began to get angry.

When Mr. Perlman walked to the front of the classroom to announce the names of the students who would read their work to the class, I was surprised. He hadn't given me back my paper yet. I wondered how it could be so bad that he wouldn't even return it, but then I remembered that he had given me back my other assignment with the huge red F on it without blinking an eye. So where was my paper now? When he called out my name, I sat frozen. He had included me with the students who would read their papers to the class.

Nancy Cicero's mouth dropped open. She seemed to be more in shock than I was.

I watched as, one by one, the four other kids whose names had been called before mine read their stories. I watched them, but I couldn't listen to them read. I was too excited.

Read the boxed section once silently and then twice aloud. Pay special attention to the two voices: Dianne's narrating voice and Mr. Perlman's voice. Be sure to infuse the words with the tone the author intended, ranging from the nervousness and anxiety the narrator feels to Mr. Perlman's friendliness toward the other students.

Notes

220
230
240
250

Anderson Ross/Getty Images.

INFER

In line 251, Dianne assumes that Mr. Perlman asks her to read her paper because he thinks it is good. Underline clues the writer gives to show you that this is not so. Pause for a moment, and make a prediction about what is actually happening.

____

____

____

____

____

____

I was going to read my story to the class! He wanted *me* to read my story to the class! I was glad that I had put so much work into the writing.

Mr. Perlman stood, holding out my paper to me. "All right, Miss Dixon, we will hear from you now."

I smiled at him as I took it from his hands. I noticed that there was no grade on it, but I didn't think much about that. I looked up at the class, smiling so hard my cheeks hurt. I looked at Nat. He raised his fist halfway and mouthed the words "Way 260 to go, Dianne!" to me. I was enjoying this.

I began reading my story to the class. It was about my genius twins. I had given them telepathic° powers, but only between each other. They had discovered a cure for cancer from their experiments with black-eyed peas. One of the girls was

____

° **telepathic** (tel'ə·path'ik) *adj.:* communicated through means other than the normal senses; in this case, through mind reading.

kidnapped by the owners of a large drug company, who tried to force her to hand over the cancer cure. They wanted to develop an expensive pharmaceutical from the natural black-eyed peas cure so that they could make a lot of money. But the girls out-smarted the kidnappers. They sent telepathic messages to each other so that the police had no trouble finding the kidnappers' hideout. At the end of the story, I had the twins broadcast their experiments on the news so that everyone would know what the cure was and no drug company would be able to cheat people out of it.

When I finished reading my story, I looked up to see the expressions on the other kids' faces. They were smiling. And then they did something that I never would have expected. They began to clap. They were actually clapping for my story! All except Nancy Cicero, of course.

I looked at Nat and watched him put two fingers in his mouth and whistle, loud. Then I turned my head to look at Mr. Perlman. I wanted to see the face that I usually tried to avoid. I wanted to see what those thin lips looked like when they formed a smile. He stood glaring at me with his hands on his hips and his head tilted to one side. He was squinting his tiny blue eyes, and his lips were pinched tightly together. He cleared his throat and then spoke.

"Well, well, well, Dianne. That was quite some story. Yes, a very good story in fact. And, as you can see, the whole class enjoyed it. They even clapped for you. So perhaps you will tell us who the author is so that we can give him or her proper credit."

At first I couldn't stop blinking my eyes, as though opening and closing them could somehow change what I had just heard. I was sure I had misunderstood.

"You heard me. We're all waiting. Whose book did you copy that story from? I know *you* couldn't have written that yourself."

IDENTIFY

In this section of the story, Dianne receives two un-expected reactions to her story. What does the reaction of the students show you about Dianne's story and about the other students in the class?

Describe Mr. Perlman's
reaction to Dianne's story
and its effect on the other
students. Is the author
comparing or contrasting
the two surprises?

____

____

____

INTERPRET

At this moment, Dianne
learns the lesson referred to
in the title of the story.
Explain what she learns and
what she does about it.

____

____

____

____

____

EXPAND

When this episode took place,
Dianne was a sixth-grader in
the 1960s, isolated in her situation and publicly shamed.
Think about the courage it
took for a young girl to challenge an adult the way she
did. How common an event
do you suppose this was?

____

____

____

I began to shake. I felt cold. My stomach churned and I half
hoped I would vomit . . . yeah, vomit right now in Mr. Perlman's
300 face.

I was holding my story in my hand at my side, and slowly
I began to crumple it between my fingers, rolling it against my
thigh until all six pages were nothing more than a huge ball in
my clenched fist.

I looked around the classroom. I could tell from my classmates' expressions that they all believed I had copied my story
out of a book. Nancy Cicero was looking smug, as if to say, "I
knew you couldn't have written it."

I looked at Nat. He was mad. He was clutching the edge
310 of his desk and staring at Mr. Perlman. I turned back to Mr.
Perlman and let out all my feelings of anger and frustration.

"I wrote this story myself," I said through clenched teeth,
softly at first. I was not even sure I had spoken.

Mr. Perlman smiled. "Excuse me, Dianne, you said something?"

"I said I wrote this story myself!" I was yelling. I couldn't
hold it in. I struggled to keep from crying in shame and embarrassment. I refused to give him that.

"That's right, Mr. Perlman . . . me, I wrote this. I know why
320 that's so hard for *you* to believe, but that's your problem. I bet if
I showed you all the drafts and rewriting I went through to get
to this story, you still wouldn't be satisfied, would you Mr.
Perlman? Do you want to ask my mother who wrote this, huh?
Would you like to ask both my parents about this? I'll tell them
to come here and see you. In fact, I want them to come. I think
it's time they talked to you—and maybe the principal too—
about the way you treat me and Nat. Is that what you want?"

The room was silent. Mr. Perlman's mouth hung open, but
he recovered quickly.

330 "There's no need to speak with your parents or anybody
else's. Evidently the homework assignment I gave you and

Nathaniel to do after the last writing assignment paid off. You see that, class? It is possible to improve your writing by paying attention to the . . . ah . . . instructions in your texts. If Dianne can improve her writing, anyone can. Thank you, Dianne. You may take your seat now."

I didn't move.

Mr. Perlman glared at me, folding his arms across his chest.

"I said you may sit down, Dianne. We've heard quite
340   enough from you for one day."

I didn't move.

"What are you waiting for, a handwritten invitation?" Mr. Perlman appeared nervous.

"No," I said. "I'm waiting for my grade. You didn't give me a grade for my story."

I walked over to him and shoved the ball of paper into his hands. He just looked at it at first, and then he looked at me. Slowly, he unwrapped the ball, smoothing out the pages. He walked over to his desk to pick up a pen. He reached out his
350   hand for the red one and then stopped. He glanced back at me and then at the class, pausing for only a moment to look at Nat. He quickly picked up his blue ballpoint pen and scribbled across the top of my paper. Then he shoved the pages back into my hand, a sneer forming at the corners of his mouth.

I took back the pages and walked slowly to my seat. Sitting down next to Nancy, I spread my story out on my desk. I looked at the mark, not quite sure what to feel, until I caught her expression. Then I smiled as I watched her quickly turn her head so as not to see the A— just above the title.

360   I can still see her now . . . Mr. Perlman too. And I have often wondered how much of my experience in that sixth-grade class has shaped the person I have become. I suppose some credit must be due to Mr. Perlman for my decision to become a civil rights lawyer, a published writer of both fiction and non-fiction, and a teacher of legal writing. Perhaps, then, I have

ANALYZE

What do you find surprising about Mr. Perlman's response? Why do you suppose he behaves the way he does?

Re-read lines 368–369, in which Dianne describes the impact of Mr. Perlman's behavior. Then, read "Meet the Writer." What do you think she means to say in this sentence?

EXPAND

learned that even the most negative of circumstances can yield positive consequences. But he deserves much more "credit" than that, for I have also learned to be deeply suspicious of an entire group of people, based solely on their skin color. In the end, that

370 is a lesson no eleven-year-old, or anyone else for that matter, should ever have to learn.

MEET THE WRITER

Dianne Dixon is currently the executive director of the Access to Justice Center, in New York City, an organization that provides legal assistance to people who cannot afford it. She says that if she had not become an attorney, she would have become a full-time writer so that she could use the power of literature to inspire people to work for change. As a sixth-grader, Dixon demanded the equality promised to her by the law; as an adult, she is committed to helping other people do the same.

The Lesson

Narrator Questionnaire   This autobiographical selection is told by a first-person narrator. Fill out this chart to examine the way **point of view** affects tone and characterization.

Literary Skills
Understand
first-person
narrator.

1. What descriptions of other people's reactions has Dixon included to add to the credibility of her account? Explain.

2. How would the **tone** of this essay be different if it were told from the point of view of an **omniscient narrator,** one who knows and can reveal the thoughts and feelings of all the characters?

3. How would the **tone** of this essay be different if it were told from the point of view of a **third-person-limited narrator** describing the thoughts and feelings *only* of Nat?

Skills Review

The Lesson

VOCABULARY AND COMPREHENSION

Word Box

transported

audacity

predominantly

agitated

pathetic

atrocious

A. Evaluating Word Connotations   Fill in each blank with a word from the Word Box. Then, decide whether the connotations of the word are positive, neutral, or negative, and check the appropriate box. Be aware that not everyone will agree on the connotation of a word.

1. Kisha's brother was amazed at her ________________ when she refused to help clear the table.
   ☐ positive   ☐ neutral   ☐ negative

2. Father left the restaurant in disgust, complaining that the food was ________________.
   ☐ positive   ☐ neutral   ☐ negative

3. The hockey coach wondered how to get the team's equipment ________________ to their out-of-state playoff game.
   ☐ positive   ☐ neutral   ☐ negative

4. Joanne thought the weak little puppy was ________________, but Marty fell in love as he gazed into its big, soulful eyes.
   ☐ positive   ☐ neutral   ☐ negative

5. Hunting in vain for her notebook, Natalie became more and more ________________.
   ☐ positive   ☐ neutral   ☐ negative

6. The audience at the rock concert was ________________ under the age of eighteen.
   ☐ positive   ☐ neutral   ☐ negative

B. Reading Comprehension   Answer each question below.

1. What is unusual about the lesson Dianne describes in this selection?

   ____

   ____

2. How did this lesson help Dianne Dixon pursue her life's work?

   ____

   ____

SKILLS FOCUS

Vocabulary Skills
Evaluate connotations.

Mr. Shaabi by Pnina Kass

LITERARY FOCUS: NARRATOR'S POINT OF VIEW

A story told from the narrator's **point of view** is told in the first person. That person is either a **credible** or an **unreliable narrator.** In the story "Mr. Shaabi," you see the world and experience events as Mahdi, the narrator, does. Because he is a first-person narrator, Mahdi can tell us only what he knows and experiences himself. As you read, think about whether Mahdi is a credible, or believable, narrator. Is what he tells you accurate?

READING SKILLS: READ FOR DETAILS

Successful readers read, and re-read, and re-read some more. They know that it's nearly impossible to understand any piece of literature fully after just one reading. There are many reasons for re-reading a text. Re-reading can help you

- refresh your memory about characters and events
- clear up any misunderstandings or confusion
- deepen your understanding of a story's symbols or themes

After you read "Mr. Shaabi," think of questions you have about the story. Then, re-read the story, looking for answers to your questions.

Literary Skills
Understand the narrator's point of view. Understand whether the person telling the story is a credible narrator.

Reading Skills
Read for details.

Vocabulary Skills
Understand archaic expressions.

VOCABULARY DEVELOPMENT

PREVIEW SELECTION VOCABULARY

The following lines from Shakespeare's play *The Tragedy of King Richard III* are quoted in "Mr. Shaabi." Look them over before you begin the story.

- Phrase: "Now is the winter of our discontent / Made glorious summer. . . ."
- Meaning: The time of unhappiness is past.

- Phrase: "To fright the souls of fearful adversaries"
- Meaning: to scare an enemy

WORD ORIGINS: ARCHAIC PHRASES

Archaic phrases are phrases that are no longer in common use. In Shakespeare's writing you will find unfamiliar phrases that have passed out of use altogether, as well as phrases that are now so well known that they have a life separate from the text. "Now is the winter of our discontent" is one of these often-quoted phrases.

Mr. Shaabi

Pnina Kass

BACKGROUND: Literature and Social Studies
This story takes place during a time of strife in Iraq, when warlike conditions were part of everyday life. It tells of an inspirational Jewish teacher who helps his Muslim students cope during these trying times.

The polished willow branch in Mr. Shaabi's hand tapped out the rhythm while we chanted the words: Now - is - the - winter - of - our - discon - tent.[1]

"No, no," he shouted in irritation. He buttoned and unbuttoned his jacket. "You say these words as if they have no meaning. This is Shakespeare, the greatest poet and playwright the world has known."

A hot wind, carrying the smell of gasoline and burnt rubber,[2] blew through the broken glass of the classroom window. My notebook pages fluttered. I laid a ruler across the two sheets of my English lesson to hold them down.

"Who was the greatest playwright, Mahdi?"

"Shay Kesa-peer," I answered.

"One word, Mahdi, one word. This great Englishman's name is one word—Shakespeare. We will recite this famous speech again."

For thirty years Mr. Shaabi had been teaching English in the Saladdin Comprehensive School. My brother and my cousins

---

1. **Now . . . discontent:** famous first line of *Richard III* by William Shakespeare.
2. **smell of gasoline and burnt rubber:** Tires are often set on fire during protests.

IDENTIFY

Circle the name of the character introduced in the opening line of this story.

IDENTIFY

In line 12, circle the name of the **narrator** of this story.

INFER

Richard III is set in England during the War of the Roses. What connection do you see between that play and this story? Explain.

had been his students. In all those years he never failed to appear, at eight o'clock in the morning, in his jacket and tie. "This is the way a teacher at Oxford greets his students," he would say. "Proper dress shows respect."

Only on the Jewish holy Day of Atonement[3] did he stay home. After the last war his wife took their two daughters and immigrated to Canada, wanting only peace and quiet. But Mr. Shaabi remained. He said nothing. Only Mr. Nurredin, the principal, received an explanation: "My family and ancestors have lived near the Euphrates[4] for centuries, as far back as 597 B.C. I will not dishonor my history by leaving this city or abandoning my students. Even if I have to live alone."

"Again," Mr. Shaabi said.

Once more eleven of us chanted to the rhythm of the willow branch going up and down: "Now - is - the - winter - of - our - dis - con - tent. Made - glori - ous - sum - mer - by . . ."

The words on my notebook page were black dots, meaningless. All I could think about was tonight. Tonight the bombs would fall again. The television and the radio said we were victorious but the foreign news announced that in twenty-four hours the foreign soldiers,[5] the conquerors, would enter the city. If they came I would shout, "There is nothing for you on my street. Look, everything has tilted or fallen or crumbled or broken or shattered or burned or cracked or twisted or exploded."

I would say to the soldiers, in the English Mr. Shaabi had taught me, "Please leave us alone. My father is an accountant, my mother does sewing at home, my brother is a university student, and I am at the Comprehensive School and my sister is a little girl of five. Only us, we are the only ones left. See, the

---

3. **Jewish holy Day of Atonement:** Yom Kippur, the holiest day of the year for Jews, on which people fast and pray.
4. **Euphrates** (yōō·frāt′ēz): longest river in western Asia, flowing from Turkey to Iraq.
5. **foreign soldiers:** American soldiers taking part in Operation Iraqi Freedom.

Nik Wheeler/CORBIS

building is empty. The other six families in our apartment house packed up what they could carry and left for villages outside the city."

But meanwhile here I was, many streets away, sitting in a classroom, listening to Mr. Shaabi drone on in his perfect English accent as if nothing was happening. By tomorrow I could be dead. And my parents, and my brother and my little sister. It was inevitable. Maybe it was even the will of Allah.

To - fright - the - souls - of - fear - ful - ad - ver - saries. Wasn't Mr. Shaabi afraid? Did he think reciting *Richard III* would save us? The air raid siren began to wail.

In lines 51–55, Mahdi expresses his belief that Mr. Shaabi behaves as if nothing is happening in the world outside the classroom. From what you have learned about Mr. Shaabi so far, do you agree with Mahdi? Explain.

60
I looked up from the page; we all looked up. The willow branch in Mr. Shaabi's hand trembled. "None of you have time to get home safely. Take your things and follow me. Quickly."

I grabbed my schoolbag, my notebook. The ruler clattered to the floor. Out of habit we formed our single class line. We ran down the stone flight of stairs, following Mr. Shaabi. I heard screams and shouts from the other classrooms. Mr. Shaabi never turned around. We followed him out the back door and down the narrow street behind our school. I saw his tie fly out to the side like a black flag and his jacket flap against his legs. Where was he taking us? Where were we running to? The high pitch of

70
the air raid siren continued.

I bumped against the other boys as I ran. I heard my breathing. My mouth was dry. I thought I would choke. Could the bombs fall here? Could a pilot in the sky see me? I saw the sign on the corner—Rashid Street. We were in the Old Town. Mr. Shaabi stopped and turned around. "Are you all here?"

"Yes," we answered.

He pushed open a thick wooden door. "Hurry, everyone inside."

When he saw we had all entered, he led us down winding

80
steps to a square whitewashed room. In the dim light I saw rows of benches, a pulpit, and two carved doors. The air raid siren was drowned out by the explosions of bombs, again and again and again. We had reached this place just in time.

I stood behind him. He did not turn to look at me. He moved forward a few steps to the two carved doors. "Now is the—"

"Oh no," I thought, "he will begin to drone his Shakespeare again."

90
"—time for me to stand before your Holy Ark, Lord, the place of the Torah scrolls."[6] His English words were slow, and spaced as if he held the willow branch in his hand, "—to beg

---

6. **the place of the Torah scrolls:** the ark; the cabinet in which the Torah is stored in a synagogue. Torah scrolls contain the first five books of the Jewish Scriptures.

you, God, to protect these children of Ishmael, and me, a son of Abraham, all of us inhabitants of this ancient land. Amen."

He bowed and stepped away. He turned around and saw me. "Yes, Mahdi?"

What could I say? Should I recite a Shakespeare line that he had taught us?

"Mahdi?"

"I want to say thank you, Mr. Shaabi."

MEET THE WRITER

Pnina Kass is an Israeli author who has written novels, short stories, radio dramatizations, and a television series for young people. She writes in both Hebrew and English. Kass is one of more than one hundred writers and artists who contributed to *Lines in the Sand,* an anthology created in response to the war in Iraq. The book's purpose is to teach children about the human cost of war.

Did you find Mahdi to be a **credible narrator**? Explain.

Notes

Mr. Shaabi

Literary Skills
Analyze the
narrator's
viewpoint.

Narrator: Point of View   "Mr. Shaabi" is a short story told in the **first person,** in the voice of Mahdi. Read the sentences from the story that appear in the left-hand column of the chart below. In the right-hand column, jot down notes on Mahdi's impressions. Describe his tone: Is he bored? frightened? impatient? angry? Also, comment on his credibility as a narrator: Does he describe the scene as it really happens, or does he exaggerate? Are his judgments fair or biased?

1. "The words on my notebook page were black dots, meaningless. All I could think about was tonight. Tonight the bombs would fall again."	
2. "But meanwhile here I was, many streets away, sitting in a classroom, listening to Mr. Shaabi drone on in his perfect English accent as if nothing was happening."	
3. "Wasn't Mr. Shaabi afraid? Did he think reciting *Richard III* would save us?"	
4. "The willow branch in Mr. Shaabi's hand trembled."	
5. "I heard my breathing. My mouth was dry. I thought I would choke. Could the bombs fall here?"	
6. "'Oh no,' I thought, 'he will begin to drone his Shakespeare again.'"	
7. "'I want to say thank you, Mr. Shaabi.'"	

Mr. Shaabi

VOCABULARY AND COMPREHENSION

A. Archaic Phrases? Maybe Not!   Not all of Shakespeare's language is archaic. In fact, Shakespeare is credited with contributing more words and phrases to the English language than any other writer. Choose the Shakespearean expressions someone might use in each of the situations described.

1. A lovesick person who has waited all night for a phone call that never comes might cry all of the following *except* —

   A "Love is blind." (*The Merchant of Venice*)

   B "Good riddance!" (*Troilus and Cressida*)

   C "I've been eaten out of house and home." (*Henry IV, Part 2*)

   D "Off with his head!" (*Richard III*)

2. Someone who did not study for an exam until the night before might say all of the following *except* —

   A "I have not slept one wink." (*Cymbeline*)

   B "I bear a charmed life." (*Macbeth*)

   C "I am a sorry sight." (*Macbeth*)

   D "I'd like to vanish into thin air." (*Othello*)

3. A scary movie is most likely to —

   A "be too much of a good thing" (*As You Like It*)

   B "set your teeth on edge" (*Henry IV, Part 1*)

   C "make your hair stand on end" (*Hamlet*)

   D "keep you in stitches" (*Twelfth Night*)

B. Reading Comprehension

1. What reason is given to explain why Mr. Shaabi has not joined his family abroad?

   ____

   ____

2. At the end of the story, what is Mahdi trying to express to Mr. Shaabi?

   ____

   ____

3. Think back to "The Lesson" by Dianne Dixon. What similarities or differences do you see between the lesson Mr. Shaabi teaches and the one Mr. Perlman teaches?

   ____

   ____

SKILLS FOCUS

Vocabulary Skills
Analyze archaic expressions.

Comparing Themes

Academic Vocabulary for Collection 4

These are the terms you should know
as you read and analyze this collection.

Subject The topic of a work of literature. The subject can usually be stated in a single word or phrase, such as *love, war, childhood, growing up, aging.*

Theme A truth about life and human nature that gives meaning to a story. Different readers may discover different themes in a story, based on their own attitudes and backgrounds. The meaning of a story comes from both the writer and the reader.

Universal themes Themes that can be found in literature from different times, countries, and cultures. Universal themes cross genres as well as national boundaries, languages, customs, and historical periods. An example of a universal theme is *A hero must sacrifice something precious in order to achieve a goal.*

Generalization A broad statement that applies to many individuals, experiences, situations, or observations. A generalization is a kind of conclusion that is drawn after considering as many facts as possible. Themes are expressed as generalizations.

Genres The different forms of literature, such as stories, novels, plays, essays, and poems.

Conflict A struggle between two forces. Usually conflict results when a character wants something strongly but encounters obstacles in trying to get it. An **external conflict** takes place between two characters, between a character and a group, or between a character and an animal or a force in nature. An **internal conflict** is a struggle that takes place within a character's mind or heart.

Main character The character who drives the action in a story. How the main character changes during the story provides clues to the story's theme.

Motivation The reason a character behaves in a certain way.

from Hunger of Memory

by Richard Rodriguez

In this excerpt from his autobiography, Richard Rodriguez remembers his child-hood years speaking mainly Spanish, the language of his parents and home. He also remembers the intimidating foreign sounds of the English spoken on the streets and in stores. In the process, Rodriguez explores what is gained—and what is lost—in trading one language for another.

LITERARY FOCUS: THEME AND CONFLICT

A **theme** is what a story reveals about life or human nature. One way to discover a theme is to pay close attention to the conflict faced by the main character in a story. A **conflict** is a struggle between opposing forces. The conflict can be **external**—between two characters or between a character and an outside force, such as society or nature—or **internal**—between the opposing desires or needs in a character's own mind or heart.

The theme of this excerpt is revealed as the author struggles with learning English and comes to understand the special place of his first language, Spanish, in his heart.

- As you read this excerpt from *Hunger of Memory,* ask yourself what **external** and **internal conflicts** the writer faces. How does he deal with these conflicts? Does he resolve them? If so, how?

READING SKILLS: FINDING THEME

Writers don't usually come right out and tell you the theme of a story or a piece of writing. Instead, as you read, you consider how the various elements of a selection work together. You make **inferences** about the title, key passages, and the characters and what they learn over the course of the story.

To identify the theme of this excerpt, use the following tips:

The title. Why might the writer have chosen this title? What ideas or readings of the work does it point to?

The characters. What does the main character discover over the course of the story? What larger, or universal, meaning might the character's discovery have?

Key passages. Look for passages of description or narration that reveal insight about the characters' experiences or about life itself.

The resolution. How does the excerpt end? What has the narrator learned about himself and the world around him?

Literary Skills
Understand theme and conflict.

Reading Skills
Find theme.

Vocabulary Skills
Understand and use context clues.

VOCABULARY DEVELOPMENT

PREVIEW SELECTION VOCABULARY

The following words appear in the excerpt you are about to read from *Hunger of Memory.* Look them over before you begin the autobiography.

intimidated (in·tim′ə·dāt′id) *v.* used as *adj.:* made timid by the force of another's threats or violence.

> *Intimidated by the loud, confident voice of the shopkeeper, the boy was afraid to place his order.*

conveyed (kən·vād′) *v.:* carried; took something from one place to another.

> *His timid, high-pitched voice conveyed fear.*

inevitably (in·ev′i·tə·blē) *adv.:* as is certain to happen.

> *Growing up in this country, he will inevitably learn English.*

repetition (rep′ə·tish′ən) *n.:* act of doing or saying the same thing many times.

> *The more he heard English spoken, the more familiar it became; the repetition helped him learn the language.*

feigned (fānd) *adj.:* pretended; faked.

> *I wasn't fooled by his feigned look of interest.*

exuberance (eg·zōō′bər·əns) *n.:* high spirits.

> *We couldn't hold in our exuberance on the last day of school.*

CONTEXT CLUES: SOLVING WORD MYSTERIES

Successful readers are like detectives looking for clues. When good readers see an unfamiliar word, they look at the **context**—the words and sentences around the word—for clues to its meaning. Look at the examples in this chart for the word "repetition" to learn more: Note that the type of context clue is indicated in italics.

Type of Context Clue	Example
Definition or restatement	Through patient **repetition,** *saying the phrase over and over again,* Cari taught her parrot to say "Good morning."
Example	*Like a constant drip from a faucet,* the bird's **repetition** of "Good morning" irritated the rest of the family.
Antonym	Practice requires **repetition,** *not merely doing something once.*
Cause and effect	*Because of her daily* **repetition** *of the monologue, Cari did well in her audition.*

from

Hunger of Memory

by Richard Rodriguez

The **title** of this autobiography is an unusual and thought-provoking phrase. What might this phrase mean?

____

____

____

intimidated (in·tim′ə·dāt′id) v. used as *adj.*: made timid by the force of another's threats or violence.

Pause at line 10. Where and when does this part of the autobiography take place? Circle the words and phrases that tell you.

In the early years of my boyhood, my parents coped very well in America. My father had steady work. My mother managed at home. They were nobody's victims. Optimism and ambition led them to a house (our home) many blocks from the Mexican south side of town. We lived among *gringos* and only a block from the biggest, whitest houses. It never occurred to my parents that they couldn't live wherever they chose. Nor was the Sacramento of the fifties bent on teaching them a contrary lesson. My mother and father were more annoyed than **intimidated** by those two or

10 three neighbors who tried initially to make us unwelcome. ('Keep your brats away from my sidewalk!') But despite all they achieved, perhaps because they had so much to achieve, any deep feeling of ease, the confidence of 'belonging' in public was withheld from them both. They regarded the people at work, the faces in crowds, as very distant from us. They were the others, *los gringos*. That term was interchangeable in their speech with another, even more telling, *los americanos*.

20 I grew up in a house where the only regular guests were my relations. For one day, enormous families of relatives would visit and there would be so many people that the noise and the bodies would spill out to the backyard and front porch. Then, for weeks, no one came by. (It was usually a salesman who rang the doorbell.) Our house stood apart. A gaudy yellow in a row of white bungalows. We were the people with the noisy dog. The people who raised pigeons and chickens. We were the foreigners on the block. A few neighbors smiled and waved. We waved back. But no one in the family knew the names of the old couple

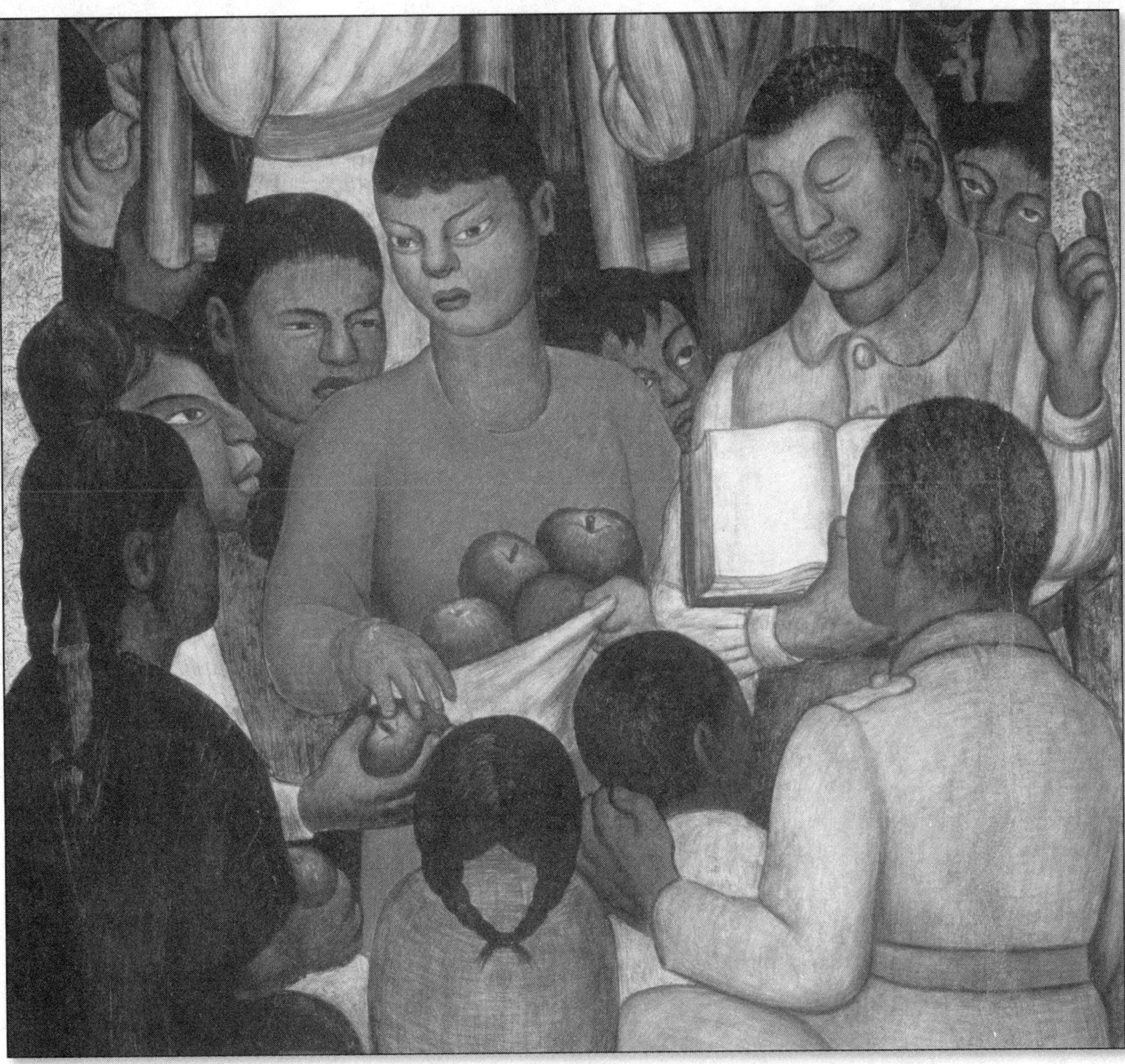

Banco de Mexico Trust

from **Hunger of Memory**   **95**

Pause at line 45. Compare
how English and Spanish
sound to the narrator. What
different associations does
the narrator have with each
language?

____

____

____

____

____

VOCABULARY

conveyed (kən·vād′) *v.:*
carried; took something
from one place to another.

INFER

Re-read lines 46–58. Underline the words and phrases
the author uses to describe
the sound of English being
spoken in public. Based on
these descriptions, what can
you infer about how the
author feels about English?

____

____

____

____

____

____

who lived next door; until I was seven years old, I did not know
the names of the kids who lived across the street.

30   In public, my father and mother spoke a hesitant, accented,
not always grammatical English. And they would have to strain—
their bodies tense—to catch the sense of what was rapidly said
by *los gringos.* At home they spoke Spanish. The language of their
Mexican past sounded in counterpoint to the English of public
society. The words would come quickly, with ease. **Conveyed**
through those sounds was the pleasing, soothing, consoling
reminder of being at home.

    During those years when I was first conscious of hearing,
my mother and father addressed me only in Spanish; in Spanish

40 I learned to reply. By contrast, English (*inglés*), rarely heard in
the house, was the language I came to associate with *gringos.* I
learned my first words of English overhearing my parents speak
to strangers. At five years of age, I knew just enough English
for my mother to trust me on errands to stores one block away.
No more.

    I was a listening child, careful to hear the very different
sounds of Spanish and English. Wide-eyed with hearing, I'd
listen to sounds more than words. First, there were English
(*gringo*) sounds. So many words were still unknown that when

50 the butcher or the lady at the drugstore said something to me,
exotic polysyllabic sounds would bloom in the midst of their
sentences. Often, the speech of people in public seemed to me
very loud, booming with confidence. The man behind the
counter would literally ask, 'What can I do for you?' But by
being so firm and so clear, the sound of his voice said that he
was a *gringo;* he belonged in public society.

    I would also hear then the high nasal notes of middle-class
American speech. The air stirred with sound. Sometimes, even
now, when I have been traveling abroad for several weeks, I

60 will hear what I heard as a boy. In hotel lobbies or airports, in
Turkey or Brazil, some Americans will pass, and suddenly I will
hear it again—the high sound of American voices. For a few

seconds I will hear it with pleasure, for it is now the sound of
my society—a reminder of home. But **inevitably**—already on
the flight headed for home—the sound fades with **repetition.**
I will be unable to hear it anymore.

When I was a boy, things were different. The accent of
los gringos was never pleasing nor was it hard to hear. Crowds at
Safeway or at bus stops would be noisy with sound. And I would
70   be forced to edge away from the chirping chatter above me.

I was unable to hear my own sounds, but I knew very well
that I spoke English poorly. My words could not stretch far
enough to form complete thoughts. And the words I did speak
I didn't know well enough to make into distinct sounds.
(Listeners would usually lower their heads, better to hear what
I was trying to say.) But it was one thing for *me* to speak English
with difficulty. It was more troubling for me to hear my parents
speak in public: their high-whining vowels and guttural con-
sonants; their sentences that got stuck with 'eh' and 'ah' sounds;
80   the confused syntax; the hesitant rhythm of sounds so different
from the way *gringos* spoke. I'd notice, moreover, that my parents'
voices were softer than those of *gringos* we'd meet.

I am tempted now to say that none of this mattered. In
adulthood I am embarrassed by childhood fears. And, in a way,
it didn't matter very much that my parents could not speak
English with ease. Their linguistic difficulties had no serious
consequences. My mother and father made themselves understood at the county hospital clinic and at government offices.
And yet, in another way, it mattered very much—it was un-
90   settling to hear my parents struggle with English. Hearing them,
I'd grow nervous, my clutching trust in their protection and
power weakened.

Read the boxed passage aloud three times, improving your speed and the smoothness of your delivery with each reading.

Re-read lines 93–107. What conflict is the author experiencing? Is it **external, internal,** or both? Explain.

____

____

____

____

feigned (fānd) *adj.:* pretended; faked.

exuberance (eg·zoō′bər·əns) *n.:* high spirits.

Re-read lines 125–128. Do these lines leave you with a positive or negative picture of the author's relationship to Spanish? What **theme,** or insight about life, is suggested by these last lines?

____

____

____

____

____

There were many times like the night at a brightly lit gasoline station (a blaring white memory) when I stood uneasily, hearing my father. He was talking to a teenaged attendant. I do not recall what they were saying, but I cannot forget the sounds my father made as he spoke. At one point his words slid together to form one word—sounds as confused as the threads of blue and green oil in the puddle next to my shoes. His voice rushed
100 through what he had left to say. And, toward the end, reached falsetto notes, appealing to his listener's understanding. I looked away to the lights of passing automobiles. I tried not to hear anymore. But I heard only too well the calm, easy tones in the attendant's reply. Shortly afterward, walking toward home with my father, I shivered when he put his hand on my shoulder. The very first chance that I got, I evaded his grasp and ran on ahead into the dark, skipping with **feigned** boyish **exuberance.**

But then there was Spanish. *Español:* my family's language. *Español:* the language that seemed to me a private language. I'd
110 hear strangers on the radio and in the Mexican Catholic church across town speaking in Spanish, but I couldn't really believe that Spanish was a public language, like English. Spanish speakers, rather, seemed related to me, for I sensed that we shared— through our language—the experience of feeling apart from *los gringos.* It was thus a ghetto Spanish that I heard and I spoke. Like those whose lives are bound by a barrio, I was reminded by Spanish of my separateness from *los otros, los gringos* in power. But more intensely than for most barrio children—because I did not live in a barrio—Spanish seemed to me the language
120 of home. (Most days it was only at home that I'd hear it.) It became the language of joyful return.

A family member would say something to me and I would feel myself specially recognized. My parents would say something to me and I would feel embraced by the sounds of their words. Those sounds said: *I am speaking with ease in Spanish. I am addressing you in words I never use with* los gringos. *I recognize you as someone special, close, like no one outside. You belong with us. In the family.*

MEET THE WRITER

Richard Rodriguez (1944–   ) entered the first grade knowing barely fifty words of English. He was the only Spanish-speaking student in his class at the Sacred Heart School in Sacramento, California. With his parents' help, he learned English and went on to earn degrees in English and philosophy as well as a doctorate in English Renaissance literature. His education prepared him for a career in academia, but he decided instead to become a writer. Using his own childhood struggles with English as inspiration, Rodriguez published *Hunger of Memory: The Education of Richard Rodriguez,* in 1982.

Notes

from Hunger of Memory

Literary Skills
Analyze theme.

Theme Chart   Nearly every literary work explores a **theme,** a truth or insight about life. Fill in the chart below with key details from *Hunger of Memory*. Then, review the details, and identify the theme of this autobiography excerpt. You may want to consider what the author is saying about living in two cultures, private versus public lives, belonging, or some other topic.

	Details from *Hunger of Memory*
Narrator's thoughts/actions:	
Key passages:	
Resolution:	
Theme	

Skills Review

from Hunger of Memory

VOCABULARY AND COMPREHENSION

A. Context Clues: Solving Word Mysteries   Complete the paragraph below by writing a word from the Word Box to fit each numbered blank. Use context clues to help you.

<table>
<tr><td>

Word Box

intimidated

conveyed

inevitably

repetition

feigned

exuberance

</td></tr>
</table>

Alicia's quietness (1) _______________________ an impression of shyness, but it was only a (2) _______________________ manner she put on to try and keep out of trouble in class. (3) _______________________, though, her natural (4) _______________________ would break out whenever something excited her. Then came a (5) _______________________ of the usual pattern: Her teacher would scold her for speaking out of turn, and Alicia would be (6) _______________________ back into quietness.

B. Reading Comprehension   Answer each question below.

1. The author describes himself as having been "a listening child." According to the excerpt, what sounds does he pay close attention to?

   ____

   ____

2. According to the author's childhood view of things, is Spanish or English the language of power? Explain.

   ____

   ____

3. According to the author as an adult, what are the benefits of Spanish in his life?

   ____

   ____

Vocabulary Skills
Analyze context clues.

Before You Read

All-American Girl by Julia Alvarez

What does it really mean to be "all-American"? Is it in what you wear, how you act, or something else? What does being "all-American" mean to the speaker of this poem?

LITERARY FOCUS: THEME AND GENRE

Theme is an insight about life conveyed in literature. All types of literature can convey a theme. How that theme is conveyed, however, depends on the category, or **genre,** of literature. Genre affects our responses to a work. To understand the role of genre, consider the following questions:

- **How does the choice of genre relate to the author's purpose for writing**? Fiction writers take readers on a journey that usually leads to some discovery through the **characters** they create. Poets, on the other hand, use **sound devices** and **imagery** to help readers see and feel things that will affect their perspective.

- **How does the writer use the characteristics of the chosen genre to develop the theme?** The theme of a short story can often be discovered by noticing how the main character changes and what he or she discovers by the end of the story. In poems a theme may be revealed by noting the **repetition** of key ideas or images, by looking at **word choice,** by listening to the sounds of the poem, and by thinking about the poem's **title.**

As you read the poem "All-American Girl," focus on the author's word choice, listen to the sounds of the poem, and pay attention to the poem's title. What theme emerges?

SKILLS FOCUS

Literary Skills
Understand theme and genre.

All-American Girl

Julia Alvarez

I wanted stockings, makeup, store-bought clothes;

I wanted to look like an American girl;

to speak my English so you couldn't tell

I'd come from somewhere else. I locked myself

5   in the bathroom, trying to match my face

with words in my new language: *grimace, leer,*

disgust, disdain—feelings I had yet to feel

in English. (And would *tristeza* even feel

the same as *sadness* with its Saxon sound?

10   Would *pity* look as soulful as *piedad*?)

I didn't know if I could ever show

genuine feeling in a borrowed tongue.

If *cortesía°* would be misunderstood

as brown-nosing or cries of *alegría°*

15   translate as terror. So, mirror in hand,

I practiced foreign faces, Anglo grins,

repressing a native Latin fluency

for the cooler mask of English ironies.

I wanted the world and words to match again

20   as when I had lived solely in Spanish.

But my face wouldn't obey—like a tide

it was pulled back by my lunatic heart

to its old habits of showing feelings.

Long after I'd lost my heavy accent,

---

13. *cortesía* (cōr′tā·sē′ä): Spanish for "courtesy."
14. *alegría* (ä′lā·grē′ä): Spanish for "happiness."

IDENTIFY

In lines 1–4, underline the words that show what the narrator wants.

INFER

Pause at line 15. What is the narrator's main **conflict**? Is it **internal** or **external**—or both? Explain.

INTERPRET

Pause at line 24. A **simile** makes a comparison between two unlike things, using words such as *like* or *as.* Explain the simile the writer uses in lines 21–23. What does the "it" refer to (line 22)?

Do you think this picture illustrates the narrator's dilemma? Why or why not?

____

____

What does the narrator mean by saying she "couldn't keep the southern continent out of the northern *vista* of my eyes" (lines 26–27)?

____

____

____

____

____

____

Pause at the end of the poem. What different meaning does "all-American girl" have in the last line? Now look back at the **title**. How does it suggest a resolution of the narrator's **conflict**?

____

____

____

____

____

____

Jose Luis Pelaez, Inc./CORBIS

25   my face showed I had come from somewhere else.

I couldn't keep the southern continent

out of the northern *vista*° of my eyes,

or cut my *cara*° off to spite my face.

I couldn't look like anybody else

30   but who I was: an all-American girl.

---

27. *vista* (vēs′tä): Spanish for "view."
28. *cara* (cä′rä): Spanish for "expression."

MEET THE WRITER

Julia Alvarez (1950–   ) was born in the United States but raised in the Dominican Republic until she was ten years old. At that point her family, fleeing political persecution, returned to the United States. Because Alvarez grew up in an oral culture, story-telling was natural for her. Alvarez loves the ways that written words—both English and Spanish—express the world of the imagination. She published her first novel, the acclaimed *How the García Girls Lost Their Accents,* in 1991.

Hunger of Memory / All-American Girl

Genre Chart *Hunger of Memory* and "All-American Girl" are different genres, or types, of literature. One is an autobiography and the other is a poem, but they both reveal something to us about what it is like to belong to two cultures. Use the Genre Chart below to examine how each text reveals its theme. Then, using your own words, state the theme that the two works have in common. Remember that there is no one correct answer.

Literary Skills
Analyze genre and theme.

Excerpt from *Hunger of Memory*	"All-American Girl"
Genre:	Genre:
Main character:	Speaker:
Setting:	Setting:
Plot:	Repeated images/key ideas:
Conflict:	Conflict:
How is the conflict resolved?	How is the conflict resolved?

Universal theme: ____

____

Kipling and I by Jesús Colón

LITERARY FOCUS: THEME AND CHARACTER

One way to identify the **theme** of a literary work—its underlying truth about life—is to pay close attention to its **main character** or **narrator.** The experiences of a story's main character—or an essay's narrator—may help you pinpoint the work's major themes. In the essay you are about to read, the narrator will change in an important way and come to a new realization about life. This change or realization is linked to the story's theme.

- As you read "Kipling and I," observe how the narrator handles his **conflicts.**
- Look for details that show how and why he changes his attitude toward life. These details may help you identify the essay's **theme.**
- As you read "Kipling and I," think about its **title.** The title of a work often hints at its theme.

READING SKILLS: MAKING INFERENCES

When you make an **inference** about a narrator, you use clues from the text and your own experiences to make a guess about why he or she makes certain choices, says certain things, and acts a certain way.

Make inferences about the narrator as you read "Kipling and I." What motivates him? You may want to list your inferences on a chart like this one. The first row has been filled in as an example.

Detail from the Essay	Inference
He buys a poem and places it prominently in his room.	He finds the poem inspiring.

Literary Skills
Understand theme and narrator.

Reading Skills
Make inferences.

Vocabulary Skills
Understand prefixes and word roots.

VOCABULARY DEVELOPMENT

PREVIEW SELECTION VOCABULARY

Before you read "Kipling and I," become familiar with the following words.

intimate (in′tə·mət) *adj.:* having or creating a feeling of closeness or privacy.

*The stove created an **intimate** circle of warmth in the room.*

profound (prō·found′) *adj.:* characterized by intellectual depth; deeply felt or considered.

*As he read the poem, he contemplated its **profound** message.*

sonorous (sə·nôr′əs) *adj.:* having a full, rich, impressive sound.

*He enjoyed the **sonorous** music of the poem.*

paltry (pôl′trē) *adj.:* wretchedly small.

*For his hard work the narrator was paid only a **paltry** sum.*

relished (rel′isht) *v.:* greatly enjoyed.

*The narrator's bosses **relished** exercising their power over him.*

PREFIXES

A **prefix** is a word part that comes before a word root and affects its meaning. Knowledge of prefixes can help you figure out the meanings of unfamiliar words. It can also help you master a wide variety of words. The word *profound,* for example, contains the prefix *pro–,* which means "forward" or "before." It also contains the root *fundus,* which means "bottom." Knowing both the prefix and the root, you may be able to guess that *profound* has something to do with depth—in this case, "intellectually deep" or "deeply felt."

Look at the prefixes in the chart at the right to see if you can identify the way they affect the meanings of some of the other Vocabulary words above.

Prefix	Meaning
in–	in; into
re–	back; again

Kipling and I

Jesús Colón

Sometimes I pass Debevoise Place at the corner of Willoughby Street . . . I look at the old wooden house, gray and ancient, the house where I used to live some forty years ago . . .

My room was on the second floor at the corner. On hot summer nights I would sit at the window reading by the electric light from the street lamp which was almost at a level with the windowsill.

It was nice to come home late during the winter, look for some scrap of old newspaper, some bits of wood and a few
10   chunks of coal, and start a sparkling fire in the chunky four-legged coal stove. I would be rewarded with an **intimate** warmth as little by little the pigmy stove became alive puffing out its sides, hot and red, like the crimson cheeks of a Santa Claus.

My few books were in a soap box nailed to the wall. But my most prized possession in those days was a poem I had bought in a five-and-ten-cent store on Fulton Street. (I wonder what has become of these poems, maxims and sayings of wise men that they used to sell at the five-and-ten-cent stores?) The poem was printed on gold paper and mounted in a gilded frame ready to
20   be hung in a conspicuous place in the house. I bought one of those fancy silken picture cords finishing in a rosette to match the color of the frame.

I was seventeen. This poem to me then seemed to summarize, in one poetical nutshell, the wisdom of all the sages that ever lived. It was what I was looking for, something to guide myself by, a way of life, a compendium[1] of the wise, the true and

---

1.   **compendium** (kəm·pen′dē·əm) *n.:* brief summary; list.

IDENTIFY

Pause at line 3. Underline the words and phrases that tell you how long ago the story the narrator is telling takes place.

VOCABULARY

intimate (in′tə·mət) *adj.:* having or creating a feeling of closeness or privacy.

INFER

Pause at line 22. From the details the narrator gives about his room, what **inferences** can you make about him and his situation?

____

____

____

____

INFER

Pause at line 25. What would you infer is this narrator's outlook on life at age seventeen? Explain.

____

____

____

the beautiful. All I had to do was to live according to the counsel
of the poem and follow the instructions and I would be a perfect
man—the useful, the good, the true human being. I was very
happy that day, forty years ago.

The poem had to have the most prominent place in the
room. Where could I hang it? I decided that the best place for
the poem was on the wall right by the entrance to the room. No
one coming in and out would miss it. Perhaps someone would
be interested enough to read it and drink the **profound** waters
of its message . . .

Every morning as I prepared to leave, I stood in front of the
poem and read it over and over again, sometimes half a dozen
times. I let the **sonorous** music of the verse carry me away. I
brought with me a handwritten copy as I stepped out every
morning looking for work, repeating verses and stanzas from
memory until the whole poem came to be part of me. Other
days my lips kept repeating a single verse of the poem at inter-
vals throughout the day.

CORBIS

In the subways I loved to compete with the shrill noises of the many wheels below by chanting the lines of the poem. People stared at me moving my lips as though I were in a trance. I looked back with pity. They were not so fortunate as I who had as a guide to direct my life a great poem to make me wise, useful and happy.

50　　And I chanted:

> *If you can keep your head when all about you*
> *Are losing theirs and blaming you . . .*
>
> *If you can wait and not be tired by waiting,*
> 　　*Or being lied about, don't deal in lies,*
> *Or being hated don't give way to hating . . .*
>
> *If you can make one heap of all your winnings;*
> 　　*And risk it on one turn of pitch-and-toss,*
> *And lose, and start again at your beginnings . . .*

"If—," by Kipling, was the poem. At seventeen, my evening
60　prayer and my first morning thought. I repeated it every day with the resolution to live up to the very last line of that poem.

I would visit the government employment office on Jay Street. The conversations among the Puerto Ricans on the large wooden benches in the employment office were always on the same subject. How to find a decent place to live. How they would not rent to Negroes or Puerto Ricans. How Negroes and Puerto Ricans were given the pink slips first at work.

From the employment office I would call door to door at the piers, factories and storage houses in the streets under the
70　Brooklyn and Manhattan bridges. "Sorry, nothing today." It seemed to me that "today" was a continuation and combination of all the yesterdays, todays and tomorrows.

From the factories I would go to the restaurants, looking for a job as a porter or dishwasher. At least I would eat and be warm in a kitchen.

"Sorry" . . . "Sorry" . . .

Sometimes I was hired at ten dollars a week, ten hours a day including Sundays and holidays. One day off during the week. My work was that of three men: dishwasher, porter, bus-
80 boy. And to clear the sidewalk of snow and slush "when you have nothing else to do." I was to be appropriately humble and grateful not only to the owner but to everybody else in the place.

If I rebelled at insults or at a pointed innuendo[2] or just the inhuman amount of work, I was unceremoniously thrown out and told to come "next week for your pay." "Next week" meant weeks of calling for the **paltry** dollars owed me. The owners **relished** this "next week."

I clung to my poem as to a faith. Like a potent amulet,[3] my precious poem was clenched in the fist of my right hand inside
90 my secondhand overcoat. Again and again I declaimed aloud a few precious lines when discouragement and disillusionment threatened to overwhelm me.

> *If you can force your heart and nerve and sinew*
> *To serve your turn long after they are gone . . .*

The weeks of unemployment and hard knocks turned into months. I continued to find two or three days of work here and there. And I continued to be thrown out when I rebelled at the ill treatment, overwork and insults. I kept pounding the streets looking for a place where they would treat me half decently,
100 where my devotion to work and faith in Kipling's poem would be appreciated. I remember the worn-out shoes I bought in a secondhand store on Myrtle Avenue at the corner of Adams Street. The round holes in the soles that I tried to cover with pieces of carton were no match for the frigid knives of the unrelenting snow.

---

2. **innuendo** (in′yo͞o·en′dō) *n.:* veiled comment on a person's character or reputation.
3. **amulet** (am′yo͞o·lit) *n.:* object thought to have magical powers, worn to protect the wearer from evil.

paltry (pôl′trē) *adj.:* wretchedly small.

relished (rel′isht) *v.:* greatly enjoyed.

WORD STUDY

Dis– is a prefix meaning "away." Look at the two words containing *dis–* in line 91. What two things are being taken away from the narrator?

PREDICT

Pause at line 92. In lines 77–87, the narrator faces hardships that test his resolution to live by the words of the poem. How long do you **predict** he will maintain his resolution? Explain.

INTERPRET

Pause at line 105. Have the narrator's hardships eased? Or have they grown worse?

Underwood & Underwood/CORBIS

THEME

Underline the actions the narrator takes in lines 115–118. What do these actions suggest about his change in attitude? What **theme,** or insight about life, is suggested by his final actions?

____

____

____

____

____

____

One night I returned late after a long day of looking for work. I was hungry. My room was dark and cold. I wanted to warm my numb body. I lit a match and began looking for some scraps of wood and a piece of paper to start a fire. I searched all

110 over the floor. No wood, no paper. As I stood up, the glimmering flicker of the dying match was reflected in the glass surface of the framed poem. I unhooked the poem from the wall. I reflected for a minute, a minute that felt like an eternity. I took the frame apart, placing the square glass upon the small table. I tore the gold paper on which the poem was printed, threw its pieces inside the stove and, placing the small bits of wood from the frame on top of the paper, I lit it, adding soft and hard coal as the fire began to gain strength and brightness.

     I watched how the lines of the poem withered into ashes

120 inside the small stove.

Jesús Colón (1901–1974) was the son of a poor baker in Puerto Rico. His childhood home was located behind the town's cigar factory, a place where Colón was exposed to philosophical and political ideas. It was at the factory that Colón learned of the teachings of Karl Marx, Émile Zola, and Honoré de Balzac. He developed a strong sense of justice and an interest in literature. At sixteen he left Puerto Rico as a stowaway on the SS *Carolina* and ended up in Brooklyn, New York, where his initial experiences provided the basis for his essay "Kipling and I." Colón eventually enjoyed a career as a journalist, publisher, and writer. He published his well-known book of essays, *A Puerto Rican in New York, and Other Sketches,* in 1961. Colón helped to lay the groundwork for the New York–based Puerto Rican literary movement known as the Nuyorican Movement.

Notes

Kipling and I

SKILLS FOCUS

Literary Skills
Analyze universal themes.

Universal Themes Chart   Universal themes can be found in the selections in Collection 4, as well as in other stories, poems, and essays you encounter in your reading. Use the following Universal Themes Chart to determine what universal themes are shared by "Kipling and I" and a selection of your choice. Fill in the first blank column with notes about "Kipling and I." In the second blank column, fill in notes about a selection from this book or another selection with which you are familiar. Then, note one or more common themes in the two works.

	"Kipling and I"	Your Selection's Title _______________
Main character/narrator:		
Conflict:		
Character's/narrator's motivation:		
What the character/ narrator discovers:		
Common themes:		

Skills Review

Kipling and I

VOCABULARY AND COMPREHENSION

A. Using Prefixes   Write words from the Word Bank to complete the paragraph below. Then, re-read the paragraph and circle words that contain the prefixes *sub–*, *un–*, and *com–*.

When he first arrived in New York, he found a job that paid a

(1) _______________________ wage and that barely allowed him to pay

his rent and subsist. His subterranean room, though small, was not un-

comfortable. It was made cozy and (2) _______________________ by the

stove and the homemade curtains. He (3) _______________________ the

peace and quiet of the late night when he read his books aloud. The

(4) _______________________ sounds of the words filled him with complete

calm. He stared out the window and contemplated the complex and

(5) _______________________ ideas competing with each other in his head.

<table>
<tr><td>Word Box</td></tr>
<tr><td>intimate</td></tr>
<tr><td>profound</td></tr>
<tr><td>sonorous</td></tr>
<tr><td>paltry</td></tr>
<tr><td>relished</td></tr>
</table>

B. Reading Comprehension   Answer each question below.

1. How old was the narrator when he came upon Kipling's poem "If—"?
How does the narrator feel at the start of the essay about this poem?

____

____

____

2. Describe the narrator's job search and his feelings about it.

____

____

____

3. What does the narrator end up using the poem for at the end of the essay?

____

____

____

SKILLS FOCUS

Vocabulary Skills
Use prefixes to determine word meanings.

Irony and Ambiguity

Three Lions/Hulton/Archive.

Academic Vocabulary for Collection 5

These are the terms you should know
as you read and analyze the texts in this collection.

———————

Irony The difference between what we expect or what seems suitable and what actually happens. There are three main types of irony:

- **Verbal irony** occurs when someone says one thing but means the opposite. "Big dog," you say as you cradle a tiny Pomeranian puppy in the palm of your hand.
- **Situational irony** refers to an event that is contrary to, or the opposite of, what we expect. The fire station burns in a fire. The winner of a wrestling match is the weakest member of the team.
- **Dramatic irony** takes place when we know what is going to happen to a character but the character does not know. We know, but the robbers speeding in the getaway car do not know, that the drawbridge ahead of them is stuck in the open position.

Ambiguity   A quality that allows something to be interpreted in different or conflicting ways. If you and a friend have completely different ideas about an ambiguous character or the ambiguous ending of a story, you both might be right. There is no single way to interpret an ambiguous story. That is part of what makes it enjoyable.

Before You Read

The New Girl by Nicole Keeter

The new girl of the selection's title is the only African American girl in the author's town besides the author herself. Until Chris joins her fifth-grade class, the author is viewed by her classmates and neighbors as different but also as special. Now, Chris's presence threatens the author's social standing.

LITERARY FOCUS: SITUATIONAL IRONY

Situational irony describes an event that is not just surprising but actually contrary to what you expected to occur. It reminds you that chance often has the last word. For example, in "The New Girl," you'd expect the author to be happy about having another African American student in her class. However, the author views the new girl, Chris, as a threat. It's this irony that makes the author's experience with Chris such a misadventure.

READING SKILLS: MAKING INFERENCES

Ambiguity is the quality that allows something to be interpreted in different ways. In "The New Girl" the author's feelings about Chris's arrival are ambiguous—they are complex and not easy to put into words. As a reader, you take the information the author gives you and compare it with your own and others' experiences in order to **make inferences.** By making these inferences, you can come to a clearer understanding of the motivations behind the author's feelings toward Chris.

To make an inference about a character or an event that you find puzzling or ambiguous, first determine what details are confusing, missing, or just plain contradictory. Next, draw on your own and others' experiences to help clarify the details. Then, apply these findings so that you better understand the character or event. Remember to revise your inferences as you acquire new information about characters or situations.

Literary Skills
Understand
irony and
ambiguity.

**Reading
Skills**
Make inferences
about
ambiguity.

**Vocabulary
Skills**
Understand
word families.

VOCABULARY DEVELOPMENT

PREVIEW SELECTION VOCABULARY

The following words appear in "The New Girl." Look them over before you read the essay.

interactive (in′tər·ak′tiv) *adj.:* acting on one another.

In coed Truth or Dare, the author receives no invitations for **interactive** *dares.*

acutely (ə·kyo͞ot′lē) *adv.:* intensely; keenly.

The author is **acutely** *aware of the limits of her "special" status.*

vicinity (və·sin′ə·tē) *n.:* area; location.

The author always knows when Chris is in her **vicinity.**

appraising (ə·prāz′iŋ) *v.* used as *adj.:* evaluating.

Chris often sends curious and **appraising** *looks in the author's direction.*

vague (vāg) *adj.:* indistinct; unclear.

When Brandon pats Chris's cheek, the author feels a **vague** *sense of panic, quickly followed by a burst of hope for her own future.*

WORD FAMILIES: LATIN AND GREEK ROOT WORDS

English contains more than 88,500 word families, or groups of words that originated from a common root. It is helpful to know word families because some form of the original meaning can usually be applied to *all* the words in a single family. For example, the word *interactive* is constructed from the Latin word *inter* (meaning "between") and a base form of the Latin word *agere* (meaning "to do"). Other members of this family are *act, actor, activist, actual, enact, exact,* and *react.* Consider the meaning these words share: All have to do with making something happen.

When you come across a word you don't know, think of words you *do* know that are similar. Ask yourself what these words have in common, and you might be able to get an idea of the unknown word's meaning. This process won't help you every time, but you have a pretty good chance of coming up with a useful connection.

The New Girl

Nicole Keeter

What sets the author apart from the rest of the students in her class?

____

____

____

In lines 1–17, we learn that the author considers herself to be special. Circle the positive things associated with being special. Underline the negative things associated with being special.

interactive (in′tər·ak′tiv) *adj.*: acting on one another.

acutely (ə·kyōōt′lē) *adv.*: intensely; keenly.

vicinity (və·sin′ə·tē) *n.*: area; location.

appraising (ə·prāz′iŋ) *v.* used as *adj.*: evaluating.

I was in the third grade when my family moved from Indianapolis in the early 80's and I became the lone black kid in a little Iowa town. At first there were stares, followed by the standard questions: Why did I call it getting a perm if it actually made my hair straighter? Did it hurt that my legs were so dry? Other kids who were different, who were fat or ugly or handicapped in some way, were ridiculed. But somehow I was special.

Special meant people were always nice to you. There were invitations to sit with the popular kids in the cafeteria and to

10 attend the best slumber parties. Parents always addressed me by name, saying how delighted they were to have me in their homes.

But I sensed the boundaries of my special status were not to be tested. So I didn't complain that none of the boys asked me to couple-skate or that I never got any thrilling **interactive** dares in coed Truth or Dare. I pretended that I was the same as the others, and I didn't ask for anything more than what they wanted to give me.

Then Chris arrived during the fall of our fifth-grade year, just before cutouts of orange pumpkins gave way to cutouts of

20 brown turkeys on the walls. She was pretty, tall and enviably developed, with neat black pigtails and creamy brown skin a shade lighter than mine. A stretch of it peeped from between the hem of her yellow coat and her long white socks.

I became **acutely** aware of when she was in my **vicinity,** but I didn't speak to her. She was usually alone. Once or twice when I watched Chris from a distance, our eyes would lock until I looked away. Her expression, at those quick moments, was curious, even **appraising,** and my stomach would flip-flop.

Tony Anderson/Getty Images

I was afraid Chris's presence would expose me as someone who
was not special at all but merely different—someone like all the
frightening or laughable black people my classmates had seen
on TV.

A week or so before Christmas vacation, however, Chris's
status took an unexpected turn. Our grade's star boy, Brandon,
missed catching the kickball, and it soared from the field. The
ball, wet and dirty from recent snows, seemed to have bruised
Chris's cheek as it landed. Brandon ran up to her, apologizing
and promising her it was an accident. He put his arm around
her and patted her cheek, and he gave her his remarkable smile,
walking backward as he left to make sure she was O.K. The other
girls gathered around her in awe and confusion.

Watching from across the schoolyard, I felt **vague** panic at
first, but then a sudden rush of hope for us both. Maybe someday I would get my hair under control, and then we'd see what
could happen. Maybe being different could be O.K.

A few days later, I found Chris slumped on the floor in the
doorway of the girl's bathroom. She was crying, with her arms
wrapped around her knees.

VISUALIZE

Re-read lines 33–41. Visualize
the situation. Can you see the
kickball soaring through the
air? Do you see the person
running up to her and apologizing? What's the expression
on his face? What do the
expressions of the onlookers
indicate?

VOCABULARY

vague (vāg) *adj.:* indistinct;
unclear.

INFER

In line 45, the author has a
momentary hope that "being
different could be O.K."
What do you think she
means by this remark?

____

____

____

The New Girl   **121**

In lines 55–56, how is the boys' treatment of Chris different from their treatment of her after she was struck by the kickball?

The word *deliver* (line 62) comes from a form of the Latin word *liberare,* meaning "to free." Other words in this family are *liberal* and *livery.* Think of another word from this family, and write it on the line below.

Re-read lines 64–67. Why does the narrator become angry? Explain what you think she means by saying that Chris got what she deserved for "asking for too much from them."

Mel Curtis/Getty Images

"How do you . . . ," she said when I stopped for our first real meeting. She gathered herself. "How do you do it here, with only them all the time?"

"Them?" I said, feeling my body stiffen. "I don't know what you mean."

She studied my face and hugged her knees more tightly. "The boys were out here laughing, saying how gross it would be to kiss a little . . ." She shuddered. And then came the N-word.

I took her hand and squeezed it, looking for words to comfort her. Chris stretched her legs out in front of her, and a white Christmas card envelope with a festive gold border fell to the floor. She quickly turned it face down, but not before I read the bold girlish script: "Brandon." I pictured Chris on the playground, at once eager and scared to deliver a card to her crush. All his friends must have been watching.

I dropped Chris's hand. Any affection I was feeling turned into anger. I wanted to shake her and make her see that she had ruined this place for both of us. It served her right, I thought, for asking for too much from them.

"What do you think I should do?" she was saying.

I refused to look her in the eye. "I don't know," I said. "I've

70 never had anything like that happen to me." And I walked away.

When I came back to school from Christmas vacation, Chris was gone. Her teacher said simply that her family moved to the nearby city. I never said anything and never heard anything more about her. In most ways, life went back to normal in my town. I was special again.

But eventually I started watching for her. I started making up reasons for my parents to drive me to the city. A few times when we drove its streets or walked through its stores, I thought I saw her. I'd spot a pair of black pigtails or a patch of brown

80 skin between a coat and knee-high sock, and I'd twist my neck around and look hard. It was never Chris, of course, just someone who looked exactly and nothing like her.

MEET THE WRITER

Nicole Keeter was born in Iowa. A lover of movies, she has worked as a film critic for *Time Out New York.* She is currently a freelance writer living in Brooklyn, New York. This essay appeared in *The New York Times Magazine.*

Read the boxed passage aloud twice. On your first read, focus on conveying the basic meaning. During the second read, focus on expressing the feelings behind the words.

Why do you think the author looks for Chris in the city?

____

____

____

____

____

Notes __________________

____

____

____

____

____

____

____

____

____

____

____

____

The New Girl

Literature Skills
Analyze irony and ambiguity.

Reading Skills
Make inferences about ambiguity.

Ambiguity Chart   "The New Girl" contains plenty of ambiguity. The events and feelings the author describes can be interpreted in different, even conflicting ways. The chart below contains details from the story that are ambiguous. Next to each detail, provide a reasonable interpretation that conflicts with the one already provided.

Details from the Story	Meaning: Interpretation 1	Meaning: Interpretation 2
1. The author sees herself as being in a "special" category.	Being *special* is better than being *different*.	
2. Brandon responds with concern when Chris is hurt by the stray kickball.	When someone is physically hurt, Brandon knows what to do.	
3. One of her male classmates calls Chris an offensive name.	This hurts Chris worse than being struck by the kickball, but the boys don't seem to know this.	
4. Some time after Chris leaves, the author makes excuses to look for her in the city.	The author wants to ask for forgiveness.	

Skills Review

The New Girl

VOCABULARY AND COMPREHENSION

A. Word Families   In the chart below, fill in the appropriate vocabulary word from the Word Box. (Note: You will not use one of the words in the Word Box.)

Word Box

interactive

acutely

vicinity

appraising

vague

Latin Root and Meaning	Word Family Examples	Vocabulary Word
agere, "to do"	actuality, counter-action, reactive	
acus, "needle"	acumen, acupressure, acupuncture	
pretium, "worth"	appreciation, praise, price	
vagus, "wandering"	vagabond	

B. Reading Comprehension   Answer each question below.

1. Why doesn't the author speak to Chris when she first joins the class?

____

____

2. With Chris no longer in the class, the author believes she is again special. Do you think she is correct? Explain.

____

____

3. If, during her searches of the city, the author had found Chris, what do you think she would have told her?

____

____

Vocabulary Skills
Analyze word families.

Three Wise Guys by Sandra Cisneros

Imagine that one day a box arrives at your house. You open the card with your family and read it aloud: *This box contains anything you want it to. The only rule is that you can only choose once, and you must choose together as a family.* Would your family easily agree, or would you all want different things? The story you are about to read, "Three Wise Guys," features just such a mysterious gift.

LITERARY FOCUS: SITUATIONAL IRONY

We love stories with good surprises—they are suspenseful and often feel true, since life can surprise us. In a well-written story there are usually elements of surprise. A writer may create suspense in a story by withholding, or not giving, important information to readers.

Often when we read a story, we think one thing will happen, only to be surprised when something entirely different takes place. Unexpected events often create **irony**—the difference between what we thought would happen and what really happens. Outcomes that are contrary to our expectations are examples of **situational irony.**

READING SKILLS: MAKING PREDICTIONS

Most readers **make predictions** as they read. This means that they make a series of guesses about what will happen next. By making predictions as you read "Three Wise Guys," you will become involved in the lives of the Gonzalez family. "Three Wise Guys" concerns a mysterious gift that is delivered to the Gonzalez family in time for Christmas but that must remain wrapped until the Day of the Kings. See if you can predict what the present will be.

To make a prediction:

- Look for clues in the story that suggest what might happen next.
- Make a prediction about future events based on clues in the story and on what you know from your own experiences.
- Read on to confirm your prediction—to see if it is correct. If necessary, revise your prediction when you learn new information.

Literary Skills
Understand situational irony.

Reading Skills
Make predictions.

Vocabulary Skills
Understand diction.

PREVIEW SELECTION VOCABULARY

Get to know these words before you read "Three Wise Guys."

obstructed (əb·strukt′id) *v.:* cut off from sight; blocked.

*The box **obstructed** the view, but it didn't matter since the TV didn't work.*

portable (pôr′tə·bəl) *adj.:* easily transported or carried.

*A **portable** washing machine she could move around would make Mama's chores easier.*

prophecy (präf′ə·sē) *n.:* prediction.

*Papa made a **prophecy** that the gift in the box would be an air conditioner.*

embossed (em·bôst′) *adj.:* raised above the surface.

*The volumes were covered in imitation leather **embossed** with gold letters.*

improvised (im′prə·vīzd′) *v.:* made or created from available materials.

*The family **improvised** new uses for the books.*

DICTION: PLAIN, FANCY, OR POETIC?

Diction is word choice. When it comes to diction, it's true that it is not what you say but how you say it. Diction is an important aspect of a writer's style. Some writers use fancy, or formal, diction. A writer who uses fancy diction might write:

The naive maiden wailed in abject misery.

On the other hand, a writer who prefers a plain style might say:

The girl cried in despair.

Cisneros is known for her poetic diction. Poetic diction can be either fancy or plain, but it is always unique and unexpected. Though Cisneros often uses simple words, she strings them together poetically. Look at this sentence from "Three Wise Guys":

The girl Rosalinda let out a sad cry, as if her hair was going to be cut again.

As you read "Three Wise Guys," be aware of Cisneros's unique, poetic style.

Three Wise Guys

Sandra Cisneros

BACKGROUND: LITERATURE AND CULTURE

According to Christian tradition, the giving of Christmas gifts began with the Three Wise Men, who brought gold, frankincense, and myrrh to the stable where the Christ child was born. The visit of the Three Wise Men is celebrated on January 6, twelve days after Christmas. In many countries, people exchange gifts on January 6 rather than on Christmas. The Mexican Americans in this story give gifts on January 6, which they call *Dia de los Reyes,* the "Day of the Kings."

INFER

Pause at line 8. Where does this story take place? Underline the clues that tell you. What suspenseful situation is being set up?

The big box came marked DO NOT OPEN TILL XMAS, but the mama said not until the Day of the Three Kings. Not until Dia de los Reyes, the sixth of January, do you hear? That is what the mama said exactly, only she said it all in Spanish. Because in Mexico where she was raised, it is the custom for boys and girls to receive their presents on January sixth, and not Christmas, even though they were living on the Texas side of the river now. Not until the sixth of January.

Yesterday the mama had risen in the dark same as always to reheat the coffee in a tin saucepan and warm the breakfast tortillas. The papa had gotten up coughing and spitting up the night, complaining how the evening before the buzzing of the chicharras[1] had kept him from sleeping. By the time the mama had the house smelling of oatmeal and cinnamon, the papa would be gone to the fields, the sun already tangled in the trees

---

1. **chicharras** (chē·chä′räs): Spanish for "cicadas," insects that make a loud, high-pitched sound.

The Three Kings: Los Tres Reyes Magos (1960) by Manuel Jiménez.
Arrazola, Oaxaca, Mexico. Painted wood, figure on left is 9¹/₄".
Girard Foundation Collection at the Museum of International Folk Art, a unit of the Museum of
New Mexico, Santa Fe. Photo by Michel Monteaux.

and the urracas[2] screeching their rubber-screech cry. The boy
Ruben and the girl Rosalinda would have to be shaken awake for
school. The mama would give the baby Gilberto his bottle and
then she would go back to sleep before getting up again to the
20   chores that were always waiting. That is how the world had been.

But today the big box had arrived. When the boy Ruben and
the girl Rosalinda came home from school, it was already sitting

---

2. **urracas** (o͞o·rä′käs): Spanish for "magpies," black and white birds
known for their noisy chattering.

Pause at line 20. From the
details of their daily lives,
how would you describe the
family in this story so far?

____

____

____

____

____

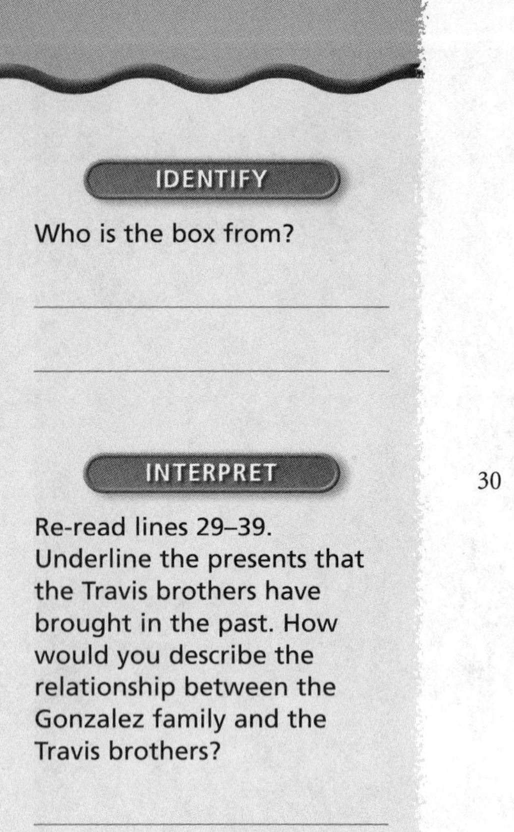

Who is the box from?

____

____

Re-read lines 29–39. Underline the presents that the Travis brothers have brought in the past. How would you describe the relationship between the Gonzalez family and the Travis brothers?

____

____

____

____

____

____

____

Read the boxed passage aloud several times until you can read it through without pausing. Pay attention to Cisneros's simple **diction** and minimal use of punctuation. Consider what effect this creates in the voice of the narrator.

obstructed (əb·strukt′id) *v.*: cut off from sight; blocked.

---

in the living room in front of the television set that no longer worked. Who had put it there? Where had it come from? A box covered with red paper with green Christmas trees and a card on top that said "Merry Christmas to the Gonzales Family. Frank, Earl, and Dwight Travis. P.S. DO NOT OPEN TILL XMAS." That's all.

30   Two times the mama was made to come into the living room, first to explain to the children and later to their father how the brothers Travis had arrived in the blue pickup, and how it had taken all three of those big men to lift the box off the back of the truck and bring it inside, and how she had had to nod and say thank-you thank-you thank-you over and over because those were the only words she knew in English. Then the brothers Travis had nodded as well, the way they always did when they came and brought the boxes of clothes, or the turkey each November, or the canned ham on Easter, ever since the children had begun to earn high grades at the school where Dwight Travis was the principal.

40   But this year the Christmas box was bigger than usual. What could be in a box so big? The boy Ruben and the girl Rosalinda begged all afternoon to be allowed to open it, and that is when the mama had said the sixth of January, the Day of the Three Kings. Not a day sooner.

It seemed the weeks stretched themselves wider and wider since the arrival of the big box. The mama got used to sweeping around it because it was too heavy for her to push in a corner. But since the television no longer worked ever since the after-noon the children had poured iced tea through the little grates in 50   the back, it really didn't matter if the box **obstructed** the view. Visitors that came inside the house were told and told again the story of how the box had arrived, and then each was made to guess what was inside.

It was the comadre[3] Elodia who suggested over coffee one afternoon that the big box held a portable washing machine that

---

3. **comadre** (kô·mä′dre): Spanish word referring to a woman relative or very close family friend. The word literally means "co-mother." It often refers to a godmother.

could be rolled away when not in use, the kind she had seen in her Sears Roebuck catalog. The mama said she hoped so

because the wringer washer she had used for the last ten years had finally gotten tired and quit. These past few weeks she had had to boil all the clothes in the big pot she used for cooking the Christmas tamales. Yes. She hoped the big box was a portable washing machine. A washing machine, even a **portable** one, would be good.

But the neighbor man Cayetano said, What foolishness, comadre. Can't you see the box is too small to hold a washing machine, even a portable one. Most likely God has heard your prayers and sent a new color TV. With a good antenna you could catch all the Mexican soap operas, the neighbor man said. You could distract yourself with the complicated troubles of the rich and then give thanks to God for the blessed simplicity of your poverty. A new TV would surely be the end to all your miseries.

Each night when the papa came home from the fields, he would spread newspapers on the cot in the living room, where the boy Ruben and the girl Rosalinda slept, and sit facing the big box in the center of the room. Each night he imagined the box held something different. The day before yesterday he guessed a new record player. Yesterday an ice chest filled with beer. Today the papa sat with his bottle of beer, fanning himself with a magazine, and said in a voice as much a plea as a **prophecy:** air conditioner.

But the boy Ruben and the girl Rosalinda were sure the big box was filled with toys. They had even punctured it in one corner with a pencil when their mother was busy cooking, but they could see nothing inside but blackness.

Only the baby Gilberto remained uninterested in the contents of the big box and seemed each day more fascinated with the exterior of the box rather than the interior. One afternoon

Re-read lines 101–115. Underline the details in these lines that help you visualize the **setting.** Describe the setting and the atmosphere that the details in these lines help create.

____

____

____

____

____

____

____

____

____

____

____

____

____

____

____

What do you think is in the box?

____

____

____

____

he tore off a fistful of paper, which he was chewing when his mother swooped him up with one arm, rushed him to the kitchen sink, and forced him to swallow handfuls of lukewarm water in case the red dye of the wrapping paper might

100 be poisonous.

When Christmas Eve finally came, the family Gonzalez put on their good clothes and went to Midnight Mass. They came home to a house that smelled of tamales and atole,[4] and everyone was allowed to open one present before going to sleep. But the big box was to remain untouched until the sixth of January.

On New Year's Eve the little house was filled with people, some related, some not, coming in and out. The friends of the papa came with bottles, and the mama set out a bowl of grapes to count off the New Year. That night the children did not sleep

110 in the living room cot as they usually did, because the living room was crowded with big-fannied ladies and fat-stomached men sashaying to the accordion music of the midget twins from McAllen.[5] Instead the children fell asleep on a lump of handbags and crumpled suit jackets on top of the mama and the papa's bed, dreaming of the contents of the big box.

Finally, the fifth of January. And the boy Ruben and the girl Rosalinda could hardly sleep. All night they whispered last-minute wishes. The boy thought perhaps if the big box held a bicycle, he would be the first to ride it, since he was the oldest.

120 This made his sister cry until the mama had to yell from her bedroom on the other side of the plastic curtains, Be quiet or I'm going to give you each the stick, which sounds worse in Spanish than it does in English. Then no one said anything. After a very long time, long after they heard the mama's wheezed

---

4. **atole** (ä·tō′lä): warm drink made with corn flour.
5. **McAllen:** small town in Texas near the Mexican border.

breathing and the papa's piped snoring, the children closed their eyes and remembered nothing.

The papa was already in the bathroom coughing up the night before from his throat when the urracas began their clownish chirping. The boy Ruben awoke and shook his sister. The mama, frying the potatoes and beans for breakfast, nodded permission for the box to be opened.

With a kitchen knife the boy Ruben cut a careful edge along the top. The girl Rosalinda tore the Christmas wrapping with her fingernails. The papa and the mama lifted the cardboard flaps and everyone peered inside to see what it was the brothers Travis had brought them on the Day of the Three Kings.

There were layers of balled newspaper packed on top. When these had been cleared the boy Ruben looked inside. The girl Rosalinda looked inside. The papa and the mama looked.

This is what they saw: the complete Britannica Junior Encyclopaedia, twenty-four volumes in red imitation leather with gold-**embossed** letters, beginning with Volume I, Aar-Bel and ending with Volume XXIV, Yel-Zyn. The girl Rosalinda let out a sad cry, as if her hair was going to be cut again. The boy Ruben pulled out Volume IV, Ded-Fem. There were many pictures and many words, but there were more words than pictures. The papa flipped through Volume XXII, but because he could not read English words, simply put the book back and grunted. What can we do with this? No one said anything, and shortly after, the screen door slammed.

Only the mama knew what to do with the contents of the big box. She withdrew Volumes VI, VII, and VIII, marched off to the dinette set in the kitchen, placed two on Rosalinda's chair so she could better reach the table, and put one underneath the plant stand that danced.

When the boy and the girl returned from school that day they found the books stacked into squat pillars against one living room wall and a board placed on top. On this were arranged several plastic doilies and framed family photographs. The rest

VOCABULARY

embossed (em·bôst′) *adj.*: raised above the surface.

IRONY

Pause at line 150. **Situational irony** occurs when things turn out differently than we expected. What **situational irony** can you find now that the box has been opened?

Pause at line 162. What is the mother using the books for? Describe the **situational irony** you find here.

____

____

____

____

____

____

____

improvised (im′prə·vīzd′) v.: made or created from available materials.

Pause at line 182. Why do you think Ruben won't touch the books? What does this reluctance suggest about him as a **character**?

____

____

____

____

____

____

160 of the volumes the baby Gilberto was playing with, and he was already rubbing his sore gums along the corners of Volume XIV.

The girl Rosalinda also grew interested in the books. She took out her colored pencils and painted blue on the eyelids of all the illustrations of women and with a red pencil dipped in spit she painted their lips and fingernails red-red. After a couple of days, when all the pictures of women

170 had been colored in this manner, she began to cut out some of the prettier pictures and paste them on looseleaf paper.

One volume suffered from being exposed to the rain when the papa **improvised** a hat during a sudden shower. He forgot it on the hood of the car when he drove off. When the children came home from school they set it on the porch to dry. But the pages puffed up and became so fat, the book was impossible to close.

Only the boy Ruben refused to touch the books. For several

180 days he avoided the principal because he didn't know what to say in case Mr. Travis were to ask how they were enjoying the Christmas present.

On the Saturday after New Year's the mama and the papa went into town for groceries and left the boy in charge of watching his sister and baby brother. The girl Rosalinda was stacking books into spiral staircases and making her paper dolls descend them in a fancy manner.

Perhaps the boy Ruben would not have bothered to open the volume left on the kitchen table if he had not seen his moth-

190 er wedge her name-day corsage in its pages. On the page where the mama's carnation lay pressed between two pieces of Kleenex was a picture of a dog in a space ship. FIRST DOG IN SPACE the caption said. The boy turned to another page and read where cashews came from. And then about the man who invent-

ed the guillotine. And then about Bengal tigers. And about clouds. All afternoon the boy read, even after the mama and the papa came home. Even after the sun set, until the mama said time to sleep and put the light out.

In their bed on the other side of the plastic curtain the mama and the papa slept. Across from them in the crib slept the baby Gilberto. The girl Rosalinda slept on her end of the cot. But the boy Ruben watched the night sky turn from violet. To blue. To gray. And then from gray. To blue. To violet once again.

MEET THE WRITER

Sandra Cisneros (1954–   ) grew up in two worlds, as her family moved back and forth between Chicago and Mexico City. Her famous book *The House on Mango Street* is a wonderful collection of vignettes about a girl named Esperanza growing up in a Hispanic neighborhood in Chicago. As a child, Cisneros says, she buried herself in books—the lives of the saints, the Doctor Doolittle books, *Alice in Wonderland,* and fairy tales. What makes her stories unique isn't just what she writes about—it's how Cisneros writes about it. Critics have praised her distinctive style. Also a poet, Cisneros often gives readings of her poems and stories. She makes her home in San Antonio, Texas, in a house that is painted purple.

Three Wise Guys

Literary Skills
Analyze
situational irony.

Irony Chart   The contrast between expectations and reality is referred to as irony. Fill in the Irony Chart below to help you understand how the events in "Three Wise Guys" create **situational irony.**

Expectation—What the Gonzalez family hopes is in the box:

Reality—What is really in the box:

Situational irony—Difference between expectations and reality:

Expectation—How the present was intended to be used:

Reality—How it is actually used:

Situational irony—Difference between expectations and reality:

Skills Review

Three Wise Guys

VOCABULARY AND COMPREHENSION

A. Diction: Plain, Formal, or Poetic?   Fill in each blank with a word from the Word Box. Then, check the box that best describes the type of diction used in each sentence.

Word Box

obstructed

portable

prophecy

embossed

improvised

1. Since we possess a utilitarian and ___________________ cat-carrier device, we could transport our ailing feline by foot to the veterinarian.
   ☐ poetic   ☐ formal   ☐ plain

2. We ___________________ an umbrella out of sticks and nylon.
   ☐ poetic   ☐ formal   ☐ plain

3. She gazed in delight at her gift—a diary bound in leather with her initials ___________________ on the cover.
   ☐ poetic   ☐ formal   ☐ plain

4. The bellhop removed the luggage because it ___________________ the hallway.
   ☐ poetic   ☐ formal   ☐ plain

5. Kwan waited for the ___________________ to be told—for his future, wrapped in the mists of the possible, to be unveiled.
   ☐ poetic   ☐ formal   ☐ plain

B. Reading Comprehension   Answer each question below.

1. What does each person in the family imagine is in the box? What actually is in the box?

   ____

   ____

2. How does each person in the house make use of the gift?

   ____

   ____

3. What does Ruben discover by the end of the story?

   ____

   ____

SKILLS FOCUS

Vocabulary Skills
Analyze diction.

Before You Read

Hurdles by Derek Kirk Kim

This is a story about jumping hurdles, both figuratively and literally.

LITERARY FOCUS: VERBAL AND SITUATIONAL IRONY

Irony is the difference between what we expect to happen and what actually happens.

Verbal irony is used when someone says something but means the opposite. You are using verbal irony when you say you can't eat another bite while piling your plate high with second helpings.

Situational irony describes an event that is not just surprising but is actually the opposite of what we expected. When we see five large people get out of a tiny car, we see situational irony.

As you read the story, think about the hurdles the narrator comes up against and how his reactions to them lead to the ironic ending of the story.

READING SKILLS: CAUSE AND EFFECT

"Hurdles" contains a series of causes and their effects. A **cause** is the reason that an action takes place. An **effect** is the result or consequence of a cause. As you read this graphic story, watch for the causes of certain events and the effects of others.

SKILLS FOCUS

Literary Skills
Understand verbal and situational irony.

Reading Skills
Understand cause and effect.

HURDLES

1.

I jump hurdles every day. While everyone else on the track team runs straight through, my fellow hurdlers and I go up and down, up and down. Some hurdlers jump over the hurdles, and others kick them down. I jump over them.

2.

Sometimes I'd like to just kick them out of my way, but I guess I'm just too polite. But who cares, I can cross the finish line and that's all that matters. Besides, my coach says either way is just fine.

3.

We call our coach "Pear-Nose". There's always a pair of black sunglasses atop that nose of his. And he always stands with his hands behind his back. Now that I think about it, I've never seen his hands. Maybe he doesn't have any hands, I don't know.

CLARIFY

In panel 1, the narrator describes two ways of dealing with hurdles. Which one does he prefer?

INFER

In panel 2, we learn that the narrator sometimes wants to kick the hurdles over but stops himself. Why doesn't he kick them over?

AMBIGUITY

In panel 3, the narrator says he has never seen his coach's hands. Do you think this statement's meaning is literal, figurative, or ambiguous?

Panel 4 acts as a hinge on which the story turns, or changes direction. From what you know of the narrator and his coach so far, predict what will happen next.

____

____

____

____

IRONY

What kind of irony does panel 6 contain?

____

____

____

____

CONNECT

In panel 2, on page 139, the narrator states that he is too polite. Do you think his re-action to his coach, described in panel 7, is too polite? Explain.

____

____

____

____

____

____

____

4.

5.

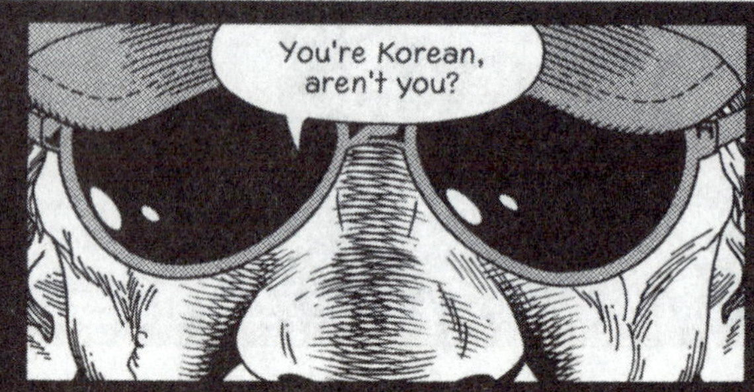

6.

7.

MEET THE WRITER

Derek Kirk Kim (1974–   ) writes and illustrates short stories that are published in books called graphic novels. He was born in South Korea, where reading comics was a normal part of learning to read. Kim remembers imitating the style of those comics as soon as he learned how to draw. At the age of eight, he moved to the United States. He grew up in Pacifica, California, where he still lives. Today he pursues his passion for writing and drawing realistic fiction.

Hurdles

**Reading
Skills**
Identify cause
and effect.

Cause-and-Effect Chart   Fill in the blanks below with the appropriate causes
or effects.

Cause	Effect
Because . . .	The narrator doesn't kick the hurdles down.
Because . . .	The narrator doesn't know if the coach has any hands.
Because they have a big meet coming up . . .	
Because . . .	The narrator runs through the grass, past the baseball field, out the main gate, and home.

Skills Review

Hurdles

COMPREHENSION

A. Reading Comprehension   Answer each question below.

1. In panel 2, the narrator argues that the end justifies the means. How does he do this?

____

____

____

____

2. The coach is notable for his nickname, for wearing a pair of black sunglasses, and for what else?

____

____

____

____

3. In panels 5 and 6, the coach sets up the narrator in order to put him down. What is the put-down?

____

____

____

____

4. What inferences can you make about the narrator's statement "I jump hurdles every day" at the end of the comic?

____

____

____

____

Collection 6

Symbolism and Allegory

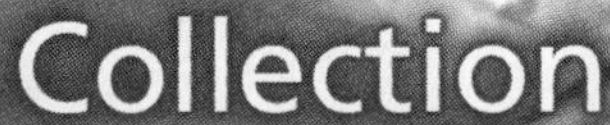

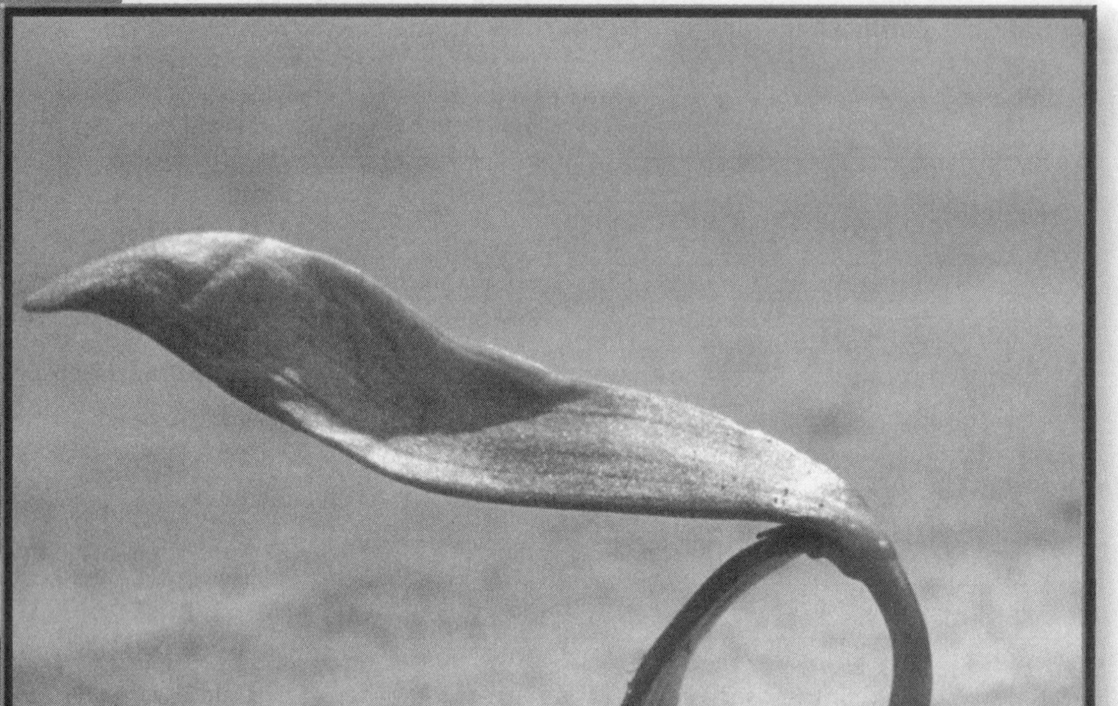

James Osmond/Alamy

Academic Vocabulary for Collection 6

These are the terms you should know
as you read and analyze the texts in this collection.

____

Symbol An object, a person, an animal, or an event that stands for something more than itself. For example, a blindfolded woman who is holding up balance scales is often used to symbolize justice, which calls for fairness in weighing the fate of the accused.

Public Symbol A symbol that has become widely recognized, such as the bald eagle (a symbol of the United States) or the olive branch (a symbol of peace).

Invented Symbol A symbol invented by a writer that usually stands for something abstract, such as evil, innocence, or love. The meanings of literary symbols must be interpreted by the reader. Use these guidelines when you are trying to interpret the meaning of a symbol:

- Symbols are often visual.
- When an object or event is used as a symbol, it usually appears several times in a text.
- A symbol is a type of figurative language. Like a metaphor, a symbol is identified with something that is very different but that shares some of the same qualities. When you are thinking about whether something is used symbolically, ask yourself, "Does this character, object, or event stand for something?" In Herman Melville's novel *Moby-Dick,* for example, readers begin to sense that the white whale being hunted by Captain Ahab is more than just a whale. From the many descriptions of the whale in the novel, readers come to see it as a symbol of random, unexplainable evil.

Allegory A story in which characters or settings stand for something beyond themselves. The underlying meaning in an allegory is usually of moral, social, religious, or political significance. The characters may personify such abstract ideas as goodness or evil, charity or greed, and may contain clues to these qualities in their names. For example, a woman who stands for goodness might be named Ms. Kind.

Prologue *from* Walking with the Wind by John Lewis

You can take this story at face value: a simple tale involving children, a wooden house, and a windstorm. However, you can also consider the symbolic meaning of the characters and settings to find the story's deeper meaning.

LITERARY FOCUS: SYMBOLS AND ALLEGORY

A **symbol** is a specific kind of metaphor in which a person, a place, a thing, or an event stands both for itself and for something beyond itself. For example, in this memoir you will read a story about a windstorm. The windstorm actually occurred, but the writer also sees it as a **symbol** that deepens the story's meaning by representing another, larger force. Because the characters, objects, and events described in this anecdote carry symbolic meanings that tell a larger story, this prologue from *Walking with the Wind* becomes a kind of extended metaphor called **allegory.**

As you read, look for clues that suggest the windstorm stands for something more than itself.

READING SKILLS: MAKING INFERENCES

An **inference** is an intelligent guess you make about the meaning of something. You form inferences by putting together several related details and then generalizing about what they might mean. In making inferences about characters, you also draw on your own experiences. For example, if you observe a character who speaks sharply to her dog, slams the door, and won't speak to her parents, you can make an inference that this character is upset about something, You make that inference based on story details and on your own experiences with people.

To make inferences about the meaning of a symbol, follow these steps:

- Pay attention to details. Does the writer keep mentioning something, such as an event or an object, throughout the story?
- Think about what the event or object represents to you. If the object is a ring, for example, it may represent love or friendship.
- Then, combine your own experience with the evidence in the story to make an inference about what this event or object might signify.

Literary Skills
Understand symbolism and allegory.

Reading Skills
Make inferences.

Vocabulary Skills
Understand connotation and denotation.

VOCABULARY DEVELOPMENT

PREVIEW SELECTION VOCABULARY

Preview the following words from the memoir before you begin reading.

monumental (män′yoo·ment′′l) *adj.:* of outstanding significance, often historical.

*John Lewis was on the front lines of one of America's **monumental** movements for change.*

dignity (dig′nə·tē) *n.:* inherent nobility or worth.

*Lewis respects the **dignity** of all people.*

essence (es′əns) *n.:* core; heart; embodiment.

*This simple anecdote, says Lewis, is the **essence** of his life.*

beacon (bē′kən) *n.:* source of guidance or inspiration.

*Martin Luther King, Jr.'s concept of the Beloved Community has guided Lewis like a **beacon** throughout his life.*

CONNOTATION AND DENOTATION: WORD INTENSITY

Every word has a denotation, or literal dictionary meaning. Some words also have connotations, or associations and emotions that have come to be attached to them. You can determine a word's connotation by its context. For example, *noteworthy, significant, major,* and *monumental* all have the same denotation: *important.* However, these words' connotations are not the same, as they represent different degrees, or intensities, of importance. Study this chart to understand the intensity of the connotations of these words:

Lowest Intensity   **Highest Intensity**

important		more important		most important
noteworthy	→	significant	→	major	→	monumental

Walking with the Wind

John Lewis

VOCABULARY

monumental
(män'yoo·ment''l) *adj.:* of outstanding significance, often historical.

IDENTIFY

In lines 3–4, underline the three things the narrator's story will be about.

CLARIFY

The war referred to in lines 10–12 is World War II, which was fought from 1939 to 1945.

I want to begin this book with a little story. It has nothing to do with a national stage, or historic figures, or **monumental** events. It's a simple story, a true story, about a group of young children, a wood-frame house and a windstorm.

The children were my cousins: Roy Lee and Jinnie Boy, Naomi and Leslie and Willie Muriel—about a dozen of them, all told—along with my older sister Ora and my brothers Edward and Adolph. And me, John Robert.

10   I was four years old at the time, too young to understand there was a war going on over in Europe and out in the Pacific as well. The grownups called it a world war, but I had no idea what that meant. The only world I knew was the one I stepped out into each morning, a place of thick pine forests and white cotton fields and red clay roads winding around my family's house in our little corner of Pike County, Alabama.

We had just moved that spring onto some land my father had bought, the first land anyone in his family had ever owned—110 acres of cotton and corn and peanut fields, along with an old but sturdy three-bedroom house, a large house for that part of the county, the biggest place for miles around. It had a well in the front yard, and pecan trees out back, and muscadine° grapevines growing wild in the woods all around us—*our* woods.

My father bought the property from a local white business-man who lived in the nearby town of Troy. The total payment was $300. Cash. That was every penny my father had to his name, money he had earned the way almost everyone we knew made what money they could in those days—by tenant farming. My father was a sharecropper, planting, raising and picking the same crops that had been grown in that soil for hundreds of years by tribes like the Choctaws and the Chickasaws and the Creeks, Native Americans who were working this land long before the place was called Alabama, long before black or white men were anywhere to be seen in those parts.

Almost every neighbor we had in those woods was a share-cropper, and most of them were our relatives. Nearly every adult I knew was an aunt or an uncle, every child my first or second cousin. That included my uncle Rabbit and aunt Seneva and their children, who lived about a half mile or so up the road from us.

On this particular afternoon—it was a Saturday, I'm almost certain—about fifteen of us children were outside my aunt Seneva's house, playing in her dirt yard. The sky began clouding over, the wind started picking up, lightning flashed far off in the distance, and suddenly I wasn't thinking about playing anymore; I was terrified. I had already seen what lightning could do. I'd seen fields catch on fire after a hit to a haystack. I'd watched trees actually explode when a bolt of lightning struck them, the sap inside rising to an instant boil, the trunk swelling until it

---

° **muscadine** (mus′kə·din) *n.:* variety of grape with small leaves and
   clusters of spherical grapes.

Why do you think the narrator's mother tells the children that the sound of thunder is the sound of God working? Explain.

____

____

____

____

In lines 59–70, the author illustrates the intensity of the storm by describing its effect on the house in which his family takes shelter. What happens after the house starts to shake?

____

____

____

____

In lines 78–80, we learn the literal meaning of the memoir's title. What is the literal meaning?

____

____

____

____

burst its bark. The sight of those snips of pine bark snaking
50 through the air like ribbons was both fascinating and horrifying.

Lightning terrified me, and so did thunder. My mother used to gather us around her whenever we heard thunder and she'd tell us to hush, be still now, because God was doing his work. That was what thunder was, my mother said. It was the sound of God doing his work.

But my mother wasn't with us on this particular afternoon. Aunt Seneva was the only adult around, and as the sky blackened and the wind grew stronger, she herded us all inside.

Her house was not the biggest place around, and it seemed
60 even smaller with so many children squeezed inside. Small and surprisingly quiet. All of the shouting and laughter that had been going on earlier, outside, had stopped. The wind was howling now, and the house was starting to shake. We were scared. Even Aunt Seneva was scared.

And then it got worse. Now the house was beginning to sway. The wood plank flooring beneath us began to bend. And then, a corner of the room started lifting up.

I couldn't believe what I was seeing. None of us could. This storm was actually pulling the house toward the sky. With us
70 inside it.

That was when Aunt Seneva told us to clasp hands. Line up and hold hands, she said, and we did as we were told. Then she had us walk as a group toward the corner of the room that was rising. From the kitchen to the front of the house we walked, the wind screaming outside, sheets of rain beating on the tin roof. Then we walked back in the other direction, as another end of the house began to lift.

And so it went, back and forth, fifteen children walking with the wind, holding that trembling house down with the
80 weight of our small bodies.

More than half a century has passed since that day, and it has struck me more than once over those many years that our society is not unlike the children in that house, rocked again and again by the winds of one storm or another, the walls around us seeming at times as if they might fly apart.

It seemed that way in the 1960s, at the height of the civil rights movement, when America itself felt as if it might burst at the seams—so much tension, so many storms. But the people of conscience never left the house. They never ran away. They stayed, they came together and they did the best they could, clasping hands and moving toward the corner of the house that was the weakest.

And then another corner would lift, and we would go there.

And eventually, inevitably, the storm would settle, and the house would still stand.

An African American student sits at a lunch counter reserved for white customers during a sit-in to protest segregation. Packages of napkins have been placed on nearby stools to discourage other protesters from joining the sit-in.

dignity (dig′nə·tē) *n.:* inherent nobility or worth.

essence (es′əns) *n.:* core; heart; embodiment.

In lines 100–104, the narrator explains the symbolic meaning of the story's title. Explain it in your own words.

But we knew another storm would come, and we would have to do it all over again.

And we did.

And we still do, all of us. You and I.

100   Children holding hands, walking with the wind. That is America to me—not just the movement for civil rights but the endless struggle to respond with decency, **dignity** and a sense of brotherhood to all the challenges that face us as a nation, as a whole.

That is the story, in **essence,** of my life, of the path to which I've been committed since I turned from a boy to a man, and to which I remain committed today. It is a path that extends

Christopher Felver/CORBIS

beyond the issue of race alone, and beyond class as well. And
gender. And age. And every other distinction that tends to separate us as human beings rather than bring us together.

That path involves nothing less than the pursuit of the
most precious and pure concept I have ever known, an ideal I
discovered as a young man and that has guided me like a **beacon**
ever since, a concept called the Beloved Community.

MEET THE WRITER

John Lewis (1940–   ) was born in Alabama to sharecropping
parents. As a child, Lewis experienced racism and its effects firsthand, which led him to participate in the many civil rights demonstrations and protests that occurred in the South during the 1950s
and '60s. He was an organizer and important member of the
Student Nonviolent Coordinating Committee (SNCC). By 1963,
despite his young age, Lewis was recognized as one of the most
important civil rights leaders in the country. Although he was
arrested, attacked, and injured on numerous occasions, he continued to support the use of nonviolent protests as a means of
ending discrimination. Lewis continues to fight for racial and
economic equality by working for change through the political
system. After first serving on the Atlanta City Council, Lewis
became a member of the U.S. House of Representatives for
Georgia's Fifth District. He is now serving his eighth term in office.

beacon (bē'kən) *n.:* source
of guidance or inspiration.

The "Beloved Community"
is a term popularized by
Dr. Martin Luther King, Jr.
that describes a community
without discrimination or
poverty in which conflicts
are resolved through non-
violent means.

Notes

Prologue *from* Walking with the Wind

SKILLS FOCUS

Literature Skills
Analyze symbolism and allegory.

Allegory Chart   In *Walking with the Wind*, the story elements stand both for themselves and for something beyond themselves. Use the following chart to explore the allegorical meanings of the symbols and how they work together to convey the author's meaning. The left-hand column summarizes literal story events. In the right-hand column, write the allegorical meaning of those events. The first row has been done for you.

Literal Story Event	Allegorical Meaning
Most of the neighbors were relatives.	All people of the world are connected.
Aunt Seneva's house was small and seemed smaller when crammed with children.	
The sky darkened, the wind picked up, lightning flashed, and the narrator grew frightened.	
The windstorm was pulling the house apart, with the narrator and his family inside it.	
The children held hands and walked as a group toward the corner of the house that was lifting.	
The children walked back and forth, holding down different corners of the house with their weight.	

    Collection 6: Symbolism and Allegory

Skills Review

Prologue *from* Walking with the Wind

VOCABULARY AND COMPREHENSION

A. Determining Connotations: Intensity   Read each sentence from the selection, paying special attention to the Word Box word in bold. Then, decide which answer choice has the *most* similar connotation.

<table>
<tr><td>

1. "It has nothing to do with . . . **monumental** events."

   A important

   B major

   C significant

   D noteworthy

</td><td>

3. "That is the story, in **essence,** of my life."

   A core

   B necessity

   C crux

   D significance

</td></tr>
<tr><td>

2. "That is America to me . . . the endless struggle to respond with decency, **dignity** and a sense of brotherhood to all . . . challenges."

   F standing

   G pride

   H grandeur

   J status

</td><td>

4. "That path involves . . . an ideal I discovered as a young man and that has guided me like a **beacon** ever since."

   F guiding light

   G North Star

   H signal fire

   J lantern

</td></tr>
</table>

> **Word Box**
>
> monumental
>
> dignity
>
> essence
>
> beacon

B. Reading Comprehension   Answer each question below.

1. How old was John Lewis when the story he relates took place?

____

2. Why did John Lewis take such pride in the area in which he lived as a child?

____

____

3. The story Lewis relates in this selection has guided him in his life. What does this story symbolize to him?

____

____

____

SKILLS FOCUS

Vocabulary Skills
Analyze connotation and denotation.

March by Clay Goss

Many authors use symbols in their writing to convey their deeper messages and emotions. As you read this monologue, think about what the changing of the seasons and "spring fever" mean to Clay Goss.

LITERARY FOCUS: SYMBOLISM AND ALLEGORY

An allegory is a story that has both a literal and a symbolic meaning. Allegories tend to use simple situations to illustrate broader ideas, but those broader meanings are not often stated directly. In the previous selection from *Walking with the Wind,* John Lewis explains the deeper meaning of his allegory. However, it is far more common for the author to leave it to you to find the meaning of a symbol, which is not always obvious at first. Deciphering an allegory usually requires reading a text more than once.

READING SKILLS: MAKING INFERENCES

To discover the meaning of most symbols and allegories, you have to think about all the elements of a work and then make an inference, or educated guess, based on the sum of the clues provided in the text and on the background knowledge you bring to your reading.

- Read "March" on a literal level to find out what happens to whom.
- Use your background knowledge to think of everything you know about kite flying, father-son relationships, and human nature.
- Consider the story elements that may be symbolic and represent broader ideas.
- Finally, consider how these elements work together to create allegory.

As you read, jot down your ideas in a chart like this:

Literal Story Event	Allegorical Meaning
loses his mind every March	loses touch with what's important

Literary Skills
Understand symbolism and allegory.

Reading Skills
Making inferences.

Vocabulary Skills
Understand figurative language.

VOCABULARY DEVELOPMENT

PREVIEW SELECTION VOCABULARY

The following words appear in "March." Look them over before you begin the monologue.

abrupt (ə·brupt′) *adj.:* unexpectedly sudden.

*Every year, with the **abrupt** arrival of spring, the narrator loses his mind.*

tether (te*th*′ər) *n.:* leash used as a restraint.

*The narrator regards the string of his kite as a **tether** that connects him to the cosmos.*

deconstructing (dē′kən·strukt′iŋ) *v.:* breaking into component parts.

*Jamaal first cries, "I love you, Amigo!" before **deconstructing** the chant to "I love the kite."*

incantation (in′kan·tā′shən) *n.:* magical charm or spell.

*Jamaal chants an **incantation** to the kite and the cosmos it connects him with.*

FIGURATIVE LANGUAGE: IDIOM, SIMILE, AND METAPHOR

In a general sense, words and phrases that describe one thing in terms of another different thing are called **figurative language.** Figurative language relies on imagery and appeals to the senses and is not meant to be taken literally. Three common types of figurative language follow:

- An **idiom** is an expression peculiar to a particular language that is not understandable in a literal sense. For example, our narrator might have a *windfall* (unexpected good luck), get a *second wind* (new burst of energy after a lag), *shoot the breeze* (chat), or be told to *go fly a kite* (go away) without even stepping outside.

- A **simile** is a figure of speech that uses comparison words, such as *like, as, than,* or *resembles.* The old saying "March comes in *like* a lion and goes out *like* a lamb" describes the sudden, abrupt change in the weather that the narrator celebrates.

- A **metaphor** is a figure of speech that compares two unlike things by saying that something *is* something else without using comparison words. You could turn the example above from a simile into a metaphor by saying "March *is* a lion" or "March *is* a lamb."

Remember that in literature, metaphors become symbols when they are used to convey a broader meaning; similarly, a group of symbols working together to tell a story within the story will make it an allegory.

As you read, note Clay Goss's rich use of figurative language.

March

Clay Goss

This story, originally a letter written to a friend, was developed into a monologue about father-son relationships.

Every year for as long as I can remember, in the month of March I lose my memory. Maybe it's just the way my body responds to the **abrupt** change of seasons. The days are longer and the sun is out more. There's an expectancy in the air, a whisper slowly growing into a warm mellow roar.

I lose my keys. I lose my money. I misplace papers. I can't remember obvious things like my telephone number. Just the other day I had to dial information to find out what my number was, this after dialing my old number (twenty-five cents), what I thought was my current number (twenty-five cents), and having to ask someone what the information number was (I thought it was still 411).

Then there's the wind. Me and the wind. Or the wind and me. I'll step outside and the wind will be up, and I'll get this feeling that the wind is going through me or inside me, straight up to my brain where it just blows whatever perception I have of myself away. My head gets to spinning, floating. It's as if I'm a leaf left over from the fall finally getting its chance to fly.

I want to fly a kite. A boyhood dream, I know. I want to fly a kite in a big open space, stand there anchored to the ground with the pull of the string as a **tether** to the cosmos. And so I get a kite and go up to Belmont Plateau where Ben Franklin flew his legendary kite with the key dangling from its string. I do this every year.

"March" by Clay Goss from *Jump Up and Say!* by Linda Goss and Clay Goss. Copyright © 1995 **Clay Goss.** Reproduced by permission of the author.

Sidebar notes:

IDENTIFY

Every year in March, the narrator loses his memory. Underline what he suspects is the cause in lines 2–5.

VOCABULARY

abrupt (ə·brupt′) *adj.:* unexpectedly sudden.

IDENTIFY

Underline the figure of speech used in lines 17–18. What type of **figurative language** is this?

VOCABULARY

tether (te*th*′ər) *n.:* leash used as a restraint.

FIGURATIVE LANGUAGE

Identify the figure of speech in line 21. Is it an idiom, a simile, or a metaphor?

Purestock/Alamy

I buy the kite, and it never flies right. The last few years I have taken my son along, and he just looks at me as I try to fly my kite. It goes up and it comes down. It never goes up very far or stays up very long. We always end up looking at all the other kites swaying in the plateau breeze. That's a lot of fun, too. The next best thing to being there.

This year I bought my kite and headed out with Jamaal for our yearly attempt at flying. We went out in the late afternoon. Monsoon[1] winds accompanied us, but still the kite wouldn't fly. We watched the others, some in the oddest shapes one can create, swoop the wind into their wings.

---

1. **monsoon** (män·sōon′) *n.* used as *adj.:* seasonal wind system that brings heavy rainfall to southern Asia.

> **INFER**
>
> What does Jamaal think about his father's kite-flying abilities?

March **159**

The next afternoon we went out again, because I had no classes to teach. It was a warm day with very little wind. I got the kite off the ground and decided to hand the controls over to Jamaal. I don't know why I did that since he was content to see me fail—by now it had become a joke between us, a fish tale, the one that always got away.

Jamaal began to run with the kite. I told him to slow down, but he kept on running. Soon he was fifty yards away and, *boom,* it was a miracle. The darn thing took flight. It looked like a bird. Then a sea gull. A hawk. An eagle. A Phantom jet fighter. A messenger from God. Jamaal stood there. It got to him. He was really moved. He told me he could feel the pull of the string from the tug. He screamed out some babble about my mother's dog— the one that was run over by a school bus last September, the dog he had named Amigo, the one we all loved. He screamed out, "Amigo, Amigo," over and over again. And then hollered, "I love you, Amigo," a couple of hundred times. By the time I got over to him, he was **deconstructing** this **incantation** back to the kite. He loved the kite now. But I know what I heard.

He handed me the controls, and I let myself be attached to the spirit of the string. It was a wonderful spirit, a pulling upward and outward at the same time. All you had to do was hold your ground and let the kite lead you around. Either way was cool. It was all about the connection.

After about five minutes I gave him back the reins. Man, the kite stayed up there for another thirty-five minutes, extended out as far as the length of the string. Jamaal said something like "This kite goes into my kite Hall of Fame."

Every year for as long as I can remember, in the month of March I lose my memory. I lose my car keys. I lose my wallet. I lose my socks and my underwear. I lose my eyeglasses. I lose my way. I lose my bearings. I lose my composure. I lose my head, and I often lose my mind. And then the March winds come

70 along, and I want to fly a kite. I want my son to tag along and watch me connect to the vastness of the universe; let him see me ride the breeze of the great googamooga,[2] drop eighteen thousand splits to the floor right dead in the lap of the alpha and the omega.[3] Recycle a boyhood dream.

This March the kite went up.

MEET THE WRITER

Clay Goss (1946–   ) was born in Philadelphia, Pennsylvania, and worked as a teacher before becoming a writer. Primarily a dramatist, Goss writes for theater and television, in addition to short fiction. He also writes books on African American traditions, such as *It's Kwanzaa Time!*, which he wrote with his wife, Linda.

---

2. **great googamooga** *n.:* expression similar to "Great God."
3. **the alpha and the omega:** first and last letters of the Greek alphabet. The expression is used to express the completeness of God.

ALLEGORY

What do you think kite flying **symbolizes** to the author? Do you think he will fly the kite the following March?

March

SKILLS FOCUS

Literature Skills
Analyze symbolism and allegory.

Allegory Chart   "March" is an allegory: It is meant to be read on both a literal and a symbolic level. Use the following chart to explore the allegorical meanings of the story events. The left-hand column summarizes the literal story events. In the right-hand column, write the allegorical meaning of those events.

Literal Story Event	Allegorical Meaning
The author loses his memory every March.	
The wind makes the author want to fly a kite.	
Each year the author buys a kite but fails to make it fly.	
The author's son finally gets the kite to soar.	
The author takes control of the kite and feels the pull of the string.	

Skills Review

March

VOCABULARY AND COMPREHENSION

A. Understanding Figurative Language   Read each sentence below. Fill in the blanks with the correct Word Box words. Then, underline the figure of speech in each sentence.

1. The ____________________ attached to the helium balloon was a slippery fish in Suraj's hand, so his mother tied it around his wrist to keep the balloon from flying away.

2. The train's stop was so ____________________ that my luggage was a missile shooting down the aisle.

3. Jan's repetition of chemical names before his science exam sounded like a magical ____________________ to his younger sister.

4. My cousin Albert, who is a very picky eater, was ____________________ his salad as carefully as if he were defusing a bomb.

B. Reading Comprehension   Answer each question below.

1. What happens to the narrator every March?

____

____

2. What does the narrator enjoy doing every March?

____

____

3. What effect does flying a kite have on Jamaal?

____

____

4. What effect does flying a kite have on the narrator?

____

____

Word Box

abrupt

tether

deconstructing

incantation

SKILLS FOCUS

Vocabulary Skills
Analyze figurative language.

Poetry

© Peter Lilja/Getty Images.

Academic Vocabulary for Collection 7

These are the terms you should know
as you read and analyze the poems in this collection.

Imagery Language that appeals to one or more of the five senses: sight, hearing, taste, touch, and smell. For example, this image—"the fish's slippery, shiny scales"—appeals to the senses of sight and touch. The words help us picture the fish and imagine how it would feel if we touched it.

Figurative Language A word or phrase that creates an imaginative comparison. Figurative language is not meant to be taken literally. There are several types of figures of speech:

- A **simile** compares two unlike things by using such words as *like* or *as:* "The many-colored fish is like a rainbow."
- A **metaphor** compares two unlike things without using such words as *like* or *as:* "The fish is a rainbow."
- **Personification** is a type of metaphor in which an object, animal, or idea is talked about as if it were human: "The fish smiles happily."

Rhyme The repetition of the sounds of the stressed vowel and of the rest of the word (*thinking, linking*).

- Words that have **approximate rhyme** repeat some sounds but are not exact echoes (*mean, fine*).
- Most rhymes—called **end rhymes**—come at the ends of lines: "Where in this *book* / Do you think I should *look*?
- Some rhymes—called **internal rhymes**—occur within a line of poetry: "I set my *hat* on the *mat.*"

Rhythm A musical quality based on the pattern of stressed and unstressed syllables that makes the voice rise and fall.

Meter The regular pattern of stressed and unstressed syllables in each line of poetry.

Free Verse Poetry that does not follow a regular pattern of rhyme and meter.

Alliteration (ə·lit′ər·ā′shən) The repetition of consonant sounds in words that appear close together: "He had horse and harness for them all."

Onomatopoeia (än′ō·mat′ō·pē′ə) The use of words that sound like that what they mean. *Beep, boom,* and *pow* are examples of onomatopoeia.

POEM

Slam, Dunk, & Hook

by Yusef Komunyakaa

The title of this poem—"Slam, Dunk, & Hook"—refers to the everyday game of basketball. For the poem's speaker, however, basketball is no ordinary game.

LITERARY FOCUS: IMAGERY

Poets help us share their experiences by using **imagery**—language that appeals to one or more of our five senses: sight, hearing, touch, smell, and taste.

- The **images** in "Slam, Dunk, & Hook" appeal to three senses—sight, hearing, and touch. As you read, think about how these images help the speaker convey his experiences.

READING SKILLS: READING A POEM

When you're reading a poem, keep the following strategies in mind:

1. **Look for punctuation in the poem telling you where sentences begin and end.** You'll notice that poets often—but not always—write in full sentences.
2. **Do not pause or make a full stop at the end of a line if there is no comma, period, semicolon, colon, or dash.** If there is no punctuation at the end of a line of poetry, most poets intend us to read right on to the next line to complete the sense of the sentence.
3. **If a passage of a poem is difficult to understand, look for the subject, verb, and complement of each sentence.** Decide what words the clauses and phrases modify.
4. **Be alert for comparisons—figures of speech.** Try to visualize what the poet is describing.
5. **Read the poem aloud.** Poets are not likely to work in silence. The sound of a poem is important.
6. **After you have read the poem, talk about it with someone, and read it again.** This time you'll see things in the poem you didn't notice before.

Literary Skills
Understand imagery.

Reading Skills
Use strategies for reading a poem.

Slam, Dunk, & Hook

Yusef Komunyakaa

BACKGROUND: LITERATURE AND SPORTS

"Slam, Dunk, & Hook" is inspired by the fast-paced, energetic game of basketball. The poem refers to several moves made on the basketball court. A fast break is a drive down the court at top speed. A slam dunk is a high jump that enables a player to slam the ball into the basket. As you read the poem, you may recognize other examples of basketball moves.

Fast breaks. Lay ups. With Mercury's°

Insignia° on our sneakers,

We outmaneuvered to footwork

Of bad angels. Nothing but a hot

5   Swish of strings like silk

Ten feet out. In the roundhouse

Labyrinth° our bodies

Created, we could almost

Last forever, poised in midair

10   Like storybook sea monsters.

A high note hung there

A long second. Off

The rim. We'd corkscrew

Up & dunk balls that exploded

15   The skullcap of hope & good

Intention. Lanky, all hands

& feet . . . sprung rhythm.

IMAGERY

Which senses does the **image** "a hot / Swish of strings" (lines 4–5) appeal to?

____

____

____

____

____

READING A POEM

Circle the subject and verb in the sentence in lines 6–10.

FLUENCY

Read lines 1–19 aloud twice. The first time, focus on deciding where to come to a full stop and where to pause. The second time, concentrate on conveying the speaker's emotions.

---

1. **Mercury's** (mʉr′kyͻor·ēz): Mercury is the messenger of the gods in Roman mythology. He is associated with agility and cleverness.
2. **insignia** (in·sig′nē·ə) *n.:* emblem or other distinguishing mark.
7. **labyrinth** (lab′ə·rinth) *n.:* complicated maze.

"Slam, Dunk, & Hook" from *Pleasure Dome: New and Collected Poems* by Yusef Komunyakaa. © 2001 by Yusef Komunyakaa. Reprinted by permission of Wesleyan University Press.

Why do you think Sonny Boy played basketball so hard all day when his mother died (lines 24–26)?

Macduff Everton/Iconica/Getty Images

We were metaphysical° when girls
Cheered on the sidelines.
20 Tangled up in a falling,
Muscles were a bright motor
Double-flashing to the metal hoop
Nailed to our oak.
When Sonny Boy's mama died
25 He played nonstop all day, so hard
Our backboard splintered.
Glistening with sweat,
We rolled the ball off
Our fingertips. Trouble
30 Was there slapping a blackjack
Against an open palm.
Dribble, drive to the inside,
& glide like a sparrow hawk.

---

18. metaphysical (met′ə·fiz′i·kəl) *adj.:* beyond the limits of physical experience.

Lay ups. Fast breaks.
35 We had moves we didn't know
    We had. Our bodies spun
    On swivels of bone & faith,
    Through a lyric slipknot
    Of joy, & we knew we were
40 Beautiful & dangerous.

MEET THE WRITER

Yusef Komunyakaa (1947–   ) has sometimes wished he were
an artist so that he could paint the images he tries to convey
through words in his poems. Komunyakaa's poetry is deeply
personal. His poems draw on his childhood days in Bogalusa,
Louisiana, his experiences as an African American man, and his
tour of duty during the Vietnam War. Although there were few
books in his childhood home, Komunyakaa grew up to become
a professor and award-winning poet.

Re-read lines 35–40. Explain
what the speaker is saying
about the experience of
playing basketball.

Slam, Dunk, & Hook

Literary Skills
Analyze
imagery.

Imagery Chart   Imagery is language that appeals to the senses: sight, hearing, touch, smell, and taste. Analyze the imagery in "Slam, Dunk, & Hook" by filling in the chart below. In the first column, list the images you find in the poem. In the second column, write down the sense or senses each image appeals to.

Image	Sense or senses it appeals to

Most Effective Image   Review the images you listed in your chart, and choose the one you think is the most effective. Then, write a few sentences explaining why you chose that particular image.

____

____

____

____

____

POEM

Dream Deferred by Langston Hughes

It is sometimes said that our hopes and dreams are our most important possessions. What do you think the poet means by the word *dream* in this poem? What is he saying about the importance of dreams?

LITERARY FOCUS: FIGURES OF SPEECH

A **figure of speech** is based on a comparison between two unlike things; it is not meant to be taken literally. Figures of speech help writers create imaginative comparisons that communicate thoughts and ideas in new and unique ways. Figures of speech are central to poetry. As you read the poems that follow, look for figures of speech. Several types of figures speech are defined below.

- A **simile** compares two unlike things by using such words as *like* or *as:* "When the dream ended, her hopes deflated like a popped balloon."
- A **metaphor** compares two unlike things without using any specific word of comparison. Metaphors are often **direct;** the two items being compared are linked by *is* or *are:* "The moon is a ghostly ship." Other metaphors are **implied;** the comparison is suggested rather than stated: "The moon sailed away on the clouds."
- **Personification** is a special type of metaphor in which objects, animals, or ideas are given human qualities or abilities: "The tree sang a song in the wind."

READING SKILLS: READING FOR MEANING

When you're reading a poem with figures of speech, keep the following strategies in mind:

- Look for such words as *like* and *as.* These words signal a **simile.** They tell you a comparison is being drawn.
- Remember that similes and metaphors, as **figures of speech,** are not meant to be taken literally, but figuratively.
- Use your imagination to **visualize** how similes and metaphors expand the meaning of words beyond their literal dictionary definitions.

SKILLS FOCUS

Literary Skills
Understand figures of speech.

Reading Skills
Read for meaning.

Dream Deferred

Langston Hughes

What happens to a dream deferred?

Does it dry up
like a raisin in the sun?
Or fester like a sore—
5   And then run?
Does it stink like rotten meat?
Or crust and sugar over—
like a syrupy sweet?

Maybe it just sags
10   Like a heavy load.

Or does it explode?

Alloy Photography/Veer

IDENTIFY

Underline the similes in lines 1–8. Number the four things that the poet compares a dream deferred to.

ANALYZE

The questions asked in this poem are rhetorical devices. That is, they are questions that are meant not to be answered but rather to provoke thought. In your opinion, what is the effect of the poet's beginning this poem with a rhetorical question?

____

____

____

INTERPRET

What is suggested about a dream deferred by the final **metaphor** of this poem? Why do you think the poet ended with this question?

____

____

____

____

____

Langston Hughes (1902–1967) was one of the major literary figures of the 1920s, a time known as the Harlem Renaissance.
Hughes is known for poetry that incorporates the idioms of blues
and jazz music and celebrates the African American experience.
Hughes began writing poetry in the eighth grade. His father
didn't think he would be able to make a living as a writer and
encouraged his son to take up a more practical career. He agreed
to pay Hughes's tuition at Columbia University if Hughes would
study engineering. Although he did well in his studies, Hughes
nevertheless decided to pursue his dream of becoming a writer.

Notes

Dream Deferred

SKILLS FOCUS

Literary Skills
Analyze figures of speech.

Figure of Speech Chart   **Figures of speech** are comparisons between two unlike things; figures of speech provide imaginative ways of thinking about ordinary things. Fill in the chart below as you analyze the use of figurative speech in "Dream Deferred." The first row has been filled in as an example.

Figure of Speech	Things Being Compared	What Comparison Suggests
"Does it dry up / like a raisin in the sun?" (lines 2–3)	A dream deferred is compared to a dried-up raisin.	A dream unrealized or put off shrivels and withers.
"Or fester like a sore— / And then run?" (lines 4–5)		
"Does it stink like rotten meat?" (line 6)		
"Or crust and sugar over— / like a syrupy sweet?" (lines 7–8)		
"Maybe it just sags / Like a heavy load." (lines 9–10)		
"Or does it explode?" (line 11)		

"jump mama" by Kurtis Lamkin

Some people mistakenly think that poetry has to be about grand subjects. But a good poem can have as its subject something as simple as a game of jump rope on a summer day.

LITERARY FOCUS: THE SOUNDS OF POETRY

Two special elements—rhyme and rhythm—give poetry a musical quality.

- **Rhyme** is the repetition of a stressed vowel (one that is strongly pronounced) and any sounds that follow: *phone* and *loan; station* and *nation.* **End rhyme** is created when the sound-alike words come at the ends of lines. **Internal rhyme** occurs when the sound-alike words come within a line or within a line and at the end of the line.

- **Rhythm** also creates a musical quality. Rhythm is created by a pattern of stressed and unstressed syllables, called **meter.** This line from a poem by John Keats, for example, has a pattern of unstressed and stressed syllables: "I set her on my pacing steed."

- Other sound effects include **onomatopoeia,** which is the use of words that sound like their meanings (for example, *meow* and *woof*). Another effect is **alliteration,** the repetition of consonant sounds in words occurring close together (for example, in this line by Henry Wadsworth Longfellow: "The day is done, and the darkness").

READING SKILLS: FINDING THE RHYTHM IN FREE VERSE

Free-verse poems do not have regular rhyme or meter. Instead, these poems sound more like everyday conversation. Poems written in free verse, however, may contain special sound effects, including **onomatopoeia** and **alliteration.** What makes free verse poetry instead of chopped up prose? It's true that free verse may not have rhymes or a regular meter, but it does make use of alliteration and other rhythmic poetic devices; even though free-verse lines are not metrical, the poet chooses words to create a wonderful rhythm. This rhythm is best heard when free verse is read aloud. If you listen carefully, it is possible to hear how the lines of free verse break up into rhythmic units.

Literary Skills
Understand rhyme, alliteration, rhythm, and free verse.

Kurtis Lamkin

IDENTIFY

Lines 1-8 can be broken into three rhythmic units. Circle each of these units.

IDENTIFY

Pause at line 11. What is the **setting** of this poem? Underline the details that tell you.

____

____

____

____

____

____

INTERPRET

Circle the examples of **alliteration** in line 22. Which sounds are repeated? What effect does this alliteration create?

____

____

____

____

____

____

____

pretty summer day

grammama sittin on her porch

easy

rockin her grandbaby in her wide lap

5   ol men sittin in their lincoln

tastin and talkin and talkin and tastin

young boys on the corner

milkin a yak yak   wild hands   baggy pants

young girls halfway up the block

10 jumpin that double dutch

singin their song

kenny kana paula

be on time

cause school begins

15 *at a quarter to nine*

jump one two three and aaaaaaah . . .

round the corner comes

this young woman

draggin herself heavy home from work

20 she sees the young boys

sees the old men

but when she sees the girls she just starts smilin

she says let me get a little bit of that

they say   you can't jump

25 you too old

"jump mama" by Kurtis Lamkin from *Fooling with Words with Bill Moyers.* Copyright © 1997 by **Kurtis Lamkin.** Reproduced by permission of the author.

Robert Brenner/PhotoEdit

why they say that
o, why they say that

she says tanya you hold my work bag
chaniqua come over here girl i want you to hold my handbag
30   josie could you hold my grocery bag
please
kebè take my purse
she starts bobbin her head, jackin her arms
tryin to catch the rhythm of the ropes
35   and when she jumps inside those turning loops
the girls crowd her   sing their song

INFER

Re-read lines 26–27. Is the young woman of line 18 asking a question? accepting a challenge? or both? Explain.

____

____

CLARIFY

Pause at line 36. What has the young woman decided to do?

____

____

Pause at line 49. Underline the example of **repetition** in lines 45–49. What is the effect of this repetition?

____

____

____

____

____

____

____

Read aloud lines 37–52. As you read them aloud, imagine the sound of the double-dutch ropes slapping the ground. Let the sound carry you as you say the words of the poem aloud.

____

____

____

____

____

____

____

____

kenny kana paula

be on time

cause school begins

40   *at a quarter to nine*

jump one two three and

aaaaaaaaaaaaaaaaaaaaaaaaaaaaaah

she jumps on one leg—aaaaah

she dances sassy saucy—aaaaah

45   jump for the girls mama

jump for the stars mama

jump for the young boys sayin

jump mama! jump mama!

jump for the old woman sayin—aww, go head baby

50   and what the young girls say

what the young girls say

aaaaaaaaaaaaaaaaaaaaaaaaaaaaaaaaaaaaaaaaaaaaah

MEET THE WRITER

Kurtis Lamkin is a poet who often accompanies his poems with the *kora,* a twenty-one-stringed West African harp-lute. The kora has been used for centuries in Africa by troubadours who recite the oral histories of their region. Lamkin continues this tradition by traveling around the world, performing poems such as "jump mama" to diverse audiences. Originally from Philadelphia, the poet has taught writing at universities and public schools in New York City. He currently lives in Charleston, South Carolina, with his family.

"jump mama"

Sounds of Poetry Diagram   A free-verse poem does not have to have a meter or rhyme scheme, but it does use many sound devices. Read the lines from "jump mama" in the left-hand column of the chart below. Then, put a check mark in the column that describes the sound device used in them. See if you can find more than one sound device in each group of lines from the poem.

Literary Skills
Analyze rhythm, rhyme, alliteration, and free verse.

Passage	Repetition	Rhythm	Rhyme	Alliteration
"kenny kana paula / be on time / cause school begins / at a quarter to nine" (lines 12–15)				
"draggin herself heavy home from work" (line 19)				
"jump for the girls mama / jump for the stars mama / jump for the young boys sayin / jump mama! jump mama!" (lines 45–48)				

Literary Criticism: Evaluating Style

Garry Wade/Getty Images

Academic Vocabulary for Collection 8

These are the terms you should know
as you read and analyze this collection.

Style The particular way a writer uses language. Style is revealed chiefly
through diction (word choice), sentence structure, and tone. A writer's
style may be described as plain, complex, ornate, simple, poetic,
conversational, and so on.

Diction The writer's choice of words—an essential element of a writer's
style. Diction has a major effect on the tone of a piece of writing.

Sentence structure The way words are put together to form sentences.
Sentences may be long and complex, plain and direct, or short and
punchy. Some writers deliberately use sentence fragments for certain
effects.

Connotations Meanings and emotions associated with a word that go
beyond its dictionary definition, or **denotation.** Words that have similar
meanings may have different connotations.

Figures of speech Imaginative comparisons in which one thing is described
in terms of another. Figures of speech are not meant to be understood
on a literal level. Common examples are **metaphor** (*The bird's song is
an aria on wing*), **simile** (*The bird sings like a piccolo*), and **personification** (*The bird wished its song would make the world happy*).

Tone The writer's attitude toward the subject of a work, its characters, or
the audience.

Mood The overall atmosphere or feeling of a work of literature. Diction and
figures of speech contribute to mood. The setting of a story also helps
create mood.

The Pocketbook Game by Alice Childress

A monologue is a long speech given by one character to another character. In this monologue, listen as a lively, clever Mildred tells her friend Marge about her day at work—and how she taught her employer a much-needed lesson.

LITERARY FOCUS: STYLE—DICTION AND TONE

Style is a writer's individual way of expressing herself or himself. Just as people have different styles in dress and in speaking, they have different writing styles as well. **Diction,** or word choice, is an important element of style. Writers select words to help communicate their feelings and thoughts—and to create an overall effect. For example, if a writer uses the phrase "get it?" instead of the question "understand?" then we say the diction is informal and streetwise.

Diction also has a strong effect on **tone,** the attitude a writer takes toward her or his characters or toward life in general. Like a person's voice, the tone of a work can be playful, sarcastic, affectionate, or full of remorse. Adjusting a word or two can affect the tone; if a writer changes the phrase "he took the biggest piece" to "he served himself generously," the tone changes.

- Some writers, like Alice Childress, have a very personal style that makes their work easily recognizable. As you read "The Pocketbook Game," notice how Childress uses sentence structure and punctuation to create her unique style.
- Also, pay close attention to Childress's diction. Is her diction formal or informal?
- Finally, think about Childress's attitude toward her characters. What is her tone in this monologue?

READING SKILLS: MONITORING YOUR COMPREHENSION

Good readers pause occasionally to make sure they understand what they have read. When you read a monologue such as this one, it is important to stay on top of events as they unfold.

Pause during your reading to ask yourself the following questions:
- What has happened so far?
- What has caused those events?
- Why are the characters reacting as they do?
- What might happen next?

Literary Skills
Understand elements of style, including diction and tone.

Reading Skills
Monitor your comprehension.

Vocabulary Skills
Understand dialect.

VOCABULARY DEVELOPMENT

PREVIEW SELECTION VOCABULARY

The following words appear in "The Pocketbook Game." Look them over before you begin the story.

peculiar (pi·kyōōl′yer) *adj.:* odd; strange.

Mildred doesn't know whether to be amused or irritated by Mrs. E's **peculiar** *habit.*

roam (rōm) *v.:* wander.

Mrs. E **roams** *aimlessly from room to room in her large apartment.*

dashed (dasht) *v.:* rushed.

Mildred **dashed** *through the door and grabbed her purse as if her life depended on it.*

distrust (dis·trust′) *v.:* have no faith in; doubt.

Mrs. E's **distrust** *of Mildred is evident in the way she clutches her purse when Mildred is around.*

DIALECT

Sometimes a writer's **diction** is distinguished by his or her use of **dialect,** which portrays the way of speaking characteristic to a particular region or group of people. A writer who uses dialect is attempting to let the reader "hear" the character speak exactly like a real person living in a particular place and time would. Dialect is usually informal and often includes slang and nonstandard English. As you read, note how Alice Childress uses dialect to bring Mildred's character to life.

THE POCKETBOOK GAME

Alice Childress

STYLE

Pause at line 7. Underline elements of Alice Childress's style that catch your attention. Watch for **descriptive phrases** and **dialect** and **slang.**

VOCABULARY

peculiar (pi·kyōōl′yer) *adj.:* odd; strange.

roam (rōm) *v.:* wander.

MONITOR YOUR COMPREHENSION

Pause at line 13. In this **monologue,** who is the **narrator** speaking to? What is the relationship between the two women?

____

____

INFER

Pause at line 20. What **inferences** can you make about Mildred and Mrs. E based on their behavior?

____

____

Marge . . . Day's work is an education! Well, I mean workin' in different homes you learn much more than if you was steady in one place. . . . I tell you, it really keeps your mind sharp tryin' to watch for what folks will put over on you.

What? . . . No, Marge, I do not want to help shell no beans, but I'd be more than glad to stay and have supper with you, and I'll wash the dishes after. Is that all right? . . .

Who put anything over on who? . . . Oh yes! It's like this. . . . I been working for Mrs. E . . . one day a week for several months
10 and I notice that she has some **peculiar** ways. Well, there was only one thing that really bothered me and that was her pocket-book habit. . . . No, not those little novels. . . . I mean her purse—her handbag.

Marge, she's got a big old pocketbook with two long straps on it . . . and whenever I'd go there, she'd be propped up in a chair with her handbag double wrapped tight around her wrist, and from room to room she'd **roam** with that purse hugged to her bosom. . . . Yes, girl! This happens every time! No, there's *nobody* there but me and her. . . . Marge, I couldn't say nothin' to
20 her! It's her purse, ain't it? She can hold onto it if she wants to!

I held my peace for months, tryin' to figure out how I'd make my point. . . . Well, bless Bess! *Today was the day!* . . . Please, Marge, keep shellin' the beans so we can eat! I know you're listenin', but you listen with your ears, not your hands. . . . Well, anyway, I was almost ready to go home when she steps in the room hangin' onto her bag as usual and says, "Mildred will you ask the super[1] to come up and fix the kitchen faucet?" "Yes,

---

1. **super** (sōō′pər) *n.:* shortened form of "superintendent," a person in charge of a building's maintenance.

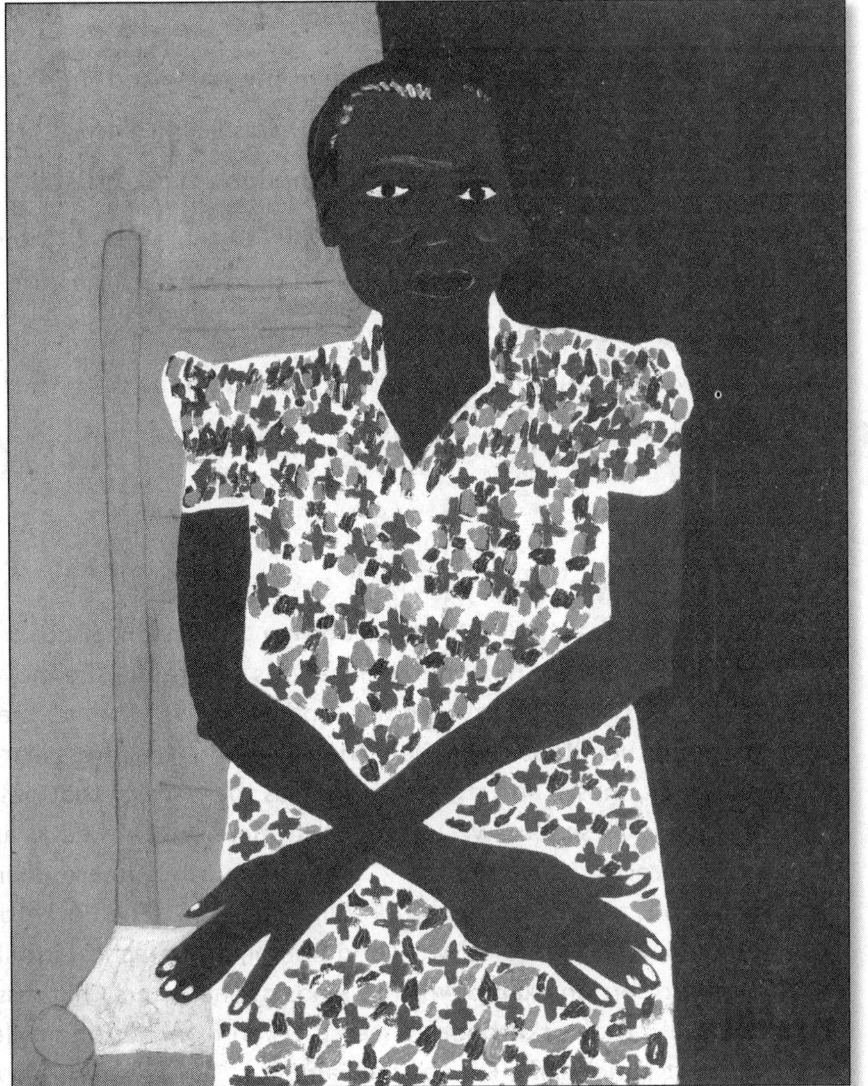

Woman in Calico (1944) by William H. Johnson. Oil.
Smithsonian American Art Museum, Washington, DC/Art Resource, NY

VISUALIZE

Study the portrait of the woman at your left. In your opinion, what qualities or aspects does she have in common with Mildred? Explain.

STYLE

Circle examples of strong verbs in lines 31–34. What effect does this word choice have on Childress's **style**?

FLUENCY

Practice reading lines 31–36 until you can read them in a voice that communicates Mildred's strong personality both in the exchange with Mrs. E and in her telling Marge about this exchange. Try to capture Mildred's enjoyment and satisfaction in retelling this scene.

Mrs. E . . . ," I says, "as soon as I leave." "Oh, no," she says, "he may be gone by then. Please go now." "All right," I says, and out

30   the door I went, still wearin' my Hoover apron.[2]

> I just went down the hall and stood there a few minutes . . . and then I rushed back to the door and knocked on it as hard and frantic as I could. She flung open the door sayin', "What's the matter? Did you see the super?" . . . "No," I says, gaspin' hard for breath, "I was almost downstairs when I remembered . . .
> *I left my pocketbook!*"

---

2. **Hoover apron:** a wraparound apron popular in the early twentieth century, often worn as part of a uniform; named after Herbert Hoover, who was head of the U.S. Food Administration before he became president in 1928.

The Pocketbook Game   **185**

dashed (dashd) *v.:* rushed.

distrust (dis·trust′) *v.:* have no faith in; doubt.

MONITOR YOUR
COMPREHENSION

Pause at line 44. In lines 21–22, Mildred says that she is looking for a way to make her point. What point—or points—has she made by the end of this monologue?

____

____

____

____

____

____

____

____

____

____

____

____

____

____

____

____

With that I **dashed** in, grabbed my purse and then went down to get the super! Later, when I was leavin' she says real timid-like, "Mildred, I hope that you don't think I **distrust**
40   you because . . ." I cut her off real quick. . . . "That's all right, Mrs. E . . . , I understand. 'Cause if I paid anybody as little as you pay me, I'd hold my pocketbook too!"

Marge, you fool . . . lookout! . . . You gonna drop the beans on the floor!

MEET THE WRITER

Alice Childress (1916–1994) was born in Charleston, South Carolina. At age nine, when her parents separated, she moved to New York City's Harlem with her mother, to live with her maternal grandmother. It was in Harlem that the young Childress learned about art, music, and theater as well as the poverty that beset many people she knew. During her lifetime she worked as an actor, director, playwright, and writer in multiple genres, winning numerous awards for her work. Mildred (from "The Pocketbook Game"), with her quick wit, good humor, and practical intelligence, offers an example of the kinds of characters Childress created. "The Pocketbook Game" is taken from her one collection of short fiction, *Like One of the Family . . . Conversations from a Domestic's Life,* published in 1956.

The Pocketbook Game

Style Chart   In this monologue, Alice Childress uses language to create the feel of a dialogue. The boxed passage below contains some of the stylistic devices used by Childress. Circle the strong verbs, underline uses of **slang** and **dialect,** and draw boxes around punctuation that helps create the feel of a spoken conversation. Then, in the space provided, describe the monologue's **tone,** or attitude toward its subject. Finally, write a few words about Childress's **style.**

Literature Skills
Analyze and evaluate style.

Passage
"Marge, she's got a big old pocketbook with two long straps on it . . . and whenever I'd go there, she'd be propped up in a chair with her handbag double wrapped tight around her wrist, and from room to room she'd roam with that purse hugged to her bosom. . . . Yes, girl! This happens every time! No, there's *nobody* there but me and her. . . . Marge, I couldn't say nothin' to her! It's her purse, ain't it? She can hold onto it if she wants to!"

Describe Monologue's Tone

____

____

____

____

____

Describe Childress's Style

____

____

____

____

____

The Pocketbook Game

VOCABULARY AND COMPREHENSION

A. Clarifying Meanings: Synonyms and Antonyms   Write the word from the Word Box that best matches a word from each synonym-antonym pair.

1. ________________________ (believe; suspect)

2. ________________________ (sauntered; hurried)

3. ________________________ (typical; unusual)

4. ________________________ (ramble; stay)

B. Dialect   Underline the dialect used in the sentence below, taken from "The Pocketbook Game." Then, rewrite this sentence in standard English.

"I tell you, it really keeps your mind sharp tryin' to watch for what folks will put over on you."

____

____

C. Reading Comprehension   Answer each question below.

1. "The Pocketbook Game" is a monologue, a speech given by a single character to another character or characters. Who is speaking in this monologue? Who is it addressed to?

____

____

2. What is the main conflict in this story, and how is it resolved?

____

____

3. What does "the pocketbook game" refer to? Who wins the game?

____

____

SKILLS FOCUS

Vocabulary Skills
Analyze elements of diction.

Codes of Conduct by Adrienne Su

In this essay, Adrienne Su examines her experiences growing up in the South and then at college in the North. She uses humor to describe situations that she really takes very seriously.

LITERARY FOCUS: STYLE AND HUMOR

Every writer has a style, though some styles are more distinctive than others. **Style** refers to the way a writer uses language. You can identify a writer's style by examining the writer's word choice (diction) and use of figurative language and imagery. When you describe a writer's style, you talk about how the writer's use of language affects the overall effect of the work.

Some writers' styles are humorous. **Humor** is generally created by a surprise of some sort. A writer might use an unusual word or make an unexpected comparison: *His handshake was as damp and squishy as a jellyfish.* Writers also create humor through **exaggeration,** or overstatement, describing something as larger, grander, or more important than it really is: *When I was elected school president, I grew to be twenty feet tall and strode through the halls like Godzilla.*

- Read "Codes of Conduct" once to enjoy Adrienne Su's humor. Then, read it again, and notice the stylistic devices Su uses to create that humor. Think about why Su chose to use humor to convey her feelings and experiences.

READING SKILLS: VISUALIZING

Writers use words to help you **visualize,** or imagine, the places, people, and situations they are describing. When you visualize, you use the writer's words to create a mental picture of what's going on—almost as if you were watching a movie. Visualizing makes it easier to "enter into" a work of literature and to understand what you are reading.

To visualize a literary work:

- Pay special attention to descriptions and word choices.
- Pause at the end of a paragraph or any other logical stopping point to imagine the scene.
- Look for imagery and sensory details. Re-read the passage to catch any details you might have missed.

Literary Skills
Understand style.

Reading Skills
Visualize.

Vocabulary Skills
Understand denotation and connotation.

VOCABULARY DEVELOPMENT

PREVIEW SELECTION VOCABULARY

Become familiar with the following words from "Codes of Conduct" before you read the selection:

innocuous (i·näk′yōō·əs) *adj.:* harmless; not controversial.

*Some people feel that telling a polite lie is an **innocuous** social convention.*

visceral (vis′ər·əl) *adj.:* instinctive; ingrained.

*Learning about her cultural heritage helped Su understand her **visceral** sense of obligation to her family.*

filial (fil′ē·əl) *adj.:* of or about a son or daughter.

*Many sons and daughters feel **filial** obligation to their parents.*

melodramatic (mel′ō·drə·mat′ik) *adj.:* sensational; overly emotional or dramatic.

*An aftermath of many dinners is a **melodramatic** struggle over who will pay the check.*

mundane (mun′dān′) *adj.:* ordinary; commonplace.

*She felt that her experiences growing up in the South were **mundane** compared with those of her parents, who grew up in China.*

ravenous (rav′ə·nəs) *adj.:* extremely hungry.

*After living in the North for a while, she was **ravenous** for southern cooking.*

DENOTATION AND CONNOTATION

Denotations are the literal meanings of words—the meanings you find in a dictionary. **Connotations** are the associations and emotions that have come to be attached to words. For example, *slender, skinny, scrawny,* and *svelte* could all be used to describe a thin person, but they have very different connotations. *Slender* and *svelte* suggest a lovely and graceful person. *Skinny* and *scrawny* imply that the person is too thin and perhaps unattractive.

Writers choose words carefully for their connotations. Writers look for the connotation that will help them create a certain mood or set the right tone. As you read "Codes of Conduct," notice how Su chooses words that add to the humor of her essay.

Codes of Conduct

Adrienne Su

Andersen Ross/Blend Images/Getty Images

In the South, where I grew up, the people have an unspoken agreement: Reality is what everyone says it is. The agreement is meant to protect others from any perceived slight. It can be as **innocuous** as complimenting an ugly outfit, but among the truly polite, you could walk into church with a horse instead of your husband, and everyone would not only fail to notice anything wrong but also exclaim, "What a beautiful hat you have on! And Harry is looking so well! The two of you must come over for dinner sometime." By the end of the day, you'd actually believe
10 that the horse was a man.

STYLE

Underline the example of **exaggeration** the author uses in lines 1–10. Circle the statement this example supports.

VOCABULARY

innocuous (i·näk′yo͞o·əs) *adj.:* harmless; not controversial.

Re-read lines 11–20. Why do you think the author hints at her Chinese heritage rather than talking about it directly?

The author uses an **extended metaphor**—a long comparison of unlike things—in lines 31–43. What point do you think she is making with this comparison?

Re-read lines 31–43. Circle the **images** that help you picture the author's extended metaphor.

In the third grade, some friends and I often re-enacted scenes from *Little House on the Prairie*.[1] My blonde friend played Mary because of the color of her hair. Another played Carrie, the youngest sister, because she was the youngest. I played Laura, "because you have dark hair," the others explained. Nobody ever pointed out that I did not in the slightest resemble a white Midwestern girl with freckles and brown pigtails. To suggest that perhaps I looked more like the long-lost daughter of a railroad worker of that time[2] was to suggest that I looked different from

20 my friends, and that simply was not done.

Not that the subject never came up—there might be a snack in my lunch that the other kids thought was strange, or a teacher might discreetly ask me about the trip my father took shortly after Nixon's visit opened China to the U.S. But most of the time, there was no language for addressing what made me different. No one asked me about Chinese culture or how to say things in Chinese, which I didn't know, anyway. Questions of the sort were considered rude, a way of pointing out that I looked Chinese, rather than like the Southern gal I was.

30 This doesn't sound too serious—just a form of Southern gentility. But imagine living your whole life in an environment where everyone says that a cat is a dog, all the time. Your perception of animals changes. You see a cat racing up a tree and remark, "My, that dog is a good climber." You hear a plaintive meow from outside and put a beef bone in the backyard. And when you yourself are a cat in this world, you grow to think you are a dog.

This is fine until you leave this world—and go to a land known as the North, where people not only recognize cathood but celebrate it. They form alliances to preserve feline culture, holding

40 fish dinners and mouse-catching lectures. They hold cat networking activities and cat social events—even writers' conferences for cats who have a way with words. For the cat who's lived her whole life thinking she's a dog, this can come as a bit of a shock.

---

1. *Little House on the Prairie:* popular book and television series depicting nineteenth-century rural American life.
2. **railroad worker . . . time:** Chinese immigrants helped build the U.S. transcontinental railroad, completed in 1869.

Up North, in college, I'd find myself in a group of Chinese Americans and think, Hey, I'm surrounded! before realizing that I blended in. I'd go to a gathering of Chinese students and wait to be discovered and thrown out. Talking with my Korean-American roommate, I found that I wasn't the only one whose lack of interest in math and science was seen as a possible birth defect.

50   One day, when I referred to myself as "Oriental," everyone in the room—white, Korean, Hispanic—pounced on me.

"It's Asian," they cried. "Oriental is offensive."

That was how I learned that there was a vocabulary for a long-unnamed aspect of my life. My **visceral** feelings of family obligation were known as **filial** piety, or, as my roommate and I described it, Asian guilt. My parents' unwillingness to contradict their friends was an act of saving face for all. And the **melodramatic** struggles to pay for dinner were not earnest fights but the desire to avoid *guanxi*, or obligation, to the other party.

60   I went home using not the big words of a kid home from college, but ordinary words for things that were familiar, in fact **mundane,** to my parents.

"I think we're making an unbalanced dinner," I said, peering into a beef stew. "Too many hot element ingredients, too few cold elements. Maybe—"

My mother, absorbed in *The Wall Street Journal*, waved a dismissive hand. My father, opening his mail, murmured, "Whatever." My brother, who was getting ready for hockey practice, was already out the door.

70   The next evening, I visited my best friend, the one who'd played Carrie, and sat down to my zillionth Southern dinner with her family.

"What classes are you taking?" her mother asked.

"I'm taking Chinese, so I can eavesdrop on my parents," I said, "and a course in East Asian religions—"

"What kind of job do you plan to get with that?" my friend's father joked.

Re-read lines 78–85. Why do you think Su's statement about learning Chinese stops the conversation?

____

____

____

____

ravenous (rav′ə·nəs) *adj.*: extremely hungry.

What are some **connotations** for the word *ravenous*? Why do you think Su uses this word instead of *hungry*?

____

____

____

____

____

Think about the **title** of the essay. How do you think Su feels about the codes of conduct that influence her life? Explain.

____

____

____

____

____

"I just want to know enough to be able to talk to my relatives in China," I said. "To find out who I really am."

80   What happened next was very strange. You could hear a crumb of cornbread drop. My friend's house had always been a second home to me, as mine was to her, but on this topic, her family, unlike mine, was stuck. And it was my fault: I had carelessly dragged the conversation into never-never land, the land of what made me different.

During that frozen silence, I busied myself eating. Then I heard myself say:

"These mashed potatoes are wonderful! I've been so homesick for them. Up North, people just don't know how to cook."

90   My friend's mother urged me to have more. My friend's father passed the gravy and made a joke about Yankees.[3] And instantly, my friend and I were eight years old again and digging into our plates, **ravenous** as puppies, because we were growing so fast.

---

3. **Yankee** (yaŋ′kē) *n.*: person who lives in a northern state in the United States.

MEET THE WRITER

Adrienne Su (1967–   ) was born and raised in Atlanta, Georgia. The daughter of Chinese immigrants, Su studied East Asian language and literature at Harvard University and creative writing at the University of Virginia. Although she is interested in exploring her Chinese heritage, Su wants her poetry and stories to appeal to everyone. Su uses her writing to reflect on all aspects of life, from the lofty to the mundane. She also enjoys making her readers laugh.

Codes of Conduct

Style Analysis Chart   Fill in the chart below to examine the style of "Codes of Conduct," providing examples from the text. Use quotation marks when you quote directly from the essay. Finally, evaluate the style of the essay.

Literary Skills
Analyze and
evaluate style.

Elements of Style
1. Give two examples of the writer's word choices, and describe their effects.
2. Give two examples of imagery in the essay, and describe their effects.
3. Describe and give one example of the writer's use of a figure of speech.

4. Describe the essay's overall style. Do you think this style effectively conveys the writer's message? Why or why not?

____

____

____

____

____

Skills Review

Codes of Conduct

VOCABULARY AND COMPREHENSION

A. Clarifying Word Meanings   On the line next to each definition, write the Word Box word that best matches that definition. You will not use all of the Word Box words.

_______________ **1.** intuitive

_______________ **2.** everyday; routine

_______________ **3.** inoffensive

_______________ **4.** famished

B. Connotations   Answer "true" or "false" by checking the correct item.

1. _____ **True** _____ **False** *I sat down to my **zillionth** Southern dinner with her family.* Replacing the boldface word with "latest" would eliminate the exaggeration in the sentence.

2. _____ **True** _____ **False** *We were as **ravenous** as puppies.* Replacing the boldface word with "hungry" would make the sentence weaker.

C. Reading Comprehension   Answer each question below.

1. How does the author use an extended metaphor about cats and dogs to describe her upbringing?

____

____

2. How do the author's feelings about being Chinese American change when she goes to college?

____

____

3. When the author shows interest in learning about Chinese culture, what reaction does she receive?

____

____

SKILLS FOCUS

Vocabulary Skills
Identify denotation and connotation.

Transformation by Lydia Minatoya

As in the Adrienne Su essay "Codes of Conduct," the writer of this selection uses humor to express her viewpoint about growing up as an Asian American girl in mainstream American society. What similarities and differences can you see in the two writers' experiences—and in their ways of telling about them?

LITERARY FOCUS: COMPARING STYLE

Style is a writer's individual way of expressing herself or himself. When you compare writers' styles, you look for similarities and differences in their use of stylistic elements. For example, you might look at each writer's use of **diction, sentence length** and complexity, **figures of speech, humor,** or any other unique elements in their use of language. When you evaluate style, also look for how extensively the writer uses precise language, **dialogue,** and description. You might find, for example, that one writer uses short, concise sentences and simple language, whereas another writer uses long, complex sentences consisting of flowery language.

- As you read "Transformation," notice how Minatoya uses complex sentence structure, ironic humor, and elegant vocabulary to create her unique style. Pay close attention to Minatoya's diction. Is it formal or informal?
- What is Minatoya's attitude toward the events she relates? What is her **tone** in this story?
- Finally, think about how Minatoya's style is similar to and different from Su's style in "Codes of Conduct."

READING SKILLS: UNDERSTANDING CAUSE AND EFFECT

A **cause** is what makes something happen. An **effect** is the result, or what happens. Imagine, for example, that a hurricane blows through a seaside town. The fierce winds overturn boats and destroy houses. The winds are the cause. The effect, or result, is the damage.

In a well-written story, the events that make up the plot are closely related. One event causes another event, which leads to another event, and so on. To find a cause, ask yourself, "Why did this event happen?" To identify an effect, ask yourself, "What happened as a result of this event?" Keep in mind that an effect, or result, can stem from several causes, and that one cause can lead to several effects.

Literary Skills
Understand and compare elements of style.

Reading Skills
Understand cause-and-effect relationships.

Vocabulary Skills
Understand prefixes.

VOCABULARY DEVELOPMENT

PREVIEW SELECTION VOCABULARY

The following words appear in "Transformation." Look them over before you begin the story.

conspicuousness (kən·spik′yoo·əs·nes) *n.:* state of attracting attention through being unusual or remarkable.

*Lydia's parents gave her a typical name so she would not be **conspicuous.***

conventional (kən·ven′shə·nəl) *adj.:* conforming to accepted rules or standards; traditional.

*Lydia wanted to be **conventional,** so she studied the way the other students acted and dressed.*

ludicrously (loo′di·krəs·lē) *adv.:* absurdly; ridiculously.

*Relocation camps were **ludicrously** positioned, often in a swamp or a desert.*

precocious (prē·kō′shəs) *adj.:* unusual in intelligence and maturity.

*Lydia's teachers liked to coo over their tiny, **precocious** doll of a student who knew the answer to any question they asked.*

ingratiate (in·grā′shē·āt′) *v.:* gain favor.

*Lydia begins a campaign to **ingratiate** herself with her favorite teacher.*

soporific (säp·ə·rif′ik) *adj.:* tending to cause sleep or sleepiness.

*When Miss Hempstead sings her **soporific** songs, her students' eyes begin to close.*

fastidious (fa·stid′ē·əs) *adj.:* careful; with great attention to detail.

*Lydia's **fastidious** grooming produces perfectly brushed hair and spotless clothing.*

tenacious (tə·nā′shəs) *adj.:* stubbornly persistent.

*Lydia is **tenacious** in her drive to get her teacher to notice her; she will not give up.*

strident (strid′′nt) *adj.:* loud; shrill.

*When Miss Hempstead becomes **strident,** her voice grows loud and anxious sounding.*

enigmatically (en′ig·mat′ik·lē) *adv.:* ambiguously; having more than one interpretation.

*Lydia smiles **enigmatically,** to the puzzlement of all except herself.*

PREFIXES: IMPORTANT BEGINNINGS

Prefixes are word parts added to the beginnings of words. Although prefixes consist of just a few letters, they are powerful and can greatly change the meaning of a word. To the right are prefixes you'll come across often in your reading. Recognizing these prefixes will help you figure out the meanings of many words that might be new to you.

Prefix	Meaning	Example
con–	with	*conspicuous,* "with observation"
dict–	speak	*diction,* "act of speaking"
in–	in, into	*ingratiate,* "into favor"
pre–	before	*precocious,* "before ripe"

Transformation

Lydia Minatoya

Perhaps it begins with my naming. During her pregnancy, my mother was reading Dr. Spock.[1] "Children need to belong," he cautioned. "An unusual name can make them the subject of ridicule." My father frowned when he heard this. He stole a worried glance at my sister. Burdened by her Japanese name, Misa played unsuspectingly on the kitchen floor.

The Japanese know full well the dangers of **conspicuousness.** "The nail that sticks out gets pounded down," cautions an old maxim. In America, Relocation[2] was all the proof they needed.

10 And so it was, with great earnestness, my parents searched for a **conventional** name. They wanted me to have the full true promise of America.

"I will ask my colleague Froilan," said my father. "He is the smartest man I know."

"And he has a poetic soul," said my mother, who cared about such things.

In due course, Father consulted Froilan. He gave Froilan his conditions for suitability.

"First, if possible, the full name should be alliterative," said

20 my father. "Like Misa Minatoya." He closed his eyes and sang my sister's name. "Second, if not an alliteration, at least the name should have assonantal rhyme."

"Like Misa Minatoya?" said Froilan with a teasing grin.

---

1. **Dr. Benjamin Spock** (1903–1998): nationally respected pediatrician and bestselling author of books on parenting.
2. **Relocation:** discriminatory policy undertaken by the U.S. government against Americans of Japanese descent. Japanese Americans living on the West Coast were forced to "relocate" to internment camps during the course of World War II.

IDENTIFY

Pause at line 12. What kind of name do the writer's parents want for her? What is their reasoning based on?

____

____

____

____

VOCABULARY

conspicuousness (kən·spik′yoo·əs·nes) *n.:* state of attracting attention through being unusual or remarkable.

conventional (kən·ven′shə·nəl) *adj.:* conforming to accepted rules or standards; traditional.

WORD STUDY

assonantal (as′ə·nən·təl) means "having repeated vowel sounds."

Circle the repeated vowel sounds in the narrator's sister's name. In what way is Misa Minatoya's name assonantal?

____

____

____

Pause at line 27. What are the requirements for a good name, according to the narrator's father?

____

____

____

____

Re-read lines 34–36. What does the narrator's father's reply suggest about the things he values?

____

____

____

____

Pause at line 45. The author's father wants his child to have a "conventional" name but not a "common" one. Explain the difference.

____

____

____

____

____

____

"Exactly," my father intoned. He gave an emphatic nod. "Finally, most importantly, the name must be readily recognizable as conventional." He peered at Froilan with hope. "Do you have any suggestions or ideas?"

Froilan, whose own American child was named Ricardito, thought a while.

30 "We already have selected the name for a boy," offered my father. "Eugene."

"Eugene?" wondered Froilan. "But it meets none of your conditions!"

"Eugene is a special case," said my father, "after Eugene, Oregon, and Eugene O'Neill.[3] The beauty of the Pacific Northwest, the power of a great writer."

"I see," said Froilan, who did not but who realized that this naming business would be more complex than he had anticipated. "How about Maria?"

40 "Too common," said my father. "We want a conventional name, not a common one."

"Hmmm," said Froilan, wondering what the distinction was. He thought some more and then brightened. "Lydia!" he declared. He rhymed the name with media. "Lydia for *la bonita infanta*!"[4]

And so I received my uncommon conventional name. It really did not provide the camouflage my parents had anticipated. I remained unalterably alien. For Dr. Spock had been addressing American families, and in those days, everyone knew all real 50 American families were white.

Call it denial, but many Japanese Americans never quite understood that the promise of America was not truly meant for them. They lived in horse stalls at the Santa Anita racetrack and

---

3. **Eugene O'Neill** (1888–1953): American playwright and winner of the 1936 Pulitzer Prize for Literature.
4. *la bonita infanta* (lä bō·nē′tä ēn·fän′tä): Spanish for "the pretty baby."

said the Pledge of Allegiance daily. They rode to Relocation Camps under armed guard, labeled with numbered tags, and sang "The Star-Spangled Banner." They lived in deserts or swamps, **ludicrously** imprisoned—where would they run if they ever escaped—and formed garden clubs, and yearbook staffs, and citizen town meetings. They even elected beauty queens.

60   My mother practiced her *okoto*[5] and was featured in a recital. She taught classes in fashion design and her students mounted a show. Into exile she had carried an *okoto* and a sewing machine. They were her past and her future. She believed in Art and Technology. My mother's camp was the third most populous city in the entire state of Wyoming. Across the barren lands, behind barbed wire, bloomed these little oases of democracy. The older generation bore the humiliation with pride. "*Kodomo no tameni,*"[6] they said. For the sake of the children. They thought that if their dignity was great, then their children

70   would be spared. Call it valor. Call it bathos.[7] Perhaps it was closer to slapstick: a sweet and bitter lunacy.

        Call it adaptive behavior. Coming from a land swept by savage typhoons, ravaged by earthquakes and volcanoes, the Japanese have evolved a view of the world: a cooperative, stoic, almost magical way of thinking. Get along, work hard, and never quite see the things that can bring you pain. Against the tyranny of nature, of feudal lords, of wartime hysteria, the charm works equally well.

        And so my parents gave me an American name and hoped

80   that I could pass. They nourished me with the American dream: Opportunity, Will, Transformation.

---

5. *okoto* (ō·kō′tō): Japanese zitherlike instrument that resembles the harp.
6. *Kodomo no tameni* (kō·dō′mō nō tă·mä′nē): popular Japanese phrase meaning "for the sake of the children."
7. **bathos** (bā′thäs′) *n.:* insincere or grossly sentimental.

ludicrously (loo′di·krəs·lē) *adv.:* absurdly; ridiculously.

STYLE

Pause at line 71. During World War II, Japanese Americans of Lydia's parents' generation bore the humiliation of being incarcerated for their ancestry with dignity. For Lydia, their behavior had "a sweet and bitter lunacy" (line 71). What **tone,** or attitude toward her subject, does the author's word choice convey? Explain.

INTERPRET

Pause at line 81. Lydia's parents gave her an American name hoping she could "pass." What does the writer mean by "pass" in this context?

When I was four and my sister was eight, Misa regularly used me as a comic foil. She would bring her playmates home from school and query me as I sat amidst the milk bottles on the front steps.

"What do you want to be when you grow up?" she would say. She would nudge her audience into attentiveness.

"A mother kitty cat!" I would enthuse. Our cat had just delivered her first litter of kittens and I was enchanted by the rasping tongue and soft mewings of motherhood.

"And what makes you think you can become a cat?" Misa would prompt, gesturing to her howling friends—wait for this; it gets better yet.

"This is America," I stoutly would declare. "I can grow up to be anything that I want!"

My faith was unshakable. I believed. Opportunity. Will. Transformation.

When we lived in Albany, I always was the teachers' pet. "So tiny, so **precocious,** so prettily dressed!" They thought I was a living doll and this was fine with me.

My father knew that the effusive praise would die. He had been through this with my sister. After five years of being a perfect darling, Misa had reached the age where students were tracked by ability. Then, the anger started. Misa had tested into the advanced track. It was impossible, the community declared. Misa was forbidden entry into advanced classes as long as there were white children being placed below her. In her defense, before an angry rabble, my father made a presentation to the Board of Education.

But I was too young to know of this. I knew only that my teachers praised and petted me. They took me to other classes as an example. "Watch now, as Lydia demonstrates attentive behavior," they would croon as I was led to an empty desk at the head of the class. I had a routine. I would sit carefully, spreading my petticoated skirt[8] neatly beneath me. I would pull my chair close to the desk, crossing my swinging legs at my snowy white anklets. I would fold my hands carefully on the desk before me and stare pensively at the blackboard.

120   This routine won me few friends. The sixth-grade boys threw rocks at me. . . . But teachers loved me. When I was in first grade, a third-grade teacher went weeping to the principal. She begged to have me skipped. She was leaving to get married and wanted her turn with the dolly.

When we moved, the greatest shock was the knowledge that I had lost my charm. From the first, my teacher failed to notice me. But to me, it did not matter. I was in love. I watched her moods, her needs, her small vanities. I was determined to **ingratiate.** . . .

DAJ/Getty Images

---

8. **petticoated skirt:** skirt with lace or ruffles sewn in at the hemline.

Miss Hempstead had a pet of her own. Her name was
130   Linda Sherlock. I watched Linda closely and plotted Miss
Hempstead's courtship. The key was the piano. Miss Hempstead
played the piano. She fancied herself a musical star. She sang
songs from Broadway revues and shaped her students' reactions.
"Getting to know you," she would sing. We would smile at her in
a staged manner and position ourselves obediently at her feet.

Miss Hempstead was famous for her ability to soothe. Each
day at rest time, she played the piano and sang **soporific** songs.
Linda Sherlock was the only child who succumbed. Routinely,
Linda's head would bend and nod until she crumpled gracefully
140   onto her folded arms. A tousled strand of blond hair would fall
across her forehead. Miss Hempstead would end her song,
would gently lower the keyboard cover. She would turn toward
the restive eyes of the class. "Isn't she sweetness itself!" Miss
Hempstead would declare. It made me want to vomit.

I was growing weary. My studiousness, my attentiveness,
my **fastidious** grooming and pert poise: all were failing me. I
changed my tactics. I became a problem. Miss Hempstead sent
me home with nasty notes in sealed envelopes: Lydia is a slow
child, a noisy child, her presence is disruptive. My mother looked
150   at me with surprise, "*Nani desu ka*?[9] Are you having problems
with your teacher?" But I was **tenacious.** I pushed harder and
harder, firmly caught in the obsessive need of the scorned.

One day I snapped. As Miss Hempstead began to sing her
wretched lullabies, my head dropped to the desk with a powerful
CRACK! It lolled there, briefly, then rolled toward the edge with
a momentum that sent my entire body catapulting to the floor.
Miss Hempstead's spine stretched slightly, like a cat that senses
danger. Otherwise, she paid no heed. The linoleum floor was
smooth and cool. It emitted a faint pleasant odor: a mixture of
160   chalk dust and wax.

---

9. ***Nani desu ka?*** (nä′nē des′′kä): Japanese for "What is it?"

I began to snore heavily. The class sat electrified. There would be no drowsing today. The music went on and on. Finally, one boy could not stand it. "Miss Hempstead," he probed plaintively, "Lydia has fallen asleep on the floor!" Miss Hempstead did not turn. Her playing grew slightly **strident** but she did not falter.

I lay on the floor through rest time. I lay on the floor through math drill. I lay on the floor while my classmates scraped around me, pushing their sturdy little wooden desks into the configuration for reading circle. It was not until penmanship practice that I finally stretched and stirred. I rose like Sleeping Beauty and slipped back to my seat. I smiled **enigmatically.** A spell had been broken. I never again had a crush on a teacher.

MEET THE WRITER

Lydia Minatoya grew up during the 1950s in upstate New York. She studied sociology in college and earned a Ph.D. in psychology. She spent two years teaching psychology and American culture on a U.S. Army base in Okinawa, Japan. This autobiographical excerpt is taken from her acclaimed 1992 memoir *Talking to High Monks in the Snow: An Asian American Odyssey,* which chronicles her journey to understand the different cultural forces that have shaped her as a Japanese American woman. She has also published a novel, *The Strangeness of Beauty,* which likewise explores the themes of identity, culture, and belonging. An honored educator and writer, Minatoya now lives and teaches in Seattle.

Transformation

SKILLS FOCUS

Literary Skills
Analyze elements of style.

Comparing Writers' Styles Chart   Writers use language to create different effects and communicate different messages. Use the chart below to compare Su's and Minatoya's writing styles. The boxed passages contain examples of each writer's style. In the space provided, make notes about these styles, considering diction, sentence patterns, tone, and use of humor. Then, write a sentence comparing Su's and Minatoya's styles.

Passage from "Codes of Conduct"	Passage from "Transformation"
"Up North, in college, I'd find myself in a group of Chinese Americans and think, Hey, I'm surrounded! before realizing that I blended in. I'd go to a gathering of Chinese students and wait to be discovered and thrown out."	"I had a routine. I would sit carefully, spreading my petticoated skirt neatly beneath me. I would pull my chair close to the desk, crossing my swinging legs at my snowy white anklets. I would fold my hands carefully on the desk before me and stare pensively at the blackboard. This routine won me few friends."

Describe Su's Style	Describe Minatoya's Style
____________________	____________________
____________________	____________________
____________________	____________________
____________________	____________________

Compare Writers' Styles
____
____
____
____

Skills Review

Transformation

VOCABULARY AND COMPREHENSION

A. Clarifying Word Meanings   On the line next to each definition, write the Word Box word that best matches that definition. You will not use all of the Word Box words.

1. ________________________ mysteriously

2. ________________________ stubborn; firm

3. ________________________ loudly; harshly

4. ________________________ meticulous; extremely careful

5. ________________________ normal; typical

Word Box

conspicuousness

conventional

ludicrously

precocious

ingratiate

soporific

fastidious

tenacious

strident

enigmatically

B. Prefixes   Below is a sentence from this selection. Use your knowledge of prefixes to choose the correct answers.

"And so I received my uncommon conventional name."

1. In the sentence above, the prefix *un–* means—

   A in; toward

   B not

   C before

   D with

2. In the sentence above, the prefix *con–* means—

   A in; toward

   B not

   C before

   D with

C. Reading Comprehension   Answer each question below.

1. What did the narrator's parents want to accomplish by naming her "Lydia"?

____

2. When does Lydia stop wanting to be the teacher's pet?

____

____

3. What is the meaning of the title "Transformation"?

____

____

SKILLS FOCUS

Vocabulary Skills
Identify prefixes and their meanings.

Collection 9

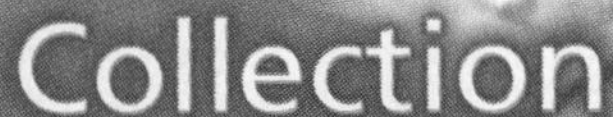

Literary Criticism: Biographical and Historical Approach

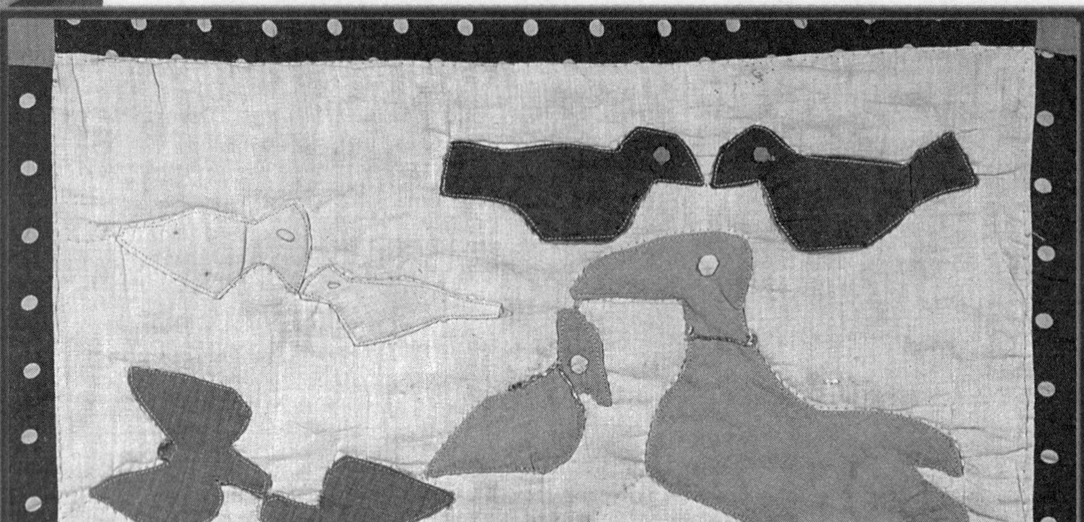

© Museum of Fine Arts, Boston, Massachusetts, USA, Bequest of Maxim Karolik/Bridgeman Art Library

Academic Vocabulary for Collection 9

These are the terms you should know
as you read and analyze the texts in this collection.

Historical setting or **historical context** The historical period that shapes
a work of literature. Understanding the historical setting helps the
reader grasp the issues that were important to people in the time
period in which the work was written.

Historical approach The use of historical context to help analyze and
respond to a text.

Biographical knowledge Information about a writer's experiences.
Understanding a writer's life, including his or her attitudes, heritage,
and traditions, adds meaning when we read his or her works.

Biographical approach The use of a writer's life experiences to help analyze
and respond to a text.

Ellis Island by Joseph Bruchac

One of America's most famous monuments, the Statue of Liberty, is widely considered to be a symbol of freedom. As Joseph Bruchac's poem reminds us, however, when it comes to the Statue of Liberty, what it personifies depends on your heritage.

LITERARY FOCUS: BIOGRAPHICAL AND HISTORICAL APPROACH

- **Historical setting** is the time and place that shape a work of literature. In "Ellis Island," Joseph Bruchac offers a view of the place from more than one point of view. In this way he can address the island's historical significance for two different groups of people.
- Notice the way Bruchac includes **biographical details** from his own life in the poem to shift the significance of this symbol from national to personal.
- Bruchac's feelings about this subject are reflected through the **tone,** or attitude, he adopts toward it. Identifying the tone will help you come to a better understanding of the poem's central insight, also called its underlying **theme.**

READING SKILLS: RECOGNIZING HISTORICAL AND BIOGRAPHICAL DETAILS

The imagery used in "Ellis Island" connects with multiple points of view. Geographical details, such as what a current visitor to Ellis Island can see, are given along with details of the experiences of immigrants in the past being screened for entry into this country. These details are then set in contrast to the experiences of people from yet another group and their past and present views of the island.

Literary Skills
Understand biographical and historical approach.

Reading Skills
Recognize historical and biographical details.

ELLIS ISLAND

Joseph Bruchac

Ellis Island, the first stop in the United States for generations of immigrants, is located in New York Harbor.
Kelly-Mooney Photography/CORBIS

Beyond the red brick of Ellis Island
where the two Slovak children
who became my grandparents
waited the long days of quarantine,°
5   after leaving the sickness,
the old Empires of Europe,
a Circle Line ship° slips easily
on its way to the island
of the tall woman,° green
10   as dreams of forests and meadows
waiting for those who'd worked
a thousand years
yet never owned their own.

---

4. **quarantine** (kwôr′ən·tēn) *n.:* period of isolation to prevent the spread of contagious diseases.
7. **Circle Line ship:** New York City sightseeing ship.
9. **tall woman:** Statue of Liberty, which stands in New York's harbor.

"Ellis Island" from *Entering Onondaga* by Joseph Bruchac. Copyright © 1976, 1977, 1978 by Joseph Bruchac. Reproduced by permission of **Barbara S. Kouts Agency, Literary Agent for Joseph Bruchac.**

HISTORICAL DETAILS

Are lines 1–6 talking about the past or the present?

____

____

IDENTIFY

In lines 8–13, who is the woman being discussed, and what does she represent?

____

____

IDENTIFY

In the first stanza, underline the line in which the setting changes from past to present.

Like millions of others,

15 I too come to this island,

nine decades the answerer

of dreams.

Yet only one part of my blood loves that memory.

Another voice speaks

20 of native lands

within this nation.

Lands invaded

when the earth became owned.

Lands of those who followed

25 the changing Moon,

knowledge of the season

in their veins.

MEET THE WRITER

Joesph Bruchac (1942–   ) was born in Saratoga Springs, New York, and was raised there by his grandmother and his grandfather, who was a member of the Abenaki people. Much of his writing is about Native American peoples and their culture. In 1999, he received the Lifetime Achievement Award from the Native Writers Circle of the Americas. In addition to writing about Native culture, Bruchac is involved with the preservation of Abenaki culture.

Ellis Island

Historical and Biographical Analysis Chart   Writers' experiences and cultural backgrounds are sometimes reflected in their works. Complete the chart below to improve your understanding of and appreciation for the poem.

Literary Skills
Analyze text using biographical and historical approach.

Reading Skills
Identify historical and biographical details.

List the two settings in stanza 1.
List the information about his heritage that Bruchac reveals in this poem.
What details in the poem reflect Bruchac's background?
What modern-day issues are reflected in the poem?

The Habit of Movement

by Judith Ortiz Cofer

What happens when you are constantly moving from one place to another? Do you eventually find a place to call home, or does the state of flux become your home?

LITERARY FOCUS: BIOGRAPHICAL APPROACH

Historical setting is the time and place that shape a work of literature. In "The Habit of Movement," the historical setting is purposely vague. Cofer is not as concerned with expressing where she is as she is with expressing what it's like to be there. This is why having **biographical information** about Cofer's life helps clarify the meaning of this poem, by giving it context. Although you could understand the poem without the biographical information provided, knowing about the circumstances that gave rise to the feelings she describes enriches and deepens your understanding.

READING SKILLS: MONITOR YOUR READING

The following tips will help you find meaning when reading poetry:

- Look for context clues to help you figure out the meanings of unfamiliar words.
- Do not pause at the end of every line. Instead, read straight through the text, pausing only at punctuation.
- Be sure you have identified the subject and verb of each sentence.
- Read the poem; then re-read it while trying to visualize, or picture, the events that are being described.

Literary Skills
Understand biographical approach to literary criticism.

Reading Skills
Monitor your reading.

The Habit of Movement

Judith Ortiz Cofer

This speaker says she and her family were nomads—that is, people who were always moving around. Judith Ortiz Cofer came to Paterson, New Jersey, from Puerto Rico when she was four years old. Her father was a career navy man, and whenever he went to sea, Judith, her mother, and her brother returned to Puerto Rico. When her father came back, they would return to New Jersey to be with him.

Nurtured in the lethargy of the tropics,°
the nomadic life did not suit us at first.
We felt like red balloons set adrift
over the wide sky of this new land.
5   Little by little we lost our will to connect
and stopped collecting anything heavier
to carry than a wish.
We took what we could from books borrowed
in Greek temples, or holes in the city walls,
10   returning them hardly handled.

We carried the idea of home on our backs
from house to house, never staying
long enough to learn the secret ways of wood

---

1. **lethargy of the tropics:** tiredness; lack of energy caused by extreme heat and humidity.

> **BIOGRAPHICAL APPROACH**
>
> Read the biographical information above. Use your background knowledge to infer what challenges Cofer faced as a child. Write your thoughts on the lines below.
>
> ______________________
>
> ______________________
>
> ______________________
>
> **INFER**
>
> In lines 5–7, underline what the speaker's family has lost. Circle the one thing they carry from place to place.
>
> **INFER**
>
> What does line 10 suggest?
>
> ______________________
>
> ______________________
>
> ______________________

DC Productions/Getty Images

Royalty-Free/CORBIS

and stone, and always the blank stare

15   of undraped windows behind us

like the eyes of the unmourned dead.

In time we grew rich in dispossession°

and fat with experience.

As we approached but did not touch others,

20   our habit of movement kept us safe

like a train in motion—

nothing could touch us.

---

17. dispossession (dis′pə·zesh′ən) *n.:* lack of property or possessions.

MEET THE WRITER

Judith Ortiz Cofer (1952–   ) was born in Puerto Rico and came to the United States when she was two years old. In grade school she understood that she needed to learn English in order to survive. Over the years, English gradually replaced Spanish as Cofer's functional language. Cofer admits that although she still speaks Spanish with her relatives, she has lost an intimacy with it and is unable to do certain types of abstract thinking in it. Cofer now uses English for all of her fiction, nonfiction, and poetry.

The Habit of Movement

Literary Criticism—Biographical Approach   Use the chart below to help you interpret the imagery used in this poem in terms of Cofer's biographical information. The first one has been done for you.

Literature Skills
Analyze biographical approach to literary criticism.

"We felt like red balloons set adrift / over the wide sky of this new land."	The family members felt as if they stuck out in their new home, to which they had no connection.
"We took what we could from books borrowed / in Greek temples . . . / returning them hardly handled."	
"We carried the idea of home on our backs / from house to house"	
"and always the blank stare / of undraped windows behind us / like the eyes of the unmourned dead."	
"In time we grew rich in dispossession / and fat with experience."	
"our habit of movement kept us safe / like a train in motion— / nothing could touch us."	

The Memory Stone by Paul Yee

In this folk tale several women suffer the consequences of the actions of a dishonorable man. Only through their own honorable actions can they end their suffering. As you read "The Memory Stone," notice how the author uses historical details to clarify the story's setting and give it context.

LITERARY FOCUS: HISTORICAL APPROACH

- **Historical setting** is the time and place that shape a work of literature. In "The Memory Stone," Paul Yee weaves historical details into his folk tale to help explain its setting and to connect the tale with his ancestors' experiences as Chinese immigrants in Canada.
- Yee also makes use of **indirect characterization** in his tale, which means he shows rather than tells what a certain character is like. As you read "The Memory Stone," look for the actions of the characters as well as their **motivations** for those actions.

READING SKILLS: MAKING INFERENCES

An **inference** is an educated guess—a guess based on good evidence. When you make an inference, you use details in the text and your own experiences to guess about something you don't know for sure.

For example, an author might say, "When the teacher called on the new girl, she smiled." The writer doesn't tell you directly that the new girl is pleased; however, you can infer that she is pleased to have been called on.

To make an inference:
- Look for details in the text.
- Relate the details to what you know about life.
- Make a careful guess.

Make inferences as you read "The Memory Stone." Look for clues that reveal information about the characters and their motivations for acting the way they do. Then, read on to see how the characters develop. Use a chart like this one to record your inferences:

Details from Story	My Inferences About Character

SKILLS FOCUS

Literary Skills
Understand historical approach.

Reading Skills
Make inferences about characters.

Vocabulary Skills
Understand figurative language.

PREVIEW SELECTION VOCABULARY

Preview the following words from the story before you begin reading:

adorning (ə·dôrn′iŋ) *v.:* decorating; enhancing.

> *People have been **adorning** themselves with jewelry since civilization began.*

essences (es′əns·ez) *n.:* crucial elements; odors.

> *It is said that cherished belongings retain the **essences** of their owners.*

trilling (tril′iŋ) *v.* used as *n.:* singing with a warble.

> *The **trilling** of her love's little bird seemed the sweetest sound on earth.*

dank (daŋk) *adj.:* disagreeably damp; clammy.

> *The constant moisture and lack of light makes many seaside buildings cold and **dank.***

ferocious (fə·rō′shəs) *adj.:* extremely violent; fierce.

> *The railroad engine belched a **ferocious** cloud of fiery soot.*

vivid (viv′id) *adj.:* intense; bright.

> *The angry scar would always be a **vivid** reminder of the forest accident.*

luster (lus′tər) *n.:* glow.

> *It was impossible to ignore the new **luster** of the jade pendant.*

FIGURATIVE LANGUAGE

The literal meaning of a word is its dictionary definition. For example, if you say, "The computer is broken," you are using the word *broken* in a literal sense: The computer doesn't work. However, if you say, "My heart is broken," you are using the word *broken* in a figurative, or imaginative, sense. Your heart is still pumping blood—it is "working" in the literal sense. What you really mean by "My heart is broken" is that you are feeling deep sorrow or hurt. You *feel* as if your heart were broken into pieces.

Figurative language is based on comparisons between unlike things. Writers use figurative language in unusual or interesting ways to create vivid images and striking comparisons.

THE MEMORY STONE

Paul Yee

To Chinese people, jade is the most magical of stones. When **adorning** human skin, it absorbs the body's oils and **essences** as well as the owner's nature, whether the person is soft or hard, warm or cold. Its healing touch can cool a fever or calm a chill. It can also be ground into powder and swallowed as a tonic.

The Chinatown museum owns a jade pendant, centuries old, the shape and size of a large coin. Cloudy green in color, its surface is as clear and smooth as water, but one side has a hairline crack running from its edge to center. For collectors, however, this feature only increases the value.

Many stories accompany this stone, but the best known comes from the turn of the century and starts in South China's Pearl River region.

Willow, a young widow, lived in a busy town where three rivers became one on their way to the ocean. Many boats passed by, so Willow and her mother-in-law opened a guesthouse that provided clean beds and hearty meals. Many men requested Willow's hand in remarriage, but she remained devoted to the memory of her husband, a kind and gentle man.

Early one morning, a beggar pounded on the back door.

"Show some heart," he shouted. "I'm going to Gold Mountain° to get rich. You'll soon be rewarded!"

Willow opened the door and her mouth dropped open. She saw a face almost identical to her husband's. Her late spouse's piercing eyes and toothy smile had stayed fresh in her memory for a long time, and she never imagined seeing them again. Her hand almost reached out to touch the stranger's face.

° **Gold Mountain:** term used for North America.

"Work for me," she said, "and I will pay you the going wage. You'll sleep in the stable and eat rice twice a day."

30   He called himself Ox, from the hill country. A blacksmith who planned to work with horses, he loved all animals. He fed exhausted packhorses slowly, to prevent stomach pains. He changed the straw in the stables every day and scrubbed the mules clean. When he whistled, wild dogs came running; when he clucked his tongue, chickens flocked at his feet. When he filled the feeding trough in the pigpen, one little piglet always nibbled at his trouser. In the fall, when the fattened hog was dispatched to the butcher, Willow saw Ox's lips tremble, and at that moment, she lost her heart to him.

40   At his departure, he said, "Wait for me, Willow, and I will return to wed you."

"Many men want me and my guesthouse," she said. "Why should I wait?"

"Because my feelings for you are the truest and the strongest." From behind his back he brought out a small bamboo cage. "This little canary will sing to our love every day."

Willow was startled. She had never owned a songbird, but the yellow-green creature had a clean sweet voice that instantly soothed her.

50   She fumbled for a return gift. Her apron pockets were empty, so from her neck she unfastened a jade pendant.

"Take this," she said, "and I will wait for you. This stone has been handed down by men and women in my family over many generations. My father claims it guards my well-being, so if you change your mind about me, you must return it."

Ox bent close and whispered, "You can trust me."

Willow kept the birdcage by her bed and listened to the **trilling** early in the morning and late at night. Every day, she fed the bird grains and greens.

60   After many months, she released the bird from its cage to see what would happen. It fluttered to the ceiling and to the four corners of the room. It danced atop the cabinet and flew by the open

---

CONNOTATION

What **images** does the word *ox* bring to mind? What qualities might a man named Ox possess?

FIGURES OF SPEECH

Underline the figure of speech used in line 39, and restate its meaning.

CLARIFY

What does Ox tell Willow the canary **symbolizes**?

PREDICT

Underline what Willow tells Ox about the jade pendant. What do her words **foreshadow**?

VOCABULARY

trilling (tril′iŋ) *v.* used as *n.:* singing with a warble.

window and the door. But it remained inside and always landed on Willow's shoulder and hands. She stroked the tiny head and wings, and delighted at its soft feathers and gentle warmth.

She sent letters to Ox, but he replied infrequently, complaining about how hard it was to find work. Then she awoke one day and found the cage empty and the bird gone. For days she searched the nearby forest and streets and waited fretfully,
70 but the canary did not return. Her heart clenched like a fighter's fist, and she could neither eat nor talk. For weeks she waited in vain for Ox's letters, but they had stopped coming.

Her mother-in-law said, "Didn't I warn you about Gold Mountain men? They leave you, and great distances cloud their memories. That man will never keep his promise. You should forget about him."

Instead, Willow decided to travel to the New World. For the first time in her life, she journeyed down the river she saw daily. At the great ocean port of Hong Kong, frantic crowds pushed at

Angelo Cavalli/zefa/CORBIS

80   her from all sides—on the docks, in the narrow streets, and even in the guarded lobby of her hotel. Never before had she seen so many people. Her room was tiny and **dank,** and she gladly boarded the steamship at sailing time. Traveling alone, she took a second-class cabin for privacy and safety.

    For days all Willow saw were blue skies and a blue ocean. Seagulls with broad wingspans hovered close, cawing and dipping by her porthole, but soon they veered away. In her cabin, she tried on the Western hats and dresses she had purchased in Hong Kong. Ox had lived in the New World for so long that she thought he

90   would probably prefer to see her dressed like a modern woman.

    When the boat docked, Willow's legs and feet felt weak and unsteady as she laced her boots. She stumbled down the gangplank, heavy bags banging at her knees, only to end up spending hours with immigration officials and translators. She pleaded she was just a visitor and not a settler who should pay the head tax, a fee that only Chinese immigrants paid to settle in the country.

    "I came to visit a friend. I have a thriving business in China. Why would I abandon it? My family is in China. Of course I want to go back."

100   When they finally released her, she headed to Chinatown in a horse-drawn buggy. The roads were jammed with wagons and horses, great metal boxes grunting on steel tracks, and small carts with black rubber wheels that ran on their own power. In Chinatown, she recognized people who had passed through her inn long ago. Some had become plump and others thin, while some had grown mustaches. But nobody recalled her face, everyone wore Western clothes, and some even spoke English.

    She stopped at a guesthouse to store her bags and comb her hair. In the mirror over the washstand, she saw deep lines

110   around her eyes and wondered if Ox would notice. Downstairs, she stopped at the front door to get her bearings. A shrill blast from the train station across the way startled her, and then the **ferocious** squeal of moving iron machinery filled the air. She clutched her hat and took a step back.

VOCABULARY

dank (daŋk) *adj.:* disagreeably damp; clammy.

INFER

What does the detail in lines 100–101 tell you about the time period in which this story is set?

CLARIFY

What is the narrator describing in lines 102–103?

VOCABULARY

ferocious (fə·rō′shəs) *adj.:* extremely violent; fierce.

The Memory Stone   **223**

CHARACTER

CHARACTER

Why do you suppose Ox married someone else? What does this suggest about his character?

____

____

____

FIGURATIVE LANGUAGE

What type of figurative language is used in lines 121–122?

____

____

PREDICT

Lines 132–136 describe significant plot events involving two objects that are important symbols in the story. Underline the objects. What do you predict these events foreshadow?

____

____

____

CONNOTATION

What images does the word *blossom* bring to mind? What qualities might a woman named Blossom possess?

____

____

____

"How will I ever find Ox in such a noisy, crowded city?" she asked herself.

At that very moment, Ox strode by, looking healthy and contented in a Western suit and polished boots. A woman's delicate hand was tucked into the crook of his arm. She was

120   as plain as a doorknob, but Ox's face glowed with pleasure.

The sighting plunged a blunt knife into Willow's heart as years of love seeped away. She retreated into the hotel and gasped, "Who is that?"

"Why, that is Ox Woo and his new bride! Her father is a gambler who made a fortune at the racetracks. Those two were married six weeks ago." The chatty innkeeper added, "Some people say she looks like a horse, too, but she does own a dozen racing steeds. She met her husband-to-be in the stables, where he was a hired hand cleaning the stalls."

130   Willow turned and dashed up the stairs. She repacked her bags and returned to the ship terminal. She vowed to never love another man, even if that meant never bearing children. At home, she flung Ox's bamboo birdcage into the stove, where it burst into crackling flames.

At this time, Ox noticed that a crack had suddenly appeared on one side of his jade pendant.

"What does this mean?" he roared, and his wife came running.

She looked closely and said, "Send it back to Willow. It is

140   not yours to keep."

"Nonsense," he declared. "This marvelous stone belongs to our firstborn child."

"No," she cried, "it will bring bad luck."

But Ox would not listen.

Soon, a daughter was born to them, named Blossom. Her features were very pleasing to the eye, and Ox gave her the jade pendant, which she wore all the time.

One day, when Blossom was five years old, Ox saddled up his favorite horse and took her riding. On the wooded trail, a bird

150 suddenly darted from the bushes and spooked the horse. It reared

up and threw off its riders. Ox hit his head on a sharp rock and

died instantly, while Blossom became tangled in the reins and was

dragged over the trail. She spent several months in a hospital, and

when the doctors removed the bandages, a scar zigzagged across

half her face. Her mother almost fainted, for its shape was iden-

tical to the crack on the jade. The doctors said nothing could be

done, for the wound was deep. In her grief, Blossom's mother

took the jade pendant and hurled it into the ocean.

Under her mother's care, Blossom grew into a good-natured

160 girl with many friends. Like her father, she was devoted to ani-

mals. She brought home birds with broken wings and tried to

nurse them back to health. Stray dogs followed her, and she

begged to keep them. When the neighbor's cat had a litter of

kittens, she pleaded for one. At school, she wrote stories about

insects and whales.

But her mother fretted about the scar, worrying that no

man would marry her. She took Blossom to doctors and sur-

geons all over North America, but they all agreed the damage

was permanent.

170 When Blossom turned seventeen, the mother asked, "What

do you want for your birthday dinner?"

"Bean-cake!"

"But that is so ordinary. How about roast chicken or bar-

becued duck?"

Blossom made a face. "You know I don't like eating meat."

The mother decided to stuff the soft bean-cake with fish-

paste, so she sent the cook to the market to buy a fresh fish. She

planned other dishes of eggs, nuts, and vegetables and invited all

of Blossom's friends.

180 Then the cook came running from the kitchen, his hands

wet and glistening. "Look what I found in the fish's stomach!"

He held up the jade pendant that had been thrown into the

ocean years ago. The mother recognized the jagged shape of the

crack right away.

Re-read lines 149–151. What caused the accident? How is this an example of irony?

What motivates the mother to throw the jade pendant into the ocean?

What can you infer about Blossom's personality from her comment to her mother in line 175?

What motivates Blossom's mother to send Blossom to China? What has the mother realized?

Blossom seems to recognize the area. What do you think this fact **foreshadows?**

vivid (viv′id) *adj.:* intense; bright.

Late that night, she sat down with Blossom. "There is something in our possession that must be returned to its rightful owner. Are you ready for a trip to China?"

So Blossom boarded a steamship and journeyed to the town where three rivers met. She passed village after village with ancient houses of blackened brick and green-tiled roofs. Barefoot children on the riverbank waved at her.

Blossom had never set foot in China before, yet somehow the bend of the river, the leafy spread of the chestnut tree, the curve of the stone bridge all seemed familiar.

Finally she reached the guesthouse where her father had worked two decades earlier, and she asked for Willow.

At the door, the mother-in-law gasped and fell against the frame. Blossom thought perhaps she had never seen a woman from Gold Mountain, and certainly not one with such a **vivid** scar.

She held out a silk pouch containing the jade. "This belongs to Willow."

The mother-in-law beckoned her to follow.

In her room, Willow knelt on the floor with her back straight and eyes closed, in front of an altar laden with flowers and fruit. The mother-in-law whispered to Blossom, "She finds peace in praying each day." Then she went and slid the jade pendant into Willow's calm hands. Willow's eyes flew open.

"Who brought this?"

Blossom stepped forward. "I did."

Willow spun around and the eyes of the two women sprang wide with amazement. Aside from the scar, Blossom looked exactly like the Willow of twenty years before. Their tapered chins, the full cheeks, and the tiny mouths were identical.

Willow gripped her jade pendant tightly. The years of anger melted as she stroked Blossom's face.

"Here," Willow said, handing her the pendant. "Rub this jade over your scar every day. You, your mother, and I, we have all suffered enough."

When Blossom took the jade, she was astounded to feel its
warmth. The stone seemed to glow with new **luster.** Holding it
to her face, she felt her cheek tingle.

Gradually her scar dissolved and she returned to the New
World with Willow's blessings. In time, she married and gave
birth to many children.

As for Willow, she worked contentedly at her guesthouse
for the rest of her life, knowing she had a daughter in Blossom.
And it was one of Blossom's grandchildren, a woman named
Jade, who donated the pendant to the Chinatown museum. It
sits in a glass case by a window, where visitors marvel at how
natural light changes the look of the stone from hour to hour.

Blossom's granddaughter left special instructions for the
care of the pendant. Once a month, the stone is removed from
the glass case. Under the watchful eyes of security guards, it is
passed by hand from one visitor to another.

And as they grip it in their palms or press it to their cheeks,
smiles fill their faces.

MEET THE WRITER

Paul Yee (1956–   ) is a third-generation Chinese Canadian who
has written many novels and short stories for young adults. Most
of his writing focuses on the experiences of Chinese immigrants
living in Canada in the late 1800s and early 1900s, when his family
immigrated. He sets his stories in the past because he wants "to
stake a claim" on Canada's history.

Yee was raised in Vancouver's Chinatown by an aunt who instilled
in him a knowledge and respect for both Chinese and Canadian
culture. As a boy, Yee was required to speak Chinese at home and
was taken to see movies made in Hong Kong on weekends. This
exposure to southern China's language, traditional stories, values,
and concepts of good and evil has allowed Yee to explore identity,
assimilation, and discrimination in his works.

SKILLS PRACTICE

The Memory Stone

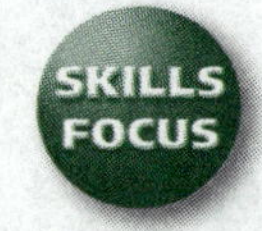

SKILLS FOCUS

Reading Skills
Make inferences about characters.

Motivation Chart The characters in "The Memory Stone" have various motivations, or reasons, for making the choices they do. Fill in the chart below by making inferences about these motivations. For each action listed, write the motivation that caused it.

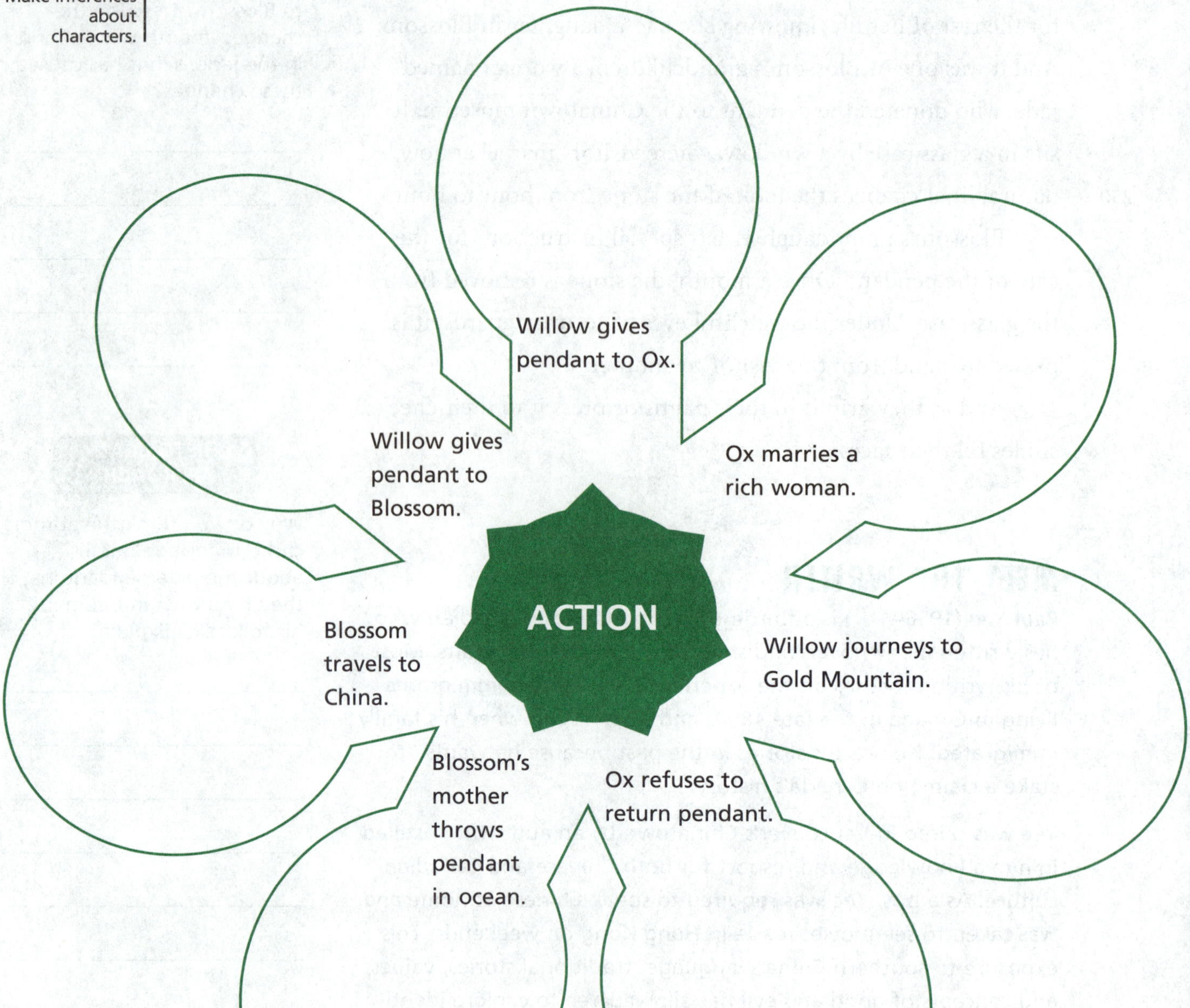

Skills Review

The Memory Stone

VOCABULARY AND COMPREHENSION

A. Vocabulary in Context   Complete the paragraph below by writing each word from the Word Box in the correct numbered blank.

Word Box

adorning

essences

trilling

dank

ferocious

vivid

Lee's favorite festival is Chinese New Year, a time for
(1) ___________________ the house with flowers and parading
through the (2) ___________________ waterside streets at dusk
with (3) ___________________ lanterns. It is a time for the
(4) ___________________, many-footed dragon to parade through
air scented with spicy (5) ___________________ and sounding of
(6) ___________________ flutes and bells.

B. Reading Comprehension

1. What makes Willow allow the beggar into her inn?

____

____

2. What makes Willow fall in love with Ox?

____

____

3. What causes Blossom's scar?

____

____

4. Why does Blossom travel to China?

____

____

Vocabulary Skills
Analyze figurative language.

Epic and Myth

Tom Bean/CORBIS

Academic Vocabulary for Collection 10

These are the terms you should know
as you read and analyze the stories in this collection.

———

Epic A long narrative poem that tells about the adventures of a great **hero.** Epics embody the values of the people who tell them.

Characters The people, animals, or creatures who take part in the action of a story. The **main character** of an epic is the hero (though in some epics, the hero's enemies are just as important). Many characters in epics are **subordinate characters;** they play lesser roles.

Conflict A struggle between opposing forces. An **external conflict** takes place between one character and another character, one character and a force of nature, or one character and society as a whole. An **internal conflict** takes place within a character's own mind or heart. In an internal conflict a character might struggle with a paralyzing fear or a need for revenge.

• • •

Myths Traditional stories, rooted in a particular culture, that usually explain a belief, a ritual, or a mysterious natural phenomenon. Most myths grew out of religious rituals.

Archetype Patterns, characters, or images that appear again and again in works of literature. Archetypes can be plots (the quest for something of value), characters (the innocent hero), places (the dragon's lair), or things (the magical gold ring).

The Story of the Eagle

by Joseph M. Marshall III

In every culture the content of myths reflects that culture's attitudes toward such human attributes as compassion, sacrifice, and duty. In the Lakota myth "The Story of the Eagle," the importance of compassion is a central theme.

LITERARY FOCUS: MYTHS

A **myth** is a traditional story rooted in a particular culture that usually explains a belief, a ritual, or a mysterious natural phenomenon. Myths might tell people where they came from, where they are going, or how they should live and are usually passed down through the generations. Many societies have myths that spring from their religious beliefs or traditions.

READING SKILLS: ANALYZING MYTH

- Myths have to do with a culture's attitudes toward reality.
- Myths have more to do with values and meanings than they do with facts.
- Myths are a way of answering such profound human questions as "Who am I?"; "Where did I come from?"; and "Where am I going?"

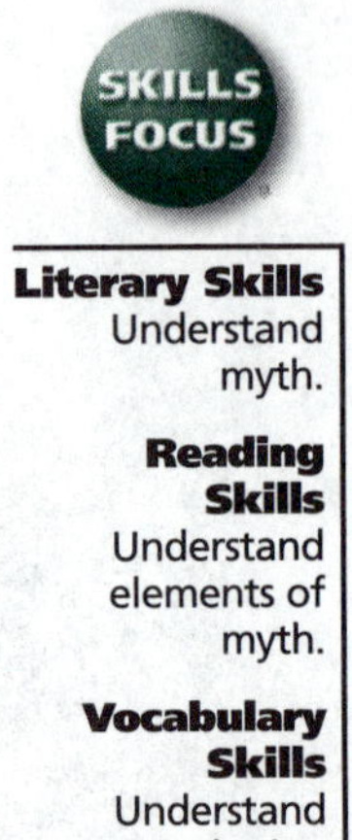

SKILLS FOCUS

Literary Skills
Understand myth.

Reading Skills
Understand elements of myth.

Vocabulary Skills
Understand analogies.

VOCABULARY DEVELOPMENT

ANALOGIES: WORD PAIRS

A word analogy is a word puzzle based on two pairs of words that have the same relationship. The words in each pair might be similar or opposite in meaning, or they might share some other relationship, such as cause and effect or whole to part. Follow this example for completing analogies:

START is to STOP as ______________________ is to love.

Start and *stop* are opposites, so the word that would show the same relationship in the second pair is *hate,* the opposite of *love.*

The analogy above is spelled out. Usually analogies are written in this form:

HUGE : ELEPHANT :: tiny : flea

The Story of the Eagle

Joseph M. Marshall III

Wautlsilapi (wah-utl-shee-lah-pee) Compassion: to care; to sympathize.

Some of our elders like to tell of how our people came up out of a hole in the Earth, in the southern edge of the Black Hills. That's a creation story. This one I'm about to tell you is a re-creation story. And it wouldn't have a good, happy ending if there were no compassion in the world.

Long ago the people were living in a land of many lakes. In the forests there were many animals, such as deer, elk, and moose, to hunt for food and clothing. The lakes were filled with fish of all kinds, and ducks and geese as well. The people were strong; their enemies were afraid of them and so there was peace. Life was very good.

Then came a particularly hard winter; the snow was deep. It came early and stayed long. All the snow finally melted in May, the Moon of Berries Ripening. Summer brought much rain and the lakes and rivers began to fill. The rains kept falling.

The people knew that the wet season always passed. They watched their round bark-and-thatch lodges to keep the water from leaking in and waited for the rains to let up. But they didn't. The lakes and rivers filled more and more until they all overflowed their banks, yet the rains kept falling. The skies stayed dark and cloudy.

The waters rose higher and higher, chasing the people out of their lodges. They found higher ground and made new lodges, but the water kept coming. Soon there was no rest from

Royalty-Free/CORBIS

the great flood; the people had to keep moving to the high hills and ridges. Even the animals fled from the waters.

Food became scarce because the hunters couldn't hunt. Many belongings were lost to the rising waters. Because there was no dry wood for fires, the people were cold. The first among them to die were the old ones who were too weak to fight the cold and hunger. Soon many people became ill with a coughing sickness. Some grew weak and died because there was no medicine to help them. Then the winds came.

Out of the north came the winds, angry and vengeful. They whipped the floods into a mean-spirited, dark being that sought out the people as they tried to flee, dragging them down into its cold darkness. Within days all but one of the people were dead.

Personification is a reference to nonhuman things or qualities as if they were human. In lines 36–39, note how the wind is personified by giving it characteristics of human behavior.

Pause at line 54. Why do you think the author chose to list the young woman's family members rather than simply saying that her family had been taken by the flood?

Pause at line 58. What do you think will happen next?

Why do you think the eagle decides to speak to the young woman?

40   A young woman clung to the rocks of a high hill. She had started climbing with her family, but the wind-driven flood had taken them all. Now she was alone, hungry and cold and dizzy with grief, huddling in the rocks waiting to die. Weakened by hunger and sadness, she fell asleep and slept for several days.

    The winds that had turned the flood into a frenzy also chased away the rain clouds. For the first time in nearly a month the sun bathed the land with its healing, soothing warmth. The great winds went away and in their place came gentle breezes that caressed the land with their softer breath.

50   The great flood was over, but it left death in its passing. Broken and uprooted trees, torn hillsides, and flattened grasses and shrubs were its trail. From the high hill the young woman could see what the flood had done. She would never forget that it had taken her mother and father and her brother and sister. It was of no matter to her that the sun was shining and the animals were beginning to return. She was alone. Her plaintive wail of grief rose over the land, causing four-leggeds and wingeds[1] to pause and listen.

    The young woman did not leave the hill. Day after day, 60 night after night, she sat overcome with grief, despair, and loneliness, growing weaker and weaker from lack of food and water. One afternoon she awoke to find a great eagle perched on a nearby rock. He was very large with dark brown, almost black feathers. She was frightened because she knew the eagle to be a great hunter with powerful talons that could rip her flesh, and she had no way to defend herself.

    The young woman was drawn to the eagle's soft brown eyes. He looked at her with curiosity. She waited, suddenly sensing that there was no danger. Then the eagle spoke.

70   "I have seen that you are alone," he said.

    She began to sob quietly, then stopped.

    "Yes," she replied. "The flood took my family; it took all of my people, the two-leggeds. I am alone."

---

1. **four-leggeds and wingeds:** creatures that walk on four legs and creatures that fly.

"You are sad. I heard you weeping."

"My family is gone. My people are gone. There is only me and all I have is sadness. It stays with me day and night."

"Then I will be your friend," the eagle said. "Tell me what I can do for you."

"You can do nothing," she lamented. "I am alone. I will die alone."

"That is not true," he replied. "Look around. Your relatives, the four-leggeds; the wingeds like me; and the crawlers:[2] They are here. We are all here."

"But my people are gone. I am the last," she sobbed. "There is no one like me left. So I am waiting to die, to rejoin my people."

"If you die, there will be no more like you on the Earth. There will be nothing but emptiness where your kind once lived. That cannot be. You must live." He stretched his wings and rose in the air.

"Where are you going?" she asked. "Are you leaving me?"

"Only to bring you food," he told her. "I will return."

And he did, bringing a large fish.

"I must make a fire to cook this," she said. "I cannot eat this without cooking it."

"What do you need for fire?" he asked.

"Wood," she said. "Dry wood."

The eagle, of course, could fly very fast, and after several flights to the forest he had collected a large pile of wood for her. The young woman first built a fire starter of wood and cord, then started a fire and cooked the fish. Even a small bite seemed to give her strength; she could feel it flowing through her. All the while the eagle had been sitting back, for he was afraid of the fire.

"You two-leggeds can do a very powerful thing," he said. "You can make fire. But, of course, we wingeds and four-leggeds do not need such a thing."

---

2. **crawlers:** creatures that crawl.

In lines 81–83, what does the eagle's comment show you about the Lakota's view of nature?

What do you think the fire mentioned in lines 100–104 **symbolizes?**

From what you've learned so far, compare and contrast the way the woman sees her situation with the way the eagle sees it.

What do the eagle's actions in line 118 reveal about his character?

Werner Forman/Art Resource, NY

"Yes. Fire cooks our food so we can eat it. It keeps us warm. There is nothing like a warm fire to chase away the darkness. A
110   good fire is like a good friend."

The eagle brought more wood so she could have a fire through the night and stay warm. In the morning when she awoke he was gone, but her fire was still smoldering. She built up her fire and wondered where he was. For a time he had eased her loneliness and she was grateful. As the morning wore on and he did not return, she thought he had only been a dream. Yet there was the fire and the dried-out skin of the fish.

He returned in the middle of the day, this time with a rabbit.

"This is a fine day," he said. "It is good to be alive."

120   The young woman was glad for the eagle's return. She skinned the rabbit, cooked it, and ate as he watched with great interest.

"There is a fine valley toward where the sun goes down—a good place to build a lodge. There is water and it is sheltered from the cold winter wind. Perhaps you should go there," he said.

"No," she replied, "I am here, and I will stay here. I can build a lodge here, if that is what I want to do."

The eagle could see that her sadness was great. He knew also that she would always be sad because she was the last of her kind. He had flown far over the lakes and valleys, but he had found no other two-leggeds. She would grow old and die alone.

He continued to bring her food and firewood day after day. And he would circle over her hill watching for any danger. Once he chased a bear away from the hill, swooping down again and again.

She grew stronger with each passing day and began to worry about her appearance. She brushed off her dress and made a comb to do her hair. Before the flood she had been the loveliest young woman in many villages, and young men had come from near and far to court her. Now, of course, she was the most beautiful young woman anywhere.

One day while waiting for the eagle, she climbed to the very top of her hill. From there she saw across a wide valley and many lakes. There was beauty all around; in time the scars from the great flood would be no more. But what could she do alone? she wondered. Like any young woman she had dreamed of marrying a fine, handsome young man and having children. They would live not far from her mother and father's lodge in their village by the lake. He would hunt and she would keep their lodge and they would grow old together. Now she was standing on a hill, a cold, terrible truth within her. She was the last of her kind. What was she to do?

One of the tiny black specks in the sky above began to grow larger and larger, and soon she heard the rush of wind under the great wings of the eagle. He landed. She marveled at the spread of his mighty wings and the power in them. But he also had a different power, the power to chase away her loneliness.

Visualize what the woman is seeing in lines 164–171 as the eagle takes her aloft.

Perspective is the ability to see things in their true relation-ship or relative importance. Another **theme** common in myths is learning to see things from a different perspective, or view of life. The eagle provides the woman the chance to see the world from a different perspective by taking her aloft. How does the woman respond?

____

____

____

____

____

____

The woman thinks about building herself a lodge. What do you think this act symbolizes to her?

____

____

____

____

____

____

"What am I to do?" she asked. "Without you I would have nothing. If only I was an eagle, I would fly with you. I could see what you see from so high in the sky. And I would not be the only one of my kind."

"Come," he said, "we shall fly. Grab my legs as I rise into the air."

She did and they rose from the hill. She was afraid at first and she hung on very tight. But as they soared upward she saw the Earth as she had never seen it before, and she trembled in awe. She felt powerful as everything on the Earth grew smaller. It was a sight she could never have imagined. Though the things on the Earth—trees, hills, lakes, and rivers—grew smaller as they went higher, the Earth itself grew larger, and the young woman was humbled by the wondrous sight of it.

They flew until her arms became tired, but she was reluctant to return to the hill.

"Thank you," she said, "I envy what you are."

"I am your friend," he replied, "and always will be."

Their friendship became stronger. He brought her food, and she scratched pictures of him on the rocks. Every day she ventured farther and farther from her camp and was soon talk-ing about building a lodge somewhere, perhaps on the very top of the hill. The eagle saw that the young woman was smiling more often. Still, he could see sadness in her eyes.

On one fine day in late summer the eagle soared on the winds high above the young woman's hill. Autumn was on the way and winter would not be far behind. Already some cold breezes were coming from the north. The young woman needed to prepare for winter or she would perish. He was troubled.

"Grandfather,"[3] he called out, "You who are most powerful, why have you not seen to her well-being?" he asked.

"I have done so," came back a voice. "I have sent you to her."

____

3. **Grandfather:** To the Lakota, Grandfather is the sky, the home of eagles. It is the place the eagle in the story goes to gain perspective.

190   "I have helped her because she is needful and a fine being,"
replied the eagle. "I can only bring her food. I cannot give her
what she truly needs. She needs others of her kind."

     "There is a way," the voice replied.

     "Tell me, Grandfather," the eagle said. "I will help her in any
way I can."

     "You are a fine being, too; you have a kind heart and you
are deserving of your place in the Great Circle of Life," said the
voice. "Few have your power. It would be difficult to lose your
place, for that is what must happen if you truly want to help

200   the two-legged."

     "I do not understand, Grandfather."

     "To help her you must become a two-legged. If you do, you
will never ride the winds again. You will never again see the Earth
from above the highest mountains. The choice is yours. You can
become a two-legged and as male and female you can together
give to the Earth more of her kind. Or you can remain as you are."

     The eagle was very quiet that night as he sat with the young
woman. He was troubled. She saw that his brown eyes had lost
their usual sparkle.

210   "Is there something on your mind?" she asked.

     "Yes," he replied. "I must go away. There is much I have to
think about."

     "You will return?" she asked. "I could not bear it if you
were lost to me."

     "I will return," he promised. "No matter what happens, I
will always be your friend. I will bring you food before I leave.
Stay on the hill; do not wander far," he cautioned.

     The next day the young woman climbed to the top of the
hill and watched the sky. There were many hawks circling and a

220   few eagles. She wondered which one of those high, black specks
was her friend. The next day was the same, and the day after
that. She was impatient for his return because loneliness stalked
her like an enemy in the night.

Explain how you know the
eagle is struggling to answer
such questions as "Who am
I?"; "What am I doing here?";
and "Where am I going?" at
this point in the story.

Underline and name the type
of figurative language used
in lines 222–223.

What do the eagle's actions and feelings described in lines 224–226 tell you about his decision?

____

____

____

____

____

What will the eagle be sacrificing if he chooses to become a human being? Explain.

____

____

____

____

____

____

From what you have learned so far about the eagle, predict what will happen next.

____

____

____

____

____

____

Library of Congress, Prints & Photographs Division, Edward S. Curtis Collection, LC-USZ62-106267

The eagle soared higher than he had ever flown and saw more of the Earth than he had ever seen. It was a sight he never wanted to forget.

"Grandfather," he called out. "I am here."

"Grandson," the voice replied, "I know what is in your heart. You have been troubled for these many days. Yet you have
230   made a choice."

"Yes," said the eagle. "I know what I must do."

"The choice you make is a road you can never turn back from," said the voice.

"There are still many of my kind," said the eagle. "She is only one, and she cannot be the last of her kind. The Earth and everything on it would feel the loss. I can see no other way."

"So be it," said the voice. "I tell you this. Two-leggeds will find a place in their hearts for your kind. They will hold you high."

Summer was ending, the young woman knew. Cold breezes
240   came down from the north. She walked the hillside to gather

wood for her fire. Now and then she looked up at the sky, but
as yet he had not returned.

> "Do you wait for someone?" came a voice from behind her.
>
> It was a familiar voice, one she knew very well. He had
> returned. The young woman turned with a smile, which became
> a frown. She could see no one.
>
> "I am here," said the familiar voice.
>
> The young woman nearly fainted as a tall, handsome young
> man stepped from behind a rock.
>
> "How can this be?" she cried. "I thought all of us were
> taken by the flood except for me!"
>
> "That is true," said the young man.
>
> "Then where do you come from?"
>
> "From the sky," the young man replied.

The young woman was shocked into silence and disbelief.
Yet the voice of the young man was familiar; it was the voice
of the eagle. Pushing aside her confusion and fear, she stepped
closer. There was something familiar in those deep, brown eyes,
also.

"Remember the day we flew together?" he asked. "I took
you up far above the Earth."

"It cannot be!" she cried. "It is you!"

"I promised I would return, and so I have. Are you not
happy to see me?"

The young woman ran and fell into his embrace, feeling
something she thought could never be. Yet she felt something
else as well: Each time she came near to him thereafter she felt
as though she were soaring.

Before that winter they built a lodge at the edge of a forest
and in time became mother and father to many children, and to
a new race of two-leggeds. She told her children who their father
was and what he had been. They would watch the sky as the
great eagles flew. They were, of course, watching their relatives.
They taught their children who taught their children, and so on,
to do the same.

FLUENCY

Read the boxed passage aloud for smoothness. Then, re-read it, being sure to express the emotions of the characters.

SYMBOLISM

What attributes does the eagle symbolize to you? Explain.

____

____

____

____

____

____

____

____

____

____

____

____

____

____

____

____

At the beginning of this selection, the author stated that "The Story of the Eagle" was a re-creation story, not a creation story. Explain how the story is a re-creation story.

Perhaps now you understand why eagle feathers are sacred to us. To this day we Lakota revere the great eagles, and each time we see one in the sky we pause to speak our thanks to those relatives for their compassion.

MEET THE WRITER

Joseph M. Marshall III (1945–   ) is a writer, teacher, actor, historian, traditional storyteller, and craftsman who is a member of the Rosebud Sioux. Marshall celebrates his Native American heritage in many ways, most notably through his writing and storytelling. The story you just read, which comes from his book *The Lakota Way,* is based on the numerous oral versions of the story he heard while growing up. In his writings he tries to capture the style and imagery the elders used when telling their versions of the traditional stories.

The Story of the Eagle

Character Traits Chart The left-hand column contains quotations about the eagle from the myth. Identify the character traits displayed in this quotation, and write them in the spaces in the right-hand column. The first one has been done for you.

Reading Skills
Analyze myth.

Quotation About the Eagle	Character Trait Described
"He was very large with dark brown, almost black feathers. She was frightened because she knew the eagle to be a great hunter with powerful talons."	powerful; able to provide food and to protect himself
"The young woman was drawn to the eagle's soft brown eyes. . . . She waited, suddenly sensing that there was no danger."	
"'If you die, there will be no more like you on the Earth. There will be nothing but emptiness where your kind once lived. That cannot be.'"	
"He continued to bring her food and firewood day after day. And he would circle over her hill watching for any danger."	
"'I will help her in any way I can.'"	
"The eagle soared higher than he had ever flown and saw more of the Earth than he had ever seen."	
"'There are still many of my kind. . . . She is only one, and she cannot be the last of her kind. The Earth and everything on it would feel the loss.'"	

The Story of the Eagle

VOCABULARY AND COMPREHENSION

A. Word Analogies   For each analogy, fill in the blank with a word that completes the puzzle.

1. OAK : TREE :: ___________________ : dog

2. COCOA : CHOCOLATE :: ___________________ : bread

3. COURAGE : BRAVERY :: sincerity : ___________________

4. GLASS : FRAGILE :: ___________________ : loud

5. CHICKEN : EGG :: tree : ___________________

6. ANGRY : IRATE :: ___________________ : elated

B. Reading Comprehension   Answer each question below.

1. What natural disaster occurs in this re-creation story?

____

____

____

2. What does the lone survivor lose as a consequence of that natural disaster?

____

____

____

3. What humanlike qualities are used to personify the eagle?

____

____

____

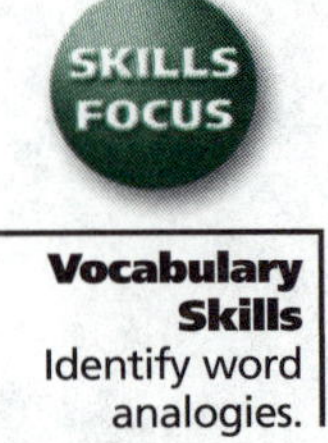

SKILLS FOCUS

Vocabulary Skills
Identify word analogies.

The Spirit Wife by Richard Erdoes and Alfonso Ortiz

"The Spirit Wife" is a traditional Zuni myth about a couple separated by death and the lengths to which the grieving husband goes to rejoin his beloved wife. As you read the story, consider the personality traits the Zuni held in high esteem and sought to foster through the telling of this myth.

LITERARY SKILLS: MYTH AND ARCHETYPES

Many archetypes (är′kə·tīps′) come from myths. **Archetypes** are very old patterns or images that occur again and again in literature. Archetypes can be characters (such as the sacrificial hero), plots (such as the heroic quest), animals (such as lambs, wolves, and serpents), or settings (such as places of perfect happiness).

In this myth you will find the archetype of the heroic quest.

READING SKILLS: IDENTIFYING CAUSE AND EFFECT

Myths are narratives, which are built on a series of causes and effects. In a narrative an event causes another event to happen, which causes another event to happen, and so on. A **cause** is why something happens. An **effect** is what happens as a result.

Writers often signal cause-and-effect relationships with words such as *because, consequently, for, if, then, so, thus, since,* and *therefore.* To find cause-and-effect relationships:

- Look for signal words that show cause and effect.
- To find an effect, ask yourself *what* has happened. You may find multiple effects.
- To find a cause, ask yourself *why* something happens. You may find multiple causes.

Literary Skills
Understand myths and archetypes.

Reading Skills
Identify cause and effect.

Vocabulary Skills
Use context clues.

VOCABULARY DEVELOPMENT

PREVIEW SELECTION VOCABULARY

The following words appear in "The Spirit Wife." Become familiar with them before you begin reading.

dissuade (di·swād') *v.:* persuade not to do something.

*Try as she might, the young spirit-wife could not **dissuade** her husband from following her.*

chasm (kaz'əm) *n.:* deep split in the earth; gorge.

*The young man faced certain death if he slipped into the rocky **chasm.***

abyss (ə·bis') *n.:* hole or space so deep that it cannot be measured.

*The great **abyss** seemed as deep as his sorrow.*

embrace (em·brās') *v.:* clasp with the arms; hug.

*The young man was forbidden to **embrace** his wife until they reached their village.*

reverently (rev'ə·rənt·lē) *adv.:* with deep respect.

*With care and respect, the young man **reverently** carved the prayer sticks.*

self-denial (self dē·nī'əl) *n.:* refusal to satisfy one's own wants; unselfishness.

*Winning his wife back required the young husband to practice **self-denial.***

USING CONTEXT CLUES

Stories like "The Spirit Wife" often contain words and expressions particular to a region or time period. When you come across an unfamiliar word in your reading, you can sometimes use **context clues**—surrounding words and phrases—to figure out its meaning. Common types of context clues include *definitions, contrasts, synonyms,* and *examples.* In the passages below, the context clues for the boldface words are underlined.

Contrast: "The spirit-wife tried to **dissuade** him, but could not overcome his determination."

Synonym: "Let not your desire to touch and **embrace** her get the better of you."

Example: "If he had not touched her, if he had practiced patience and **self-denial** for only a short time, then death would have been overcome."

As you read "The Spirit Wife," look for context clues that might help you define unfamiliar words. If you are not sure that you have defined a word correctly, use a dictionary to check its meaning.

The Spirit Wife

Richard Erdoes and Alfonso Ortiz

> ### BACKGROUND NOTE
> The Zuni people have lived in the area of the Arizona–New Mexico border since about A.D. 700. They believe that spirits protect humans and grant them health and long life. Sometimes the spirits visit humans, but usually they dwell at the bottom of the Lake of the Dead. This lake is thought to lie at the bottom of an actual lake near the Colorado River. Many Zuni today keep their ancient beliefs alive and prefer to live apart from the modern world.
>
> A strikingly similar myth, "Orpheus and Eurydice," appears in Greek mythology.

A young man was grieving because the beautiful young wife whom he loved was dead. As he sat at the graveside weeping, he decided to follow her to the Land of the Dead. He made many prayer sticks and sprinkled sacred corn pollen. He took a downy eagle plume and colored it with red earth color. He waited until nightfall, when the spirit of his departed wife came out of the grave and sat beside him. She was not sad, but smiling. The spirit-maiden told her husband: "I am just leaving one life for another. Therefore do not weep for me."

10   "I cannot let you go," said the young man, "I love you so much that I will go with you to the land of the dead."

The spirit-wife tried to **dissuade** him, but could not overcome his determination. So at last she gave in to his wishes, saying: "If you must follow me, know that I shall be invisible to you as long as the sun shines. You must tie this red eagle plume to my hair. It will be visible in the daylight, and if you want to come with me, you must follow the plume."

INFER

Pause at line 9. What does the wife's attitude tell you about the Zuni view of death?

____

____

____

____

____

____

____

VOCABULARY

dissuade (di·swād′) *v.:* persuade not to do something.

In line 20, the sun is personified—it is given human characteristics. What does this tell you about the Zuni view of nature?

Underline the figure of speech used in line 25. What is this device called?

© AGE/Fotostock

The young husband tied the red plume to his spirit-wife's hair, and at daybreak, as the sun slowly began to light up the world, bathing the mountaintops in a pale pink light, the spirit-wife started to fade from his view. The lighter it became, the more the form of his wife dissolved and grew transparent, until at last it vanished altogether. But the red plume did not disappear. It waved before the young man, a mere arm's-length away, and then, as if rising and falling on a dancer's head, began leading the way out of the village, moving through the streets out into the cornfields, moving through a shallow stream, moving into the foothills of the mountains, leading the young husband ever westward toward the land of the evening.

The red plume moved swiftly, evenly, floating without effort over the roughest trails, and soon the young man had trouble following it. He grew tireder and tireder and finally

was totally exhausted as the plume left him farther behind.
Then he called out, panting: "Beloved wife, wait for me. I can't
run any longer."

The red plume stopped, waiting for him to catch up, and
when he did so, hastened on. For many days the young man
traveled, following the plume by day, resting during the nights,
when his spirit-bride would sometimes appear to him, speaking
encouraging words. Most of the time, however, he was merely
aware of her presence in some mysterious way. Day by day the
trail became rougher and rougher. The days were long, the nights
short, and the young man grew wearier and wearier, until at last
he had hardly enough strength to set one foot before the other.

One day the trail led to a deep, almost bottomless **chasm,**
and as the husband came to its edge, the red plume began to
float away from him into nothingness. He reached out to seize it,
but the plume was already beyond his
reach, floating straight across the
canyon, because spirits can fly
through the air.

The young man called
across the chasm: "Dear wife
of mine, I love you. Wait!"

He tried to descend one
side of the canyon, hoping to
climb up the opposite side, but
the rock walls were sheer, with
nothing to hold on to. Soon he
found himself on a ledge barely
wider than a thumb, from which
he could go neither forward nor
back. It seemed that he must fall
into the **abyss** and be dashed into
pieces. His foot had already begun to
slip, when a tiny striped squirrel scooted

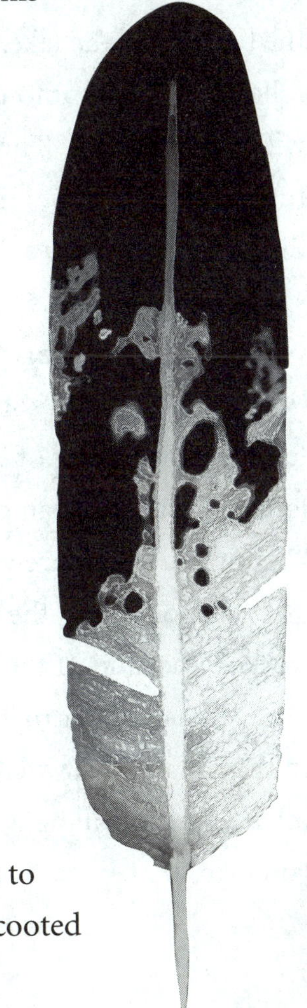

Turtle Heart/Getty Images

chasm (kaz′əm) *n.:* deep split
in the earth; gorge.

Pause at line 51. What do
you think the chasm symbolizes? Name another **myth** or
legend in which a hero faces
a seemingly insurmountable
obstacle.

abyss (ə·bis′) *n.:* hole or
space so deep that it cannot
be measured.

Pause at line 69. The hero in this myth is saved from falling by a squirrel. Who or what usually intervenes on behalf of a hero in Greek myths?

Re-read lines 77–89. Underline the details that help you visualize the scene.

Why do you think this owl can talk and knows the young man's problem?

up the cliff, chattering: "You young fool, do you think you have the wings of a bird or the feet of a spirit? Hold on for just a little while and I'll help you." The little creature reached into its cheek

70 pouch and brought out a little seed, which it moistened with saliva and stuck into a crack in the wall. With his tiny feet the squirrel danced above the crack, singing: "Tsithl, tsithl, tsithl, tall stalk, tall stalk, tall stalk, sprout, sprout quickly." Out of the crack sprouted a long, slender stalk, growing quickly in length and breadth, sprouting leaves and tendrils, spanning the chasm so that the young man could cross over without any trouble.

On the other side of the canyon, the young man found the red plume waiting, dancing before him as ever. Again he followed it at a pace so fast that it often seemed that his heart

80 would burst. At last the plume led him to a large, dark, deep lake, and the plume plunged into the water to disappear below the surface. Then the husband knew that the spirit land lay at the bottom of the lake. He was in despair because he could not follow the plume into the deep. In vain did he call for his spirit-wife to come back. The surface of the lake remained undisturbed and unruffled like a sheet of mica.[1] Not even at night did his spirit-wife reappear. The lake, the land of the dead, had swallowed her up. As the sun rose above the mountains, the young man buried his face in his hands and wept.

90 Then he heard someone gently calling: "Hu-hu-hu," and felt the soft beating of wings on his back and shoulders. He looked up and saw an owl hovering above him. The owl said: "Young man, why are you weeping?"

He pointed to the lake, saying: "My beloved wife is down there in the land of the dead, where I cannot follow her."

"I know, poor man," said the owl. "Follow me to my house in the mountains, where I will tell you what to do. If you follow my advice, all will be well and you will be reunited with the one you love."

---

1. **mica** (mī′kə) *n.:* mineral made up of very thin, flat crystal-like sheets.

100   The owl led the husband to a cave in the mountains and, as they entered, the young man found himself in a large room full of owl-men and owl-women. The owls greeted him warmly, inviting him to sit down and rest, to eat and drink. Gratefully he took his seat.

The old owl who had brought him took his owl clothing off, hanging it on an antler jutting out from the wall, and revealed himself as a manlike spirit. From a bundle in the wall this mysterious being took a small bag, showing it to the young man, telling him: "I will give this to you, but first I must instruct
110   you in what you must do and must not do."

The young man eagerly stretched out his hand to grasp the medicine bag, but the owl drew back. "Foolish fellow, suffering from the impatience of youth! If you cannot curb your eagerness and your youthful desires, then even this medicine will be of no help to you."

"I promise to be patient," said the husband.

"Well then," said the owl-man, "this is sleep medicine. It will make you fall into a deep sleep and transport you to some other place. When you awake, you will walk toward the Morning Star.
120   Following the trail to the middle anthill, you will find your spirit-wife there. As the sun rises, so she will rise and smile at you, rise in the flesh, a spirit no more, and so you will live happily."

"But remember to be patient; remember to curb your eagerness. Let not your desire to touch and **embrace** her get the better of you, for if you touch her before bringing her safely home to the village of your birth, she will be lost to you forever."

Having finished this speech, the old owl-man blew some of the medicine on the young husband's face, who instantly fell into a deep sleep. Then all the strange owl-men put on their
130   owl coats and, lifting the sleeper, flew with him to a place at the beginning of the trail to the middle anthill. There they laid him down underneath some trees.

Then the strange owl-beings flew on to the big lake at the bottom of which the land of the dead was located. The old owl-

---

Pause at line 115. What do you think this warning foreshadows?

embrace (em·brās′) v.: clasp with the arms; hug.

The owl-man warns the young man to be patient and to exercise self-control. What does this warning suggest about Zuni values?

Acoma Pueblo jar.
Chuck Place/Alamy

man's magic sleep medicine, and the feathered prayer sticks which the young man had carved, enabled them to dive down to the bottom of the lake and enter the land of the dead. Once inside, they used the sleep medicine to put to sleep the spirits who are in charge of that strange land beneath the waters. The

140 owl-beings **reverently** laid their feathered prayer sticks before the altar of that netherworld,[2] took up the beautiful young spirit-wife, and lifted her gently to the surface of the lake. Then, taking her upon their wings, they flew with her to the place where the young husband was sleeping.

When the husband awoke, he saw first the Morning Star, then the middle anthill, and then his wife at his side, still in deep slumber. Then she too awoke and opened her eyes wide, at first not knowing where she was or what had happened to her. When she discovered her husband right by her side, she smiled at him,

150 saying: "Truly, your love for me is strong, stronger than love has ever been, otherwise we would not be here."

---

2. **netherworld** (ne*th*′ər·wurld′) *n.:* world of the dead.

Zuni tribesman (1854). Color lithograph. American
School (19th century). Private collection.
Peter Newark American Pictures/Bridgeman Art Library.

They got up and began to walk toward the pueblo[3] of their
birth. The young man did not forget the advice the old owl-man
had given him, especially the warning to not touch his wife until
they had safely arrived at their home. In that way they traveled
for four days, and all was well.

On the fourth day they arrived at Thunder Mountain and
came to the river that flows by Salt Town. Then the young wife
said: "My husband, I am very tired. The journey has been long
and the days hot. Let me rest here awhile, let me sleep awhile,
and then, refreshed, we can walk the last short distance home
together." And her husband said: "We will do as you say."

---

3. **pueblo** (pweb′lō) *n.:* village made up of stone or adobe buildings,
    often arranged in terraces.

Pause at line 156. Note the
suspense that the repetition
of the owl-man's warning is
creating.

Why does the young man touch his wife?

____

____

____

self-denial (self dē·nī′əl) *n.*: refusal to satisfy one's own wants; unselfishness.

What mysterious event does this myth help the Zuni explain?

____

____

____

Most **myths** end after the hero learns his lesson. This myth contains a concluding paragraph stating that everything works out for the best. What does this tell you about the way the Zuni see themselves and their place in the circle of life?

____

____

____

The wife lay down and fell asleep. As her husband was watching over her, gazing at her loveliness, love so strong that he could not resist it overcame him, and he stretched out his hand and touched her.

She awoke instantly with a start, and, looking at him and at his hand upon her body, began to weep, the tears streaming down her face. At last she said: "You loved me, but you did not love me enough; otherwise you would have waited. Now I shall die again." And before his eyes her form faded and became transparent, and at the place where she had rested a few moments before, there was nothing. On a branch of a tree above him the old owl-man hooted mournfully: "Shame, shame, shame." Then the young man sank down in despair, burying his face in his hands, and ever after his mind wandered as his eyes stared vacantly.

If the young husband had controlled himself, if he had not longed to embrace his beautiful wife, if he had not touched her, if he had practiced patience and **self-denial** for only a short time, then death would have been overcome. There would be no journeying to the land below the lake, and no mourning for others lost.

But then, if there were no death, men would crowd each other with more people on this earth than the earth can hold. Then there would be hunger and war, with people fighting over a tiny patch of earth, over an ear of corn, over a scrap of meat. So maybe what happened was for the best.

MEET THE WRITERS

Richard Erdoes (1912–   ) is an Austrian-born illustrator, photographer, and writer. While photographing a Sioux reservation for *Life* magazine in the 1970s, Erdoes saw firsthand the conditions under which the residents were forced to live. This led him to campaign actively for the rights of Native Americans. While campaigning, he was befriended by a Sioux medicine man named Lame Deer, who asked Erdoes to write his life story. This collaboration helped launch Erdoes's writing career. Erdoes has written dozens of books, most of them about Native Americans and the colonization of the West.

Alfonso Ortiz (1939–1997) was an anthropologist, educator, and author born in New Mexico. As an anthropologist, Ortiz pioneered programs that brought academic scholars into contact with the communities they were studying, making the Native American peoples equal partners in the research. In addition to practicing and teaching anthropology, Ortiz edited several books on the Native Americans of North America. Active in fostering Native American culture and rights, he served as the president of the Association on American Indian Affairs for fifteen years.

Notes

The Spirit Wife

SKILLS FOCUS

Reading Skills
Identify cause and effect.

Cause-and-Effect Chart   "The Spirit Wife" explains the Zuni view of how death came about. It also emphasizes the importance the Zuni place on self-control and patience. The selection contains a series of causes and effects, describing the actions of the young man and the results of those actions. Some of those causes and effects are filled in on the chart below. Complete the chart by filling in the rest.

Cause— why something happens	Effect— what happens as a result
The young man places eagle feathers and prayer sticks by his wife's grave.	
	The spirit-wife tells the young man to follow the feather tied to her hair.
The young man tries to descend a wall of the canyon.	
	A large plant stalk spans the canyon.
The owl-man asks the young man why he is crying.	
	The young man promises to be patient.
The young man touches his sleeping wife.	
	The young man lives his life in a kind of trance.

Skills Review

The Spirit Wife

VOCABULARY AND COMPREHENSION

A. Vocabulary in Context   Complete the paragraph below by writing a word from the Word Box in each numbered blank.

The spirit-wife tries unsuccessfully to _________________ the young man from following her to the netherworld. He comes to a _________________ in the rock and nearly falls into the _________________ but is saved by a helpful squirrel. The owl-people offer to help the young man rejoin his wife on the condition that he practice _________________ by waiting until he returns home to _________________ her. The young man _________________ agrees to the demands of these godlike creatures but then goes back on his word.

Word Box

dissuade

chasm

abyss

embrace

reverently

self-denial

B. Reading Comprehension   Answer each question below.

1. Why does the owl-man approach the young husband?

   ____

   ____

2. What warning does the owl-man give the young man after agreeing to help him?

   ____

   ____

3. What causes the spirit-wife to return to the netherworld?

   ____

   ____

4. What do you think the Zuni hoped to teach by telling this story?

   ____

   ____

SKILLS FOCUS

Vocabulary Skills
Use context clues.

Before You Read

Orpheus and Eurydice by William F. Russell

In ancient Greece, myths—traditional stories about gods and heroes—were much more than entertaining tales. Myths were part of the Greek religion and defined the culture of the people who believed in them. Myths told people who they were, where they came from, and what they should value in life.

LITERARY FOCUS: HERO MYTHS

By means of myths, people were able to deal with the mysteries they encountered in life—mysteries they saw in the outside world and in their own inner worlds as well. Though they often have supernatural powers, the heroes in Greek myths are recognizably human. They are not divine, although some of them are the offspring of gods and humans.

In a typical hero myth, a man is sent on a quest to find something of great value, including self-knowledge and self-control. Hero stories reveal the qualities that the ancient Greeks valued and tried to instill in their children. The tales of Greek heroes tell of people who are not always noble. The characters are sometimes selfish, stubborn, or even cruel. They sometimes disobey the gods, with grave, even tragic, consequences.

READING SKILLS: SUMMARIZING

A **summary** is a short restatement of the important ideas in a work. When you summarize a story, you retell just the main events. Summarizing helps you keep track of the characters and the plot. It also increases your ability to understand and remember what you read.

To summarize as you read:	To summarize after you read:
• Pause occasionally. • Review who the characters are. • Retell what has happened to them so far.	• Briefly describe the story's beginning, middle, and end. • Focus on the main characters and events.

SKILLS FOCUS

Literary Skills
Understand characteristics of myth, including heroes and their external conflicts.

Reading Skills
Understand summarizing.

Vocabulary Skills
Learn words from Greek and Roman myths.

PREVIEW SELECTION VOCABULARY

The following words appear in "Orpheus and Eurydice." Become familiar with them before you begin reading.

shrouded (shroud′id) *v.* used as *adj.:* covered as if with a shroud, a cloth in which a body is wrapped for burial.

*The souls of Hades stood silent, **shrouded** in shadows.*

gnashing (nash′iŋ) *v.* used as *adj.:* grinding together.

*Orpheus leapt back from the **gnashing** jaws of the three-headed dog.*

insolence (in′sə·ləns) *n.:* bold disrespect.

*What at first seemed like **insolence** to King Hades was Orpheus's determination.*

WORDS FROM GREEK AND ROMAN MYTHS

Many words we use in English today come from Greek and Roman myths. For example, a journey or quest is often called an odyssey, after the title of the epic poem *Odyssey.* Some words used in "Orpheus and Eurydice" that have become part of the English language are listed in the chart below.

Words from Greek and Roman Myths	English Words
Muse, one of the nine goddesses of literature, arts, and sciences	museum; music
Mercury, the messenger god—god of commerce, cleverness, and travel	mercurial
Calliope, one of the Muses and Orpheus's mother	calliope
Styx, the river surrounding Hades	stygian

Orpheus and Eurydice

William F. Russell

IDENTIFY

Underline the literary device used in line 1. What is this device called?

IDENTIFY

Underline the literary device used in lines 4–5. What is this device called?

Long ago, when the earth was very young, there were only two kinds of musical instruments: the pipes, which were invented by the god Pan and made musical tones when a person blew into them, and the lyre, which was a stringed instrument, rather like a small harp. It is said that the lyre was invented by Mercury* while he was still just a baby. He fastened a few strings of various lengths across the hollow of a tortoise shell, and he entertained himself by plucking the strings and listening to the pretty sounds that would come out of the shell. These pretty sounds

10 were soon heard by the great and glorious god Apollo, who bought the instrument; and, being the god of music as well as the god of the sun, Apollo soon mastered all its artistic possibilities and composed many songs, each of which was more beautiful than any music that had been heard before.

Now the first mortal to play upon the lyre was a poet named Orpheus, whose mother, a Muse called Calliope, was also the goddess of epic poetry. Orpheus used the artistic talents given him by his mother to compose sweet melodies, which he played upon his lyre so beautifully that all nature seemed to

---

* Pronunciations of Greek mythological names:

Mercury (mur′kyoor·ē) Charon (ker′ən)
Orpheus (ôr′fē·əs) Cerberus (sur′bər·əs)
Eurydice (yoo·rid′i·sē′) Hades (hā′dēz′)
Calliope (kə·lī′ə·pē′) Persephone (pər·sef′ə·nē)
Styx (stiks)

20   draw near and listen. The buds on spring flowers would open
to the sound of his singing and playing; the fiercest wild beasts
became tame and gentle and would follow Orpheus about like
lambs; storms would cease to toss the seas; and even the evil
thoughts that were in the minds of the mortals who heard him
play would be transformed to thoughts of love and kindness.

When this master singer and musician returned from helping Jason and the Argonauts[1] on their quest for the Golden
Fleece,[2] he wooed and wed a beautiful maiden named Eurydice,
whom he loved so deeply that he could scarcely bear to have

30   her out of his sight. And all could see that Eurydice was in love
with him, too, as she would sit in the sunshine listening to
Orpheus's beautiful music, while the beasts came round to hear
the soothing sounds, and the trees bowed down their heads to
hear him play.

These two dwelt in perfect sweetness and bliss until, as the
Fates[3] sometimes decree, the heights of their happiness became
matched by the depths of their woe. For one day, as Eurydice
walked in the woods alone, she happened to step on a serpent
that had been hidden by the long grass; its fangs pierced her

40   dainty foot, and its venom oozed into her body and mixed with
her blood. She cried out to Orpheus, though he was far away at
the time and so did not know that his beloved bride was dying.
She slowly laid her head down on the soft grass and, before long,
she died.

When this tragic news reached Orpheus, his grief was terrible to see. He took up his golden lyre but did not play a note,
nor did he open his lips to sing. The animals that used to listen
to him wondered why Orpheus sat all alone on the green bank
where Eurydice used to sit with him, and why it was that he

---

1. **Jason and the Argonauts:** Jason was the leader of quest for the
   Golden Fleece. He and his men, the Argonauts, traveled on a ship
   called the *Argo*.
2. **Golden Fleece:** pelt of a winged ram whose wool was made of gold.
3. **Fates:** three sisters who control a person's birth, lifespan, and death
   symbolically by spinning, measuring, and then cutting thread.

IDENTIFY

Underline the supernatural
powers Orpheus displays in
lines 20–25.

HISTORICAL
CONTEXT

Pause at line 37. What does
this sentence show you
about the way the ancient
Greeks viewed destiny?

ARCHETYPE

Pause at line 54. What
archetype found in most
hero myths appears here?

Re-read lines 55–59, and then look back at "The Spirit Wife." What forms the border between the land of the living and the netherworld in that Zuni myth? How is the border between those two lands similar in this Greek myth?

____

____

____

____

Who helps Orpheus cross the river? In "The Spirit Wife," who helps the young man cross the chasm? What do these details tell you about the heroes of each story?

____

____

____

____

shrouded (shroud'id) *v.* used as *adj.:* covered as if with a shroud, a cloth in which a body is wrapped for burial.

gnashing (nash'iŋ) *v.* used as *adj.:* grinding together.

insolence (in'sə·ləns) *n.:* bold disrespect.

---

50   never made any more beautiful music. Day after day he sat there, and his cheeks were often wet with tears. Finally, he could bear his loneliness no longer, and he decided to go to the Lower World, the land of the dead, to find his bride and to bring her back.

For many long days, with his lyre in hand, Orpheus persisted on his gloomy journey, down and down from the mouth of a distant cave into the blackness of the earth. At last he came to the black waters of the river Styx, which marks the border of the land of the dead. But he could not cross it alone, and the ferry-

60   man, Charon, refused to take him in his boat. Orpheus was, after all, still alive, and only the souls of the dead were allowed beyond the river's edge. But Orpheus began to strum his lyre and to sing so sweetly that the boatman melted with tears and agreed not only to take him across, but to do so without the payment of a coin, which he usually charged for his efforts.

After some travel along shadowy paths **shrouded** in mist, Orpheus arrived at an imposing iron gateway that was guarded by a monstrous dog like no dog ever seen on earth, for this beast had three large heads, each with fiery eyes and **gnashing** teeth.

70   The dog—who was called Cerberus—roared terribly as Orpheus approached, and rose up ready to pounce on the unfortunate mortal and tear him to pieces. But again, Orpheus began to pluck the strings of his lyre, and the melodious sounds that came forth instantly soothed the beast, and Cerberus became as gentle as a house pet. Even the iron gate sprang open to allow Orpheus to continue on his journey.

Finally Orpheus arrived at the gloomy palace of Hades, lord of the Underworld, king of the land of the dead (a land that, itself, is often called Hades). He made his way to the great

80   hall, and there, on the throne, were King Hades and his youthful queen, Persephone. Hades bellowed out in a terrible voice, "Who are you, and how dare you to come here? Don't you know that only the dead are permitted here? For your **insolence** I will chain you in a dungeon here until you are one of us!"

The Granger Collection, New York

Orpheus said nothing, but once more put his fingers to the lyre and began to sing more sweetly and gently than ever. And as he sang, the face of the king began to look almost glad, and his anger passed so thoroughly that, when the song ended, Hades proclaimed: "Your music has made me feel happy—a feeling I have never had before. Ask of me what you will and I shall grant your wish."

"O King," replied Orpheus, "give me back my dear Eurydice, and let her go from this gloomy place to live with me on the bright earth again." King Hades thought awhile and said, "I will give you what you ask, but under one condition: When you leave this land for earth, you will lead and your wife will follow; but you must never look back at her until she has reached the surface, else she will be lost to you forever, and not even your sweetest songs will allow you to see her again."

Notes ______________

____

____

____

____

____

____

CONNECT

Note the similarity between the warning the owl-man gives to the young man in "The Spirit Wife" and the warning Hades gives to Orpheus.

____

____

____

____

What is the result of Orpheus's disobeying Hades?

____

____

____

____

____

____

On the lines below, write a summary of the last paragraph.

____

____

____

____

____

____

100 So Orpheus promised the king that he would go up to earth without stopping to look behind and see whether Eurydice was coming after him. And this he did, passing back through the great iron gateway (for Cerberus knew that the king had permitted Orpheus to leave), across the river Styx, and then climbing higher and higher through the gloomy passages until he came near the land of the living, and he saw just a little streak of light above him, made by the glorious sun. He had almost reached the surface when a sudden fear struck him that Eurydice might have stumbled or fallen victim to one of the dangers that

110 lay along the way. Before he could think of what he was doing, he turned his head quickly to see whether she was still following. But alas! he caught only a glimpse of her, as, with her arms stretched toward him and her lips speaking a last farewell, Eurydice was seized by hundreds of unseen hands that reached out from the dreary walls and snatched her back down into the Land of the Shades, to dwell in the Underworld forever.

Orpheus sat down at the mouth of the cave, weeping over his loss, mourning his beloved Eurydice. There he stayed day after day, without eating or sleeping, and his cheeks became

120 paler and his body weaker, till at last he knew that he must be dying. And Orpheus was not sorry, for although he loved the bright earth, with all its flowers and grass and sunny streams, he knew that he could not be with Eurydice again until he had left it. So at last he laid his head upon the earth, and fell asleep and died.

Though all of nature mourned and grieved over the death of this sweet singer, Orpheus, himself, was of happy heart as his soul made its way toward the land of the dead. This time Charon gladly ferried him across the Styx, and the ferocious

130 Cerberus wagged his tail in a friendly greeting. Soon he saw Eurydice, waiting to welcome him, and he rushed forward to meet his dear wife and put his arms about her, happy in the thought that they would never again be parted.

MEET THE WRITER

William F. Russell (1945–   ) is an educator, writer, and editor whose research and writing focuses on involving parents in their children's education. His books include *The Parents' Handbook of Grammar and Usage, Classic Myths to Read Aloud, Classics to Read Aloud to Your Children,* and the popular book *Family Learning,* which he compiled from the syndicated education column that he wrote for several years. Dr. Russell lives in Carmichael, California, and lectures widely on language and education.

Notes

Orpheus and Eurydice

SKILLS FOCUS

Literary Skills
Analyze characteristics of myth, including heroes and their external conflicts.

Hero Chart What makes someone a hero? Listed in the left-hand column of the chart below are some heroic traits. Give examples from "Orpheus and Eurydice" to show whether or not Orpheus displays these traits. At the bottom of the chart, list Orpheus's weaknesses.

Key Traits of a Hero	Details from "Orpheus and Eurydice"
Intelligence and resourcefulness	
Bravery	
Loyalty	
Weaknesses	

Skills Review

Orpheus and Eurydice

VOCABULARY AND COMPREHENSION

Word Box

shrouded

gnashing

insolence

A. Vocabulary in Context Complete the paragraph below by filling in each blank with a word from the Word Box. Then, circle the English words that come from Greek myths. (Can you find six?)

Orpheus's odyssey began along gloomy paths, __________________ in stygian shadows. His herculean journey first brought him to the river of the dead. After persuading the ferryman to take him across, he was confronted with three jaws full of sharp, __________________ teeth. Only Orpheus's sweet, lyrical music stopped Cerberus from tearing him apart. He passed the monster dog and entered the Underworld palace, where King Hades raged like a volcano at the young husband's __________________. Quickly, however, the ruler's mercurial temper was charmed by the lyre of Orpheus.

B. Reading Comprehension

1. Why does Orpheus make his journey?

   ____

   ____

2. What obstacles must Orpheus overcome in order to find Eurydice?

   ____

   ____

3. What warning does King Hades give to Orpheus?

   ____

   ____

4. What is the result of Orpheus's disobedience to King Hades?

   ____

   ____

SKILLS FOCUS

Vocabulary Skills
Identify words from Greek myths.

Drama

Hank Walker/Getty Images

Academic Vocabulary for Collection 11

These are the terms you should know
as you read and analyze this collection.

Play A story acted out, live and usually on a stage, using dialogue and
action.

Tragedy A play that presents serious and important events and ends
unhappily for the main character.

Comedy A play that ends happily, in which the main character gets what
he or she wants.

Modern Drama A play that deals with a serious subject, usually addressing
the concerns of modern, ordinary people, as opposed to gods or
royalty, and often containing elements of both comedy and tragedy.

● ● ●

Dialogue Conversations between characters in a play.

Monologue A long speech made by one character to one or more characters
onstage or to the audience.

Soliloquy A speech made by a character who is alone onstage, speaking to
himself or herself or to the audience.

● ● ●

Stage Directions Instructions telling actors how to move onstage and how
to speak their lines.

Props The portable items (properties) that actors carry or handle onstage.

Before You Read

from **Now Let Me Fly** by Marcia Cebulska

The excerpt of the play you will read in this collection is set in the years leading up to the tumultuous civil rights era, during which people fought legal discrimination against African Americans. Drama finds its home in the great tragedies and challenges of any era, whether they concern a love affair (such as Romeo and Juliet's) or a politician's death (such as Julius Caesar's) or the heroic struggles of a group of high school students to stand up for what is right.

LITERARY FOCUS: DRAMA

Drama is a form of literature that is acted out live and onstage. A drama has many of the elements of written narratives—**characters, settings, conflict,** and a **climax.** However, it is a story that is meant to be performed by actors in front of an audience. A **play** is a script that consists of the characters' words and descriptions of their actions.

Key elements of plays include **dialogue** (conversation between characters), **monologues** (long speeches delivered by a character alone onstage), **stage directions** (notes telling actors when to enter and exit and how to speak their lines), **sets** (scenery and other items used onstage that establish the place and time of the action), **costumes,** and **props.**

Drama is one of the oldest forms of storytelling, with roots in ancient Greek religious festivals. There are as many types of plays as there are types of stories—a play can be a comedy, a tragedy, a mystery, or a fantasy. Or it can be a historical play, a drama based on important events in history, like the play excerpt you are about to read.

READING SKILLS: PARAPHRASING

When you paraphrase a text, you restate it using your own words. Note that a paraphrase differs from a summary. A paraphrase is a detail-by-detail retelling; a summary is a condensed form of the original text made up of only the main details. Here is a checklist for paraphrasing:

- Have you replaced difficult words with simpler words?
- Have you restated figures of speech (similes and metaphors) in your own words? Have you clarified what is being compared with what?
- Have you restructured sentences to make them clearer? For example, you might paraphrase the sentence "Bury me not on the lone prairie" as "Don't bury me on the lonely prairie."
- Does your paraphrase include all the details in the original text?

SKILLS FOCUS

Literary Skills
Understand characteristics of drama.

Reading Skills
Paraphrase a text.

Vocabulary Skills
Understand idioms.

VOCABULARY DEVELOPMENT

PREVIEW SELECTION VOCABULARY

The following words appear in *Now Let Me Fly.* Look them over before you begin the play.

prerogative (prē·räg′ə·tiv) *n.:* right or privilege.

*The students have researched their legal rights and know it is their **prerogative** to confront the school board with their demands.*

grievance (grēv′əns) *n.:* situation that gives cause for complaint.

*The students decide that they can no longer tolerate the inferior conditions in their school, and they bring their **grievance** to the school board.*

alleviated (ə·lē′vē·āt′id) *v.:* relieved; lessened.

*The students believe that their hardships will be **alleviated** if the school board is made to hear their complaints.*

consorting (kən·sôrt′iŋ) *v.* used as *adj.:* associating.

*Segregation in schools meant that white students and black students were not often seen **consorting**.*

FIGURATIVE LANGUAGE: IDIOM

Modern dramatists use dialect—informal speech that sounds like ordinary conversation—to create a realistic and believable experience. *Now Let Me Fly* makes use of idioms. An **idiom** is an expression that is particular to a language or dialect and whose meaning differs from the literal meaning of the words. "It's raining cats and dogs" is an idiom of American English. Sometimes idioms are shortened expressions of ideas. For example, the idiom "sleep tight" comes from a time when mattresses were supported by rope slings that would loosen, causing uncomfortable sagging. Tightening the ropes would give a person a better night's sleep. Most idioms can be understood through context.

The playwright Marcia Cebulska uses idioms to create subtle but noticeable shifts in tone. As you read *Now Let Me Fly,* note where idioms are used and by whom.

Barbara Johns: Carrying on the Speaking

Flo Ota De Lange

The 1954 Supreme Court case *Brown* v. *Board of Education* was a landmark ruling that declared racial segregation in public schools to be unconstitutional. In the years leading up to this case, many local battles were fought over the very unequal facilities that often existed under the "separate but equal" policy that held sway in some states. One of the cases that the court reviewed in *Brown* v. *Board of Education* involved an African American high school student named Barbara Johns, who spoke out against the unjust and humiliating conditions under which she and other African American students in her hometown of Farmville studied and learned. In the process, Johns stood up to decades of injustice, with 450 students standing beside her. In the essay and the excerpt of the play that follow, you will read about this remarkable young woman.

[Brown *v.* Board of Education] *remained muffled in white consciousness, and the student origins of the lawsuit were lost as well on nearly all blacks outside Prince Edward County. The idea that non-adults of any race might play a leading role in political events had simply failed to register on anyone . . .*

—*Taylor Branch*

Pause at line 7. Underline the words and phrases the writer uses to describe Barbara Johns. What qualities seem unusual or noteworthy to you?

____

____

____

____

Barbara Johns says that her life began to change when, in 1948, she entered Robert R. Moton High School in Farmville, Prince Edward County, Virginia. Barbara was described by her classmates as an intelligent and quiet girl while in her freshman and sophomore years, but underneath that quietness, a social consciousness was maturing. In her junior year that social consciousness would lead her to take and hold center stage. Under her leadership the student body of Moton High would take the kind of concerted action that had never before occurred in Farmville, action that
10   triggered gawking and talking but little interference, so puzzled were the onlookers by what they were witnessing.

Farmville is a tobacco and lumber town. In 1950, its population was 4,375. The history of African Americans in Prince Edward County goes as far back as that of whites. The difference is that out of every eighteen blacks, one was free and seventeen were enslaved until the Civil War and emancipation. And though the ending of enslavement was accomplished through law, freedom from the prejudice in the minds and hearts of those who supported slavery could not be accomplished by law.
20 This made achieving equality as arduous a task as enduring slavery itself. It also raised the question of whether slavery was truly a practice of the past when its spirit persisted.

For example, in Prince Edward County, segregation was the law at drugstore soda counters and in restaurants. It would have been the law in the county's one movie theater, except for the fact that African Americans were not permitted entrance at all.

Like many small communities in the South at that time, Farmville was a town torn between its past and its present. The Prince Edward Hotel on Main Street was once host to Generals
30 Grant and Lee, as each traveled separately to the historic meeting at Appomattox Courthouse[1] a few miles down the road. There were those in the county for whom the Civil War was still as hauntingly vivid as was World War II.

When Barbara Johns's father came back to Prince Edward County in 1948 after serving in the army in World War II, he took over her uncle Vernon Johns's[2] general store. In the summers of her thirteenth and fourteenth years, Barbara worked in what was then her father's store. She remembers feeling proud to provide this service to whites. One of her customers was a white girl with whom Barbara often talked and whom Barbara thought
40 was beautiful. Later, when that same girl got a job in Farmville's

---

1. **historic meeting at Appomattox Courthouse:** meeting in which Robert E. Lee officially surrendered to Ulysses S. Grant to end the Civil War.
2. **Vernon Johns's:** Vernon Johns (1892–1965) was a civil rights pioneer and the minister of a church that would later become Martin Luther King, Jr.'s congregation.

Rephrase in your own words what the writer is saying in lines 16–19.

Re-read lines 23–33. Underline the details of historical **setting** provided by the writer of this essay. What do these details tell you about the time and place in which Barbara John lived?

Pause at line 43. What **external conflicts** does young Barbara face as a result of the racism in her society? What **internal conflicts** does she face?

____

____

____

____

____

____

____

Pause at line 54. How does Mrs. Croner respond to the racism she faces in her youth? Underline the lines that tell you.

Explain what the writer means by "It was asking for the impossible" (line 63).

____

____

____

____

____

____

five-and-dime,[3] and Barbara went into that store one day, the girl turned away and refused to acknowledge her.

Barbara's maternal grandmother, Mrs. Croner, knew about such experiences firsthand. When she herself was coming of age, she read in her every spare moment. She took what she learned from her reading and went out among the trees to do what she called her "speaking." There she could say aloud what was too dangerous for her to voice elsewhere. Speaking out, she pretended the trees were listening.

Mrs. Croner gave voice to the hardships of her people. Later, when she had children of her own, she hoped one of them would pick up on the speaking. When this didn't happen, she set her hope aside.

For years, African American parents in Prince Edward County had been petitioning for a high school for their children. Until 1939, there was no building in Prince Edward County dedicated to black secondary education. One of the arguments used to justify this lapse was that the tax contributions from African Americans were too low. However, there was no way for African Americans to increase their income, and therefore their tax contributions, without improving their education. It was asking for the impossible.

In 1939, the first African American high school in Prince Edward County opened its doors. It was the Robert R. Moton High School, and it opened with 167 students, 13 shy of its maximum capacity. Thus, by the time Barbara Johns entered Moton High, the issue of overcrowding was not a new one.

In an attempt to relieve overcrowding at Moton, three additional classroom units were built on the site in 1948. These classrooms were what the students referred to as the "tar-paper shacks." When it rained, their roofs leaked, and the students had to protect their work with opened umbrellas, lest the ink on their papers run. In cold weather each was heated by a wood-burning potbellied stove. This meant that those seated nearest

---

3. **five-and-dime** n.: store that sells a large selection of inexpensive merchandise, with many items priced at five and ten cents.

the stove wore light garments, and those seated farthest away
kept wrapped up in their overcoats.

In a sense, the problem of public school finding was similar
to the problem of the potbellied stove. To some, it was a source
of privilege, while to others, it was a source of want.

When Barbara Johns entered Moton High in 1948, an educational policy known as "separate but equal" still held sway in many
Southern states. In places like rural Prince Edward County, the
separate-but-equal policy was an added burden for the black population, many of whom were poor. It cost more to build a dual
school system than it would have to build one that accommodated
all. And when funds were squeezed, there was no such thing as separate and equal—certain projects slid to the bottom of the budget.

For example, Farmville High School, the white high school
across the way from Moton, likely had its own problems, but
whatever they were, they weren't the result of make-dos and
hand-me-downs. No one at Moton had observed anyone at
Farmville attending class in a dilapidated school bus, and in-
sofar as Moton's students knew, Farmville's auditorium was an
auditorium and not a combination of lunch area, gym, and
multiple-classroom space.

So there were good reasons for Moton's students to regard
their school as second-rate compared with the one across the
way, just as there were reasons for Farmville's students to regard
their school as superior. And given this scenario, it also wasn't
hard for Moton's students to imagine the dim view Farmville's
students took of both them and their school, as though they were
somehow responsible for the conditions under which they labored.

At any rate, it was a situation that got Barbara Johns's ire up.
Active in student affairs since entering Moton High, Barbara often
talked with her peers about conditions at their school. She knew
that their talking led nowhere because they couldn't conceive of
what to do. They were aware that their parents, the PTA,[4] and
various committees had all made ongoing attempts to solve the

---

4. **PTA:** Parent-Teacher Association.

Pause at line 123. What are Barbara's concerns? What is her main frustration?

110 overcrowding at Moton High, and all had been stymied in their attempts. If the adults couldn't find a solution, what could the students do?

Because she was elected to student council in her junior year, Barbara traveled a fair amount. She had the chance to see better-equipped high schools for African Americans in other Virginia counties, and what she saw stayed with her.

M. Boyd Jones, the principal of Moton High, was a man respected by his students. He taught fair play. He didn't pretend that theirs was the best of all possible worlds. Barbara wanted to
120 talk with him about conditions at her school and about what she had seen in her travels, but she found this too difficult to do. Instead, she spoke to her favorite teacher, Miss Davenport, who happened to be engaged to Principal Jones.

Miss Davenport listened to Barbara and then suggested Barbara do something about her concerns. Barbara remembers giving Miss Davenport a smile by way of an answer and then going about her duties of the day. But Miss Davenport's sug-

gestion stuck in her mind, and from it arose an idea that just
could be turned into a plan of action.

130   As a first step, in the fall of 1950, Barbara met with two other
student leaders, John Stokes and his sister Carrie Stokes. They met
after school behind the school's bleachers. When Barbara told
them about her idea, John and Carrie endorsed it enthusiasti-
cally, eager to act for change instead of just talking about the
issue. Barbara scheduled their next meeting for the coming winter and asked each of them to bring one other student leader who
could be trusted to keep matters confidential. Later, people would
ask Barbara why she hadn't consulted any adults before embark-
ing on her plan. Barbara would answer that she knew the adults
140 had no alternatives that didn't require her to wait, and waiting
was something everyone had already tried.

     At the winter meeting the student leaders finished develop-
ing Barbara's idea into a detailed plan of action. Building on
consensus, Barbara then asked each of them to bring one or two
other student leaders to a spring meeting. There were placards
to be made, assembly slips to be forged, and a scheme to be
devised for getting Principal Jones off campus so that he
wouldn't be blamed for what would take place.

     The morning of April 23, 1951, dawned much like any other
150 school day, but before it was over, an event would take place with
far-reaching repercussions. What started as the Moton High
student leaders' hope for school improvements at worst and a
new school at best was turned by others into a full-scale battle
to end segregation in public schools. After the Supreme Court
ruling ended public school segregation in 1954, the State of
Virginia responded by turning its separate-but-equal educational
policy into one of "massive resistance" to this ruling. Students
who would have attended Moton High from 1959 to 1964 saw
the shutting down of the one high school available to them in
160 Prince Edward County. It was as if the hands on the clock had
been pushed back, trapping them in a pre-1939 time warp.

Pause at line 141. What plan
of action do you think Barbara is forming? What might
its goals be? its methods for
achieving these goals?

Re-read lines 149–161. What
are the repercussions of the
actions taken by Barbara and
the other students?

Notes

IDENTIFY

Pause at line 190. What actions does Barbara ask the students to take?

But on the morning of April 23, 1951, the scent of spring was in the air as some ten student leaders gathered onstage behind closed curtains in Moton's auditorium. The placards were on hand, the forged assembly slips had been delivered, the student body had gathered, and when the curtains parted a few minutes after eleven, Principal Jones was nowhere in sight.

170   Instead, at center stage, speaking into the microphone, was Barbara Johns, who announced to those assembled that the meeting was for students only. She asked the teachers who were present to excuse themselves. In the subsequent confusion most teachers left voluntarily, but one had to be booed out of the room and another had to be escorted. When order was restored, Barbara began what John Stokes would call her soliloquy. She outlined for those assembled the hopes of those onstage—that no one present would continue to accept conditions as they were at Moton High. She asked the students to stay out of school for as long as necessary to bring about the needed changes. She

180   said that none of them would get into trouble as long as they all acted together; the Farmville jail wasn't large enough to house all of them.

   Showing the students the placards, Barbara explained that the students could march with them on the school grounds. The students were also given the option of simply sitting inside their classrooms without opening their books. Under no circumstances were they to leave school property during school hours and risk getting in trouble with the police. If anyone asked them why they weren't in class, they were to say that they weren't in school

190   because of the unequal facilities.

   By the time Barbara completed her speech, she had the assembled students solidly behind her. She had awakened in them the sense that enough was enough. The students began by passing up their lunch hour. Barbara took this as an encouraging sign, a symbol of their determination. After she left school that day, Barbara went to her grandmother Croner's house and told her, "Grandmother, I walked out of school this morning and carried 450 students with me."

Barbara's announcement took her grandmother's breath away. Later, she would talk about "the surprise and pride and even chagrin in the adult ranks at the actions of the children," but in that moment of first hearing Barbara's words, what Mrs. Croner most immediately registered was that her grandchild had picked up on the speaking. Only Barbara wasn't out there pretending the trees were listening. Barbara was in there talking into a microphone. And was she good? The people in the audience had nodded their heads while allowing Barbara to carry them with her.

Pause at line 208. In what ways has Barbara continued her grandmother's "speaking"?

from

Now Let Me Fly

The Struggle Toward *Brown* v. *Board*

Marcia Cebulska

SCENE 7

SETTING: *This scene takes place at a school auditorium and then at the offices of the school board.*

Houston. Farmville, Virginia. The R. R. Moton High School auditorium. It is the spring of 1951 and a young woman, Barbara Johns, age 16, is about to speak. Listen to the people, Mr. Marshall.

[HOUSTON *escorts* BARBARA JOHNS *forward to address a school assembly.*]

Barbara. Every morning I get on a bus thrown away by the white high school on the hill. I sit on a torn seat and look out a broken window. And when my bus passes the shiny new bus that the white high schoolers have, I hide my face because I'm embarrassed in my raggedy bus. And when we get to R. R.

10 Moton High, the bus driver gets off with us, because he's also our history teacher.

He comes in the classroom and fires up the stove and I sit in my winter coat waiting for the room to get warm. You know the rooms, the ones in the "addition" as they call it. We call them "the tar paper shacks" because that's what they are, am I right?

I'm embarrassed that I go to school in tar paper shacks and when it rains I have to open an umbrella so the leaks from the roof won't make the ink run on my paper. And later

20 in the day I have a hygiene class out in that broken-down bus and a biology class in a corner of the auditorium with one

From "Now Let Me Fly" by Marcia Cebulska from *A Nation Acts,* 2005. Copyright © 2005 by **Marcia Cebulska**. Reproduced by permission of the author.

Carl Iwasaki/Getty Images

microscope for the whole school. I'm embarrassed that our water fountains are broken and our wash basins are broken and it seems our whole school is broken and crowded and poor. And I'm embarrassed. But my embarrassment is nothing compared to my hunger. I'm not talking about my hunger for food. No, I'm hungry for those shiny books they have up at Farmville High. I want the page of the Constitution that is torn out of my social studies book. I want a chance at that *Romeo and Juliet* I've heard about but they tell me I'm not fit to read. Our teachers say we can fly just as high as anyone else. That's what I want to do. Fly just as high. I said, fly. You know, I've been sitting in my embarrassment and my hunger for so long that I forgot about standing up. So, today, I'm going to ask you to stand with me.

    Before we fly, before we fly just as high as anyone else, we gotta walk just as proud as anyone else. And that's what we're going to do! We're gonna walk out of this school and over to the courthouse. Do you hear me? We're gonna walk with our heads high and go talk to the school board. Are you with me?

Pause at line 45. What are the student strikers seeking? Explain.

____
____
____
____
____
____
____
____
____
____
____
____

In what way does this picture help you picture the **setting,** or time and place, of this play?

____
____
____
____
____
____
____
____
____
____

We're gonna walk out in a strike, yes, I said strike, and we won't come back until we get a real school with a gymnasium and library and whole books. And we will get them. And it'll be grand. Are you with me? Are we gonna walk? Are we gonna fly? [BARBARA *starts walking and singing.*]

[*Music: "This Little Light of Mine." The chorus of actors joins in.*]

This little light of mine I'm gonna let it shine
This little light of mine I'm gonna let it shine
This little light of mine I'm gonna let it shine
Let it shine, let it shine, let it shine

[BARBARA, *as if leading a large group, walks across the stage.* MRS. GATES *blocks her way.*]

Public Domain, National Archives and Records Administration

Barbara. As citizens of Prince Edward County, we would like to exercise our **prerogative** to address the school board.

Mrs. Gates. "Prerogative" is a mighty big word, little girl.

Barbara. My name is . . .

Mrs. Gates. I know who you are. They know who you are. You would be wise to turn tail and head home. I'm sure your grandmother would rather you were in school, not stirring up any trouble.

Barbara. We have a document to deliver . . .

Mrs. Gates. I wouldn't leave anything in writing if I were you.

Barbara. To the board of education, ma'am.

Mrs. Gates. I am Mrs. Gates, secretary to the judge. I must tell you it would be considerable unwise to leave anything in writing, Barbara Rose.

Barbara. There are four hundred students, ma'am. We are citizens . . .

Mrs. Gates. You are children in over your heads.

Barbara. We are citizens with a just **grievance** to voice. We are protected by the Constitution and . . .

Mrs. Gates [*to students*]. Hold your tongues, turn around in an orderly fashion and return to your classrooms.

Barbara. No, ma'am.

Mrs. Gates. Pardon me?

Barbara. With all due respect, no, ma'am. We are certain that members of the school board are not aware of the conditions of our school and if only they knew, our grievance would be **alleviated.** We are citizens . . .

Mrs. Gates. You are children. You have no idea what you are up against. Three hundred years of tradition. I am telling you this for your own good. You walk in there and you are throwing oil on a fire. And trust me, you will be the ones to get burned.

Barbara. We'll take that chance, ma'am. We figure the Farmville jail is too small to hold us all . . .

Mrs. Gates. Jail would be the least of your problems, girl. You walk in there and a plan of action will be set in motion . . .

---

prerogative (prē·räg′ə·tiv) *n.:* right or privilege.

Re-read lines 50–68. Notice each character's choice of words, phrasing, and speech mannerisms. From this dialogue between Mrs. Gates and Barbara, what can you **infer** about each character?

Rephrase what Mrs. Gates is saying to Barbara and the other students in lines 77–80.

grievance (grēv′əns) *n.:* situation that gives cause for complaint.

alleviated (ə·lē′vē·āt′id) *v.:* relieved; lessened.

---

from Now Let Me Fly   **285**

Barbara. Pardon me, ma'am, I don't see how there can be an action. Our assembly was a total secret. We planned it down to a gnat's eyebrow.

Mrs. Gates. Even secrets have a way of getting out. You don't want to be starting a second Civil War now, do you?

90 **Barbara.** I'm not afraid. I am standing up for my rights and I am not afraid.

Mrs. Gates. You are shaking in your Mary Janes° and I can see it. Turn around, child . . .

Barbara. As a citizen of Prince Edward County . . .

Mrs. Gates. You walk in there, Barbara Rose, and they will close your school. Now isn't it better to have some schooling than none?

Barbara. They can't do that, ma'am.

Mrs. Gates. They *will* do it. They have been talking about it for

100 months.

Barbara. I cannot believe that, ma'am. Public education is a right . . .

Mrs. Gates. Barbara Rose, you have a responsibility to the children who've followed you. They followed *you.* Are you going to lead them into disaster? They will close your school.

Barbara. No one would do that. You stop me from being educated, you stop me from being an informed citizen.

Mrs. Gates. This is reality, Barbara Rose, not a high school debate. These people don't want you **consorting** with white

110 children or taking their jobs. Go home or you'll get burned.

Barbara. We, as citizens of Prince Edward County, would like to exercise our prerogative to address the school board . . .

Voice. Let them in, Margaret . . .

[MRS. GATES *steps aside.* BARBARA *walks.*]

[HOUSTON *gives a "thumbs up" sign.*]

[*End of Scene 7.*]

° **Mary Janes:** flat shoes with a rounded toe and ankle strap.

MEET THE WRITER

Before she became a writer, **Marcia Cebulska** was a sociologist who studied race relations. Since turning to writing, she has had two books published and a screenplay produced. She has also written several successful plays, including *Now Let Me Fly*. *Now Let Me Fly* was commissioned for the fiftieth anniversary of the Supreme Court decision *Brown* v. *Board of Education of Topeka*. Cebulska wrote it while she was playwright-in-residence at the William Inge Center for the Arts in Independence, Kansas. In 2004, the play was performed at forty-eight venues across the country, including the National Constitution Center and the National Center for the Study of Civil Rights.

Cebulska has lived in cities all over the world, including Copenhagen, Denmark; Lima, Peru; Athens, Greece; Bloomington, Indiana; Chicago; Miami; and Pasadena, California. She now lives in Topeka, Kansas.

Notes

from Now Let Me Fly

SKILLS FOCUS

Literary Skills
Analyze elements of drama.

Drama Chart   In drama many elements, including **props, scene design,** and **costumes,** play a part in creating a scene's effect. Fill in the chart below. Look through the play excerpt carefully, and fill in details for each category. If details for any category are missing, think about how you would stage this play if you were directing it, and use your imagination to complete the chart. You may include sketches if you like.

Props (items used by the play's characters)

Set Design (room furnishings)

Costumes

Skills Review

from Now Let Me Fly

VOCABULARY AND COMPREHENSION

A. Figurative Language: Idioms   Match each idiom in italics with its meaning.
Write the letter of the correct answer on the line provided.

_____ 1. "You would be wise *to turn tail and head home.*"

_____ 2. "*Hold your tongues,* . . . and return to your classrooms."

_____ 3. "You are *throwing oil on a fire.*"

_____ 4. "*We planned it down to a gnat's eyebrow.*"

_____ 5. "You are *shaking in your Mary Janes* and I can see it."

a. to the smallest detail

b. making a bad situation worse

c. frightened

d. reverse yourself

e. be quiet

B. Reading Comprehension   Answer each question below.

1. At which high school is this play set? Where is the school located?

____

____

2. In which time period is the play set?

____

____

3. Which character delivers the dramatic monologue? What leads her to do so?

____

____

4. What conditions are the students seeking to change?

____

____

**Vocabulary
Skills**
Identify idioms.

Part Two

Reading Informational Texts

Informational Articles

Academic Vocabulary

These are the terms you should know
as you read and analyze these selections.

———————

Source A person, book, or document that provides information on a topic.

Elaboration The addition of details to support the ideas already presented in a work.

Synthesis The merging of information gathered from more than one source.

• • •

Argument A series of statements designed to persuade the reader to accept a claim, or opinion.

Claim An opinion on a topic or issue, which is often stated as a generalization, or broad statement that covers many situations.

Evidence Material presented as proof of a claim or an idea. Evidence includes facts, statistics, examples, anecdotes (brief stories about real people), and quotations.

Credibility The believability of an argument or statement.

Interview with Mae by Mae Jemison

In this interview, you will meet Mae Jemison, the first African American woman to travel to outer space. After you read about Jemison's journey, think of questions you'd like to have answered.

INFORMATIONAL FOCUS: HOW TO GENERATE RESEARCH QUESTIONS

Research involves finding answers to questions. To develop good questions for research based on informational materials:

- Start by filling out a KWL chart, like the one below.
- Ask *5W-How?* questions rather than simple yes-or-no questions. Who was involved? What happened? When and where did it happen? Why and how did it happen?
- Ask specific questions that can be answered within the scope of your research. You can answer the question "What courses should I take if I want to be an astronaut?" It would be more difficult to answer the question "What are the personal characteristics of most astronauts?"

READING SKILLS: MAKE A KWL CHART

Prepare to read this selection by reading the background feature on page 294. Then, fill out the first two columns of the KWL chart. In the first column, list what you know about Mae Jemison. In the second column, list some questions about Mae Jemison that you would like to have answered. After you read the article, fill out the last column. Some items in the first two columns have been filled in for you.

Mae Jemison

What I Already KNOW	What I WANT to Find Out	What I LEARNED
Mae Jemison was aboard the space shuttle *Endeavor*.	What challenges did Jemison confront on her way to becoming an astronaut?	

Reading Skills
Generate research questions. Make a KWL chart.

Vocabulary Skills
Understand synonyms and connotations.

VOCABULARY DEVELOPMENT

PREVIEW SELECTION VOCABULARY

Preview the following words from the story before you begin reading:

misconceptions (mis′kən·sep′shənz) *n.:* wrong or untrue ideas that many people believe.

*Jemison points out that the public holds onto many **misconceptions** about what astronauts do.*

neutral (nōō′trəl) *adj.:* without strong characteristics; indefinite.

*If you have **neutral** feelings about space travel, reading this interview may make you feel differently.*

buoyant (boi′ənt) *adj.:* able to rise.

When the astronauts are in space, they appear to be buoyant as they move around the spaceship.

doctorate (däk′tər·it) *n.:* highest level of university degree.

*Most people who become astronauts first receive a **doctorate** from a well-known school.*

SYNONYMS AND CONNOTATIONS

The English language is rich in **synonyms**—words that have the same or nearly the same meaning. When you choose a word or examine why someone else has chosen a word, you should think about the word's precise meaning and also about the word's **connotations,** or emotional overtones. If you are *curious* about space travel, for example, you may or may not enjoy reading this interview. However, if you are *interested* in space travel, then it's more likely that you will like the interview. As you read the selection, keep the connotations of the words you read in mind.

Interview with Mae

(an excerpt from a live online interview conducted on March 15, 2001)

Mae Jemison

GENERATE QUESTIONS

Pause at line 8. What questions do you have about what you've read so far? Think of at least two.

____

____

____

____

____

VOCABULARY

misconceptions (mis′kən·sep′shənz) *n.:* wrong or untrue ideas that many people believe.

neutral (noo′trəl) *adj.:* without strong characteristics; indefinite.

buoyant (boi′ənt) *adj.:* able to rise.

MODERATOR: What was it like being up in space? Was it scary, was it fun, or was it magical?

MAE JEMISON: Being in space has many qualities to it. I was not afraid, I was very excited and happy. The biggest thing is you can look out the window and you can see Earth, and you can see the sun, and you can see the stars, and they are very clear. So that's magical. On the other hand, you can also float around—it's a lot of fun. It feels very different from being on Earth.

Q. What antigravity training did you have to go through?

10 **A.** There's no such thing as antigravity training. That's one of those **misconceptions** that people have. Gravity is everywhere—it's just that we're *weightless* when we're flying on the shuttle. But gravity is all around you.

We do several things to train for weightlessness. Sometimes we train in a big pool of water called the "**neutral** buoyancy trainer." We put on our extra-vehicular-activity suits (the big white suits), and then we remain neutrally **buoyant**—we don't float and we don't sink. All the astronauts who are up in space are now

Mae Jemison.
Time Life Pictures/Getty Images

trained this way. There is a trainer we use that makes us truly
20   weightless. It's a big airplane called the KC-135. It flies in
parabolas—big **U**-shapes—up and down. It's like a big roller
coaster. At the top of the loop, you have about twenty seconds
of weightlessness.

Q. What did you eat in space?
A. We actually eat food that we carry up—different types. Some
is regular food (people carried up chocolate!). We also take up
things that are freeze-dried—you add water and it plumps when
you cook it. Things like oatmeal, chili, shrimp cocktail, chicken
à la king. We also carry food in foil pouches that's like canned
30   food, and we heat that up. Lots of different food! But there's no
Tang, and there's no space ice cream!

Re-read lines 34–44. Think about the information you have learned so far. Go back and underline details you have questions about.

____

____

____

____

____

doctorate (däk′tər·it) *n.:* highest level of university degree.

Information in articles is also conveyed in **photographs.** Do you have any questions about what you see in the photograph? Write them below.

____

____

____

____

____

____

Q. How long did it take you to become an astronaut? What courses did you study to become one?

A. Well, it depends on how you look at it! In one sense, I was in training from when I was born until I became an astronaut, because as an astronaut, you use all the skills you learn in life. There are certain requirements to be an astronaut: You have to have a Bachelor of Science degree in a science field—for example, chemistry, biology, physics, or engineering. To be a pilot, you also need to have at least one thousand hours of flight time in high-performance aircraft. To be a mission specialist—the ones who do the space walks and experiments—you need at least three years of experiments in your chosen field. Most astronauts have a **doctorate**—either a Ph.D. or an M.D.

Mae Jemison floating in a space lab.
NASA/Roger Ressmeyer/CORBIS

Q. What course should I take in high school if I want to go to space?

A. As we talked about before, in order to be an astronaut right now, you need a Bachelor of Science degree in a science field. So you need to take science classes like biology, chemistry, and physics. You also need to take math. But the most important thing is to be well-rounded—you need to know what's going on in the world around you.

Q. What did it feel like to be the only African American female in your NASA class?

A. In college, very often I was the only African American woman in many of my classes and work environments. There hadn't been many African American women in some of the schools I attended—in engineering, for example. So, at NASA I felt fine because I'm used to working with other people, and I'm comfortable with myself. It would be nice—and I think it *will* be nice—to have more and more people of all kinds involved with space exploration.

Q. What tips can you give young girls about achieving their dreams?

A. First of all, I think people have to stop using the word *dream,* because it implies something you can't do. I like to say, "What do you intend to do?" So, the question becomes, "How will you do what you intend to do?"

First of all, understand that sometimes other people won't have the same vision of you that you have of yourself. Don't accept other people's limitations as being reality. Also, understand that you have as much right as anyone else to be in this world, and to be in any profession you want. That's the most important thing—you don't have to wait for permission.

Q. Do you have a motto?

A. Purpose.

Interview with Mae

SKILLS FOCUS

Reading Skills
Synthesize information from several sources on a single topic.

5W-How? Good research starts with good questions. Imagine you are doing research on Mae Jemison's career. Think about the information you learned from the article. Then, using the investigation guide below, generate research questions to shape your investigation.

A good way to frame questions is to ask *5W-How?* questions. These questions ask *Who? What? When? Where? Why?* and *How?* Remember, you can ask more than one of each type of question. Some sample questions are filled in.

Investigation Guide	
Who?	Who is Mae Jemison?
What?	What has she accomplished?
When?	
Where?	
Why?	
How?	

Interview with Mae

VOCABULARY AND COMPREHENSION

A. Synonyms   Test your skills at identifying the differences in meaning among synonyms. Below, explain the difference between each Vocabulary word and its synonym. Feel free to go back to the interview and read the word in its context.

Word Box

misconceptions

neutral

buoyant

doctorate

1. *misunderstanding* and *misconception*

   ____

   ____

2. *indifferent* and *neutral*

   ____

   ____

3. *floating* and *buoyant*

   ____

   ____

4. *degree* and *doctorate*

   ____

   ____

B. Reading Comprehension   Answer each question below.

1. What feelings did Mae Jemison have about being in space?

   ____

   ____

   ____

2. Why does Jemison prefer not to use the word *dream*?

   ____

   ____

   ____

Vocabulary Skills
Analyze synonyms.

Homecoming by Richard Rodriguez
Ishi Apparently Wasn't the Last Yahi by Gretchen Kell
The Repatriation of Ishi by the Smithsonian National Museum of Natural History

In these three articles you'll read about Ishi, an American Indian often considered the last of the Yahi-Yana people. He died in 1916 in San Francisco.

INFORMATIONAL FOCUS: SYNTHESIZING SOURCES

When you **synthesize,** you pull together information on a topic from a variety of sources. Here are guidelines for synthesizing sources:

- **Find the main ideas** and **supporting evidence,** such as facts, statistics, examples, anecdotes (brief stories about real people), or quotations.
- **Compare and contrast** the information in your sources. If any information is conflicting, do additional research to explain the conflict.
- **Connect to other sources.** To make connections to other sources, gather together main ideas and supporting details in a chart like the one below. Then, use what you've learned to come to a **conclusion** about the topic.

Source 1	Source 2	Source 3
Main ideas	Main ideas	Main ideas
Details	Details	Details
Synthesis, or connecting of ideas		

READING SKILLS: AUTHOR'S PURPOSE

When reading an informational document, be sure to consider the **author's purpose,** the reason the author wrote the piece. For example, was the piece written to entertain readers, to persuade them, or simply to provide them with information? Authors usually do not state their purpose for writing directly. To determine the author's purpose, identify and examine the main ideas of a text and the details that support them.

SKILLS FOCUS

Reading Skills
Synthesize information from several sources on a single topic. Identify an author's purpose.

Vocabulary Skills
Understand word families.

VOCABULARY DEVELOPMENT

PREVIEW SELECTION VOCABULARY

Preview the following words from the story before you begin reading:

diminished (də·min′ishd) *v.* used as *adj.:* made smaller or less.

*It was thought that the **diminished** Yahi tribe further declined to one last member.*

accumulated (ə·kyōōm′yōō lāt′id) *v.:* collected over a period of time.

*The Smithsonian **accumulated** thousands of American Indian remains throughout the twentieth century.*

perpetuate (pər·pech′ōō āt′) *v.:* cause to continue.

*Ishi's family members tried to **perpetuate** their own existence by adapting to a new situation.*

ideology (ī′dē·äl′ə·jē) *n.:* set of doctrines and beliefs held by an individual or group.

*The **ideology** of the Yahi people called for them to marry other Yahi only, not outsiders.*

linguistic (liŋ·gwis′tik) *adj.:* of or relating to the study of language.

*Recordings of Ishi's speech are of **linguistic** importance to scientists.*

enmeshed (en·meshd′) *v.* used as *adj.:* caught, as in the mesh of a net.

*Most Yahi, like other American Indian peoples, had become **enmeshed** in white American culture.*

WORD FAMILIES

Most words are members of **word families,** groups of words having the same root that take slightly different forms and that function as different parts of speech.

To broaden your understanding of word usage, you can list different members of a Vocabulary word's family, using a dictionary for help. For instance, words related to the verb *perpetuate* include the adjective *perpetual*, the adverb *perpetually*, and the noun *perpetuity*. Additionally, when you come across an unfamiliar word, you can use related words that you already know to help you figure out the unknown word's meaning.

Homecoming

Richard Rodriguez

Richard Rodriguez considers an Indian named Ishi.

What is the purpose of the statement that appears below the essay's title?

____

____

____

____

____

Pause at line 8. What is the **main idea** of the first paragraph?

____

____

____

____

____

____

____

____

A few months ago, the ashes of one of America's most famous Indians, a man who never told us his name, but whom generations of schoolchildren knew simply as Ishi, were finally buried, eighty-three years after his death. When white Californians first saw Ishi in 1911, he was naked and nearly starved, crouching behind a slaughterhouse in Oroville. He was late in his forties. More notably, he was the lone survivor of the Yahi Indians, a tribe that had lived in California for thousands of years.

10   As a boy, as a young reader, I came to think of Ishi as a kind of saving remnant from the pages of Theodora Kroeber's wonderful book *Ishi, the Last of His Tribe.* In those same years, I did not recognize the living Indian staring back at me, my reflection in the mirror, but I did recognize that Ishi turned the story of California inside out. It was Ishi's luck to be guided into his new life by two anthropologists,[1] T. T. Waterman and Alfred Kroeber, although neither man would be able to protect him from his immediate notoriety[2] as the last wild Indian of North America. A train, a ferry, a streetcar brought Ishi to the University of California's anthropology museum, then in San Francisco. There 20 he would be on display, for many Californians wanted to see the Stone Age man, the archer, the man who made fire by rubbing wood together. Californians wanted to hear him sing.

---

1. **anthropologists** (an′thrō·päl′ə·jists) *n.:* scientists who study people, their customs, and their beliefs.
2. **notoriety** (nōt′ə·rī′ə·tē) *n.:* state of being famous for unfavorable reasons.

Ishi: the last Yahi?
National Anthropological Archives, Smithsonian Institution

What do you learn in lines 23–28 about the relationship between Ishi and the people who came to see him?

But Ishi was just as interested in the people who came to see him. He recognized regular visitors, distinguished, for example, a Chinese visitor from the white faces. Once, when he got invited to the theater, he spent the entire performance staring at the audience. When he went to the ocean, it was the bathers on the beach who fascinated him more than the surf.

For five years, Ishi lived here in San Francisco. He wore the white man's clothes. He made a small living as a janitor in the museum where he lived, a few blocks away. He used to come down here to the avenues just off Judah to do his shopping. In those years he spoke a kind of pidgin[3] English, and the scientists who studied him spoke enough of his native Yahi to call him Ishi, which means, simply, "man." He tolerated our custom of handshakes, but he always said that the scent of the white man reminded him of deer hide.

It was from Ishi that Californians would hear about those last decades of the nineteenth century, when the already **diminished** Yahi tribe found itself under attack and pressed in by white settlers who'd come West looking for bright dust with their murderous fire sticks. To hear Ishi's account of those cruel years is to have every history of the old West, every John Ford[4] movie, turned inside out: The Indian becomes the perceiver of history. But Ishi's last years, the San Francisco years, are as important for Americans to consider as his tribe's last frenzied decades, running, hiding, and diseased. In San Francisco, the so-called Stone Age man showed himself remarkably capable of adaptation.

Ishi was not, as myth has it, the last Indian in America; he was an example of the Indian who survives. In 1916, Ishi died of tuberculosis.[5] His body, not his spirit, was defenseless against modern infection. Despite the protests of his friend Kroeber, Ishi's body was defiled by an autopsy,[6] and his brain went into a jar, all the way back to the Smithsonian in Washington. It will remain the shame of the Smithsonian that throughout the twentieth century it **accumulated** thousands of Indian remains. Only in 1989 did the Congress require the museum to begin to

3. **pidgin:** (pij′in) adj.: mixture of two languages, simplified so people who can't speak each other's language can communicate.
4. **John Ford** (1895–1973): famous Hollywood movie director, best known for westerns.
5. **tuberculosis:** (tŏŏ·bʉr′kyə·lō′sis) n.: serious contagious disease that affects mainly the lungs.
6. **autopsy:** (ô′täp′sē) n.: medical examination of a dead body to determine cause of death.

repatriate[7] the bones and body parts and skulls that the museum
60   has kept in jars and boxes.

      Thus was Ishi's brain returned to California in a jar. At a
time when Californians drove SUV's nicknamed "Aztec" and
"Cherokee," and when an Indian tribe announced plans to erect
a casino near the entrance of Yosemite, and at a time when
many living Californians looked like Ishi, though the United
States prefers to call us Hispanics, Ishi returned home. After
his long journey, his remains were buried by a neighboring
tribe near Mount Shasta, in a location where outsiders will
never find him.

70   May you rest in peace, dear Ishi.

---

7. **repatriate:** (rē·pā′trē·āt′) *v.:* return someone to his or her own country.

Ishi Apparently Wasn't the Last Yahi

excerpt from a University of California–Berkeley press release

Gretchen Kell

IDENTIFY

Pause at line 10. What is the **main idea** presented in the first three paragraphs?

EVALUATE

Underline the text that tells you who Steven Shackley is. Do you think he is a credible source? Why or why not?

SYNTHESIZE SOURCES

What new information about Theodora Kroeber do you learn in lines 16–21 that was not in the previous piece, "Homecoming"?

Berkeley, CA—Ishi is a household name in Northern California, where schoolchildren have been taught for eighty-five years that he was the last Yahi, a subgroup of the Yana Indians.

"Ishi, the Last Yana Indian, 1916," is etched into the small black jar containing his cremated remains.

But by studying the arrowpoints Ishi made, Steven Shackley, a research archaeologist at the University of California at Berkeley's Hearst Museum of Anthropology, has discovered that Ishi apparently wasn't the last full-blooded Yahi, or Yana, after all.

Instead, Shackley said that Ishi, who was found, starving and afraid, near Oroville in 1911, was of mixed Indian blood—a finding that revises Ishi's famous history, which many Californians learned by reading *Ishi in Two Worlds* by Theodora Kroeber.

Shackley said that, in light of this new evidence on Ishi, teachers educating children about California history "should be more aware of the complexity of Ishi's situation. It's more complex than Kroeber imagined."

Her book was "simplistic," he said, "not based completely on hard research."

An analysis by Shackley of a large UC Berkeley collection of Ishi's arrowpoints indicates that although he spoke Yahi and had lived in the ancestral Yahi homeland in the Mount Lassen foothills, he also had either Wintu or Nomlaki blood.

"Arrowpoints made in the historic Yahi sites excavated by the Department of Anthropology in the 1950s and housed at the museum are quite different from Ishi's products," said Shackley. "But tools and arrowpoints made at historic Nomlaki or Wintu

30   sites also housed at the museum bear striking resemblance to those made by Ishi."

Although Ishi was culturally Yahi, said Shackley, "it appears he was not the last purely Yahi Indian. He learned to produce arrowpoints not from Yahi relatives, but very possibly from a Nomlaki or Wintu male relative.

"This makes Ishi's story even more romantic and sad," he said. "Being of mixed blood, his is an example of the cultural pressure the Anglos placed on the dwindling number of Indians in the mid- to late-1800s to marry their enemies."

40   The Wintu, Nomlaki, and Maidu belonged to a large group of Indians in the Sacramento Valley who spoke a language called Penutian. They lived adjacent to their enemies, the Yana, who were in the Lassen foothills. The Yana had four subgroups—the northern, central, and southern Yana, and the Yahi—and each had its own dialect, territory, and culture.

Ishi was born into an extended family that, in order to **perpetuate** life, was forced to intermarry with outsiders, with enemies, said Shackley, and one of Ishi's parents may have been Wintu or Nomlaki.

50   "We always thought that Ishi was a survivor who was extremely adaptive," said Shackley. "Now we know he was even more adaptive because he was the product of a society that had to adapt to a situation that was not part of its cultural **ideology.**

"Ishi didn't talk about his ancestors because his religious beliefs prevented him from doing that. But that's my job as an archaeologist," he said. "And Ishi would have wanted the truth known."

CLARIFY

Re-read lines 22–35. What details support the idea that Ishi was not a full-blooded Yahi?

IDENTIFY CAUSE & EFFECT

Re-read lines 36–39 and 46–49. According to Shackley, what caused the Yahi people to marry outsiders?

VOCABULARY

perpetuate (pər·pech′o͞o āt′) v.: cause to continue.

ideology (ī′dē·äl′ə·jē) n.: set of doctrines and beliefs held by an individual or group.

Underline the details in lines 63–70 that explain why anthropologists considered Ishi to be the last Yahi.

Pause at line 83. What probably happened to the three people with whom Ishi was seen in 1908?

Ishi first made headlines on August 29, 1911, when butchers found him outside a slaughterhouse near Oroville. Initially, he was jailed by the Butte County sheriff. But two UC Berkeley anthropologists, Alfred Kroeber and Thomas Talbot Waterman, befriended Ishi and gave him shelter at the campus's anthropology museum, then in San Francisco.

Kroeber's wife, the author of *Ishi in Two Worlds,* wrote that Ishi was "the last wild Indian in North America, a man of Stone Age culture."

The anthropologists pronounced Ishi a Yahi because he spoke Yahi and was found near Yahi territory. They also considered him the last Yahi, said Shackley, since "the only Yahi left in the hinterlands° were believed to have been exterminated by Indian killers brought in by whites."

Furthermore, they believed Ishi was the last Indian to have lived in the wild. Massacres, starvation, and disease had taken the lives of countless Indians in Northern California during the mid- to late-1800s. Many others had been forced into reservations.

In 1908, surveyors did spot four Indians in Yahi territory. But in 1909, Waterman and two guides failed to find the group. Two years later, Ishi, who verified that he had been one of the four, appeared alone near Oroville.

"That Ishi was wearing his hair burned short in sign of mourning in August, 1911, was evidence of a death or deaths in his family," wrote Theodora Kroeber, "but his mourning may well have been a prolonged one."

Under pressure from reporters who wanted to know the stranger's name, Alfred Kroeber called him "Ishi," which means "man" in Yana. Ishi never uttered his real name.

"A California Indian almost never speaks his own name," wrote Kroeber's wife, "using it but rarely with those who already know it, and he would never tell it in reply to a direct question."

° **hinterlands** (hin′tər·landz′) *n.:* interior areas of a country, away from cities and coasts.

90   Ishi was given a home at the University of California's anthropology museum—then on the UCSF campus in an old law school building. He lived there for most of the rest of his life, except for the summer of 1915, when he lived in Berkeley with Waterman and his family.

      While at the museum, Ishi often worked on native crafts, such as the arrowpoints Shackley analyzed. By his own choice, he often did these crafts for museum audiences and would give some of his work away.

      Ishi formed close friendships with Waterman and Kroeber
100   and with Saxton Pope, a teacher at the university's medical school, which was next door to the museum. He also agreed to record **linguistic** material on the Yahi language for UC Berkeley.

      In December 1914, Ishi developed what doctors felt was tuberculosis. After several hospitalizations, his friends moved him back to the museum to spend his last days. He died there on March 25, 1916.

linguistic (lin·gwis′tik) *adj.:* of or relating to the study of language.

What are some words in the same word family as *linguistic*?

____

____

____

How is the focus of "Ishi Apparently Wasn't the Last Yahi" similar to and different from the focus of "Homecoming"?

The Repatriation of Ishi, the Last Yahi Indian

Smithsonian National Museum of Natural History

> **INTERPRET**
>
> What do you learn from the time line and the map with this selection? How are they a clue to the **purpose** of the piece?
>
> ________________________
>
> ________________________
>
> ________________________
>
> ________________________
>
> ________________________
>
> ________________________

From "The Repatriation of Ishi, the Last Yahi Indian" from *Repatriation Office, Smithsonian National Museum of Natural History.* Reproduced by permission of **Smithsonian Institution.**

The National Museum of Natural History committed in March of 1999 to return the brain of Ishi to his descendants at the Redding Rancheria and Pit River Indian Tribe of California, and held it until they could recover cremated remains from the cemetery in Colma, California, where they were held by a private mortuary. The state of California released those remains, and the brain and cremated remains of Ishi have since been reunited. Ishi's remains were repatriated on August 10, 2000. The remains were reinterred[1] shortly thereafter at an undisclosed location.

10   **HISTORICAL POINTS**

- Ishi always identified himself as a Yahi-Yana person. These are terms made up by anthropologists and refer to the two closely related dialects of the Yana language: "Yana" and "Yahi" both mean *man,* in the northern and southern dialects respectively.

---

1.   **reinterred:** (rē′in·tʉrd′) *v.:* reburied.

ISHI TIME LINE

c. 1864   Born

1908   Seen when surveyors disturbed his home; he was living with three other Yahi survivors: a woman thought to be Ishi's mother and another thought to be his sister; they probably died shortly afterward. An old man was also seen and probably died.

August 29, 1911   Found at a slaughterhouse in Oroville, CA

1911–16   Lived at University of California Anthropology Museum; employed as a janitor in the museum and gave demonstrations of archery, flintknapping, house construction, fire making, and other crafts and skills; worked with anthropologists to document Yana culture and language

March 23, 1916   Dies from tuberculosis; autopsy performed at University of California medical school. His body was cremated along with some possessions and placed in a Pueblo jar in Mount Olivet Cemetery, Colma, CA

1917   Alfred Kroeber sent Ishi's preserved brain to Smithsonian Institution; it is identified as donation from the "University of California"

1860	1880	1900	1920

Ishi communicated easily with other Yana and with linguists by using Yana-Yahi.

- The Yana had a distinctive language, with different dialects: one used a distinctive pronunciation when speaking to men or women. This gender-specific dialect pattern is highly unusual in any language, and demonstrates the close common identity of all Yana speakers (including Ishi as a Yahi speaker).

- The notion that Ishi was the "last of his people" comes from the fact that Ishi was the last-known Yana to live a life essentially outside of direct contact with whites. There always were many of his tribe still alive, but they had become **enmeshed** in the larger "American" society. One might say that the early anthropologists thought of him as the last "real Indian"—a notion that is largely defunct[2] today.

- Descendants of the Yana are members of the Redding Rancheria and the Pit River Tribe. Representatives of the tribe traveled to Washington, D.C., in August 2000, and the remains of Ishi were formally repatriated to them on August 10, 2000.

---

2. **defunct:** (dē·fuŋkt′) *adj.:* out-of-date; no longer in use.

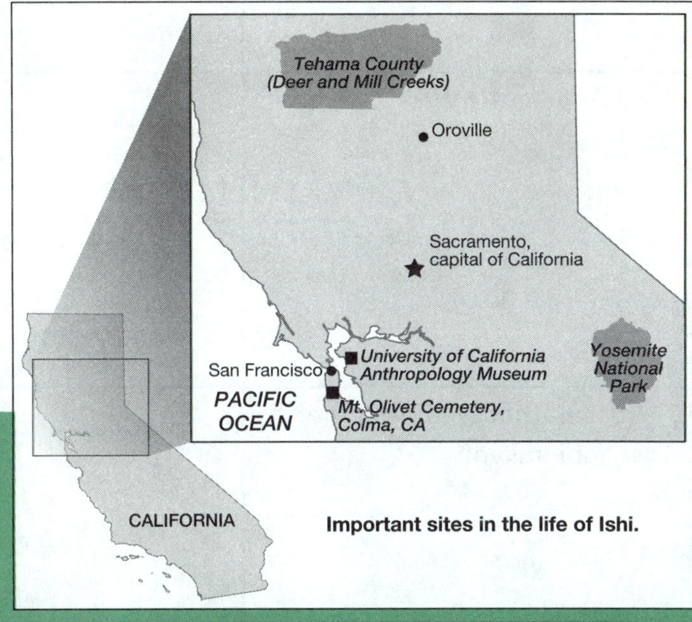

Homecoming; Ishi Apparently Wasn't the Last Yahi; The Repatriation of Ishi

Reading Skills
Synthesize information from several sources on a single topic.

Synthesizing Sources   In the chart below, list the main ideas and supporting details from the three articles you have just read. In the lines below the chart, **synthesize** the information from all three sources into one overall **conclusion.**

Source	Main Idea	Supporting Evidence
"Homecoming"		
"Ishi Apparently Wasn't the Last Yahi"		
"The Repatriation of Ishi, the Last Yahi Indian"		

Synthesis: ____

____

____

____

Skills Review

Homecoming; Ishi Apparently Wasn't the Last Yahi; The Repatriation of Ishi

VOCABULARY AND COMPREHENSION

A. Word Families   Fill out the chart with the word from the Word Box that is in the same family as the word listed. Then, explain how the two words are related.

Word Box

diminished

accumulated

perpetuate

ideology

linguistic

enmeshed

Vocabulary Word	Related Word	Explanation
	idealist	
	cumulative	
	language	
	diminutive	
	mesh	
	perpetual	

B. Reading Comprehension   Answer each question below.

1. What happened to Ishi's brain after he died? Where is it now?

____

____

2. According to Steven Shackley, what did Ishi's extended family begin doing that diverged from its cultural traditions?

____

____

3. Why is Ishi often considered the last of his people?

____

____

SKILLS FOCUS

Vocabulary Skills
Understand word families.

Free Minds and Hearts at Work
by Jackie Robinson

Jackie Changed the Face of Sports
by Larry Schwartz

In 1947, Jack Roosevelt (Jackie) Robinson became the first African American to play baseball in the major leagues in the twentieth century. In the first article that follows, you'll read some of Robinson's reflections on his sometimes difficult experiences. Then, in the second, you'll read a sports journalist's take on Robinson's importance to sports and to our nation in general.

INFORMATIONAL FOCUS: PRIMARY AND SECONDARY SOURCES

When researching a topic, you gather information from a variety of **sources**—books, magazines, newspapers, Web sites, and more. Research sources typically fall into two basic categories:

- **Primary sources** are firsthand accounts. They include interviews, letters, autobiographies, eyewitness news reports, oral histories, editorials, and speeches. In primary sources, people often present opinions about their own experiences or events that they have witnessed.
- **Secondary sources** are secondhand accounts. In secondary sources, writers summarize, interpret, or analyze events in which they did not participate. Examples of secondary sources include encyclopedias, textbooks, biographies, many magazine articles, and most newspaper articles.

READING SKILLS: IDENTIFYING AND ELABORATING ON MAIN IDEAS

You're about to read one primary source and one secondary source about Jackie Robinson. To be sure you understand these sources, pause occasionally as you read to identify the **main idea** of the passage—the main message or insight the author is trying to convey—by looking for statements that express the writer's opinion and by examining key details in the text.

Once you identify a main idea, **elaborate** on it. To elaborate on an idea:
- Connect the main idea to your own prior knowledge.
- Formulate questions you may still have.
- Do further research or develop your own opinions about the subject.

Reading Skills
Analyze primary and secondary sources. Identify and elaborate on main ideas.

Vocabulary Skills
Clarify word meanings.

VOCABULARY DEVELOPMENT

PREVIEW SELECTION VOCABULARY

Preview these vocabulary words before you begin to read:

probability (präb′ə·bil′ə·tē) *n.:* likelihood.

> The **probability** of his success motivated Robinson.

static (stat′ik) *adj.:* not moving or changing.

> Society is not **static**—positive changes take place frequently.

prone (prōn) *adj.:* having a tendency.

> Robinson was **prone** to standing up for himself, but he learned to endure abuse so that others could succeed.

epithets (ep′ə·thets′) *n.:* terms, often insulting, used to characterize a person or thing.

> Opposing players and fans shouted racial **epithets** at Robinson.

instilling (in·stil′ēŋ) *v.* used as *adj.:* gradually implanting an idea or belief.

> Robinson competed fiercely through the years, **instilling** the Dodgers with a winning attitude.

WORD KNOWLEDGE: WHAT'S THE DIFFERENCE?

You can gain a better understanding of words by distinguishing them from their **antonyms** (words that have opposite meanings) as well as from **synonyms** that have different **connotations** (associations). If you are able to express the exact difference between similar words, you'll convey just the right shade of meaning, and your writing will be more precise.

Consider the meaning of the italicized word in the following sentence from "Jackie Changed the Face of Sports": "He was an aggressive man, *outraged* at injustice, and quick to stand up for his rights." How would the meaning of the sentence change if *outraged* were replaced by *offended*? What is an antonym of *outraged*?

Free Minds and Hearts at Work

Jackie Robinson

IDENTIFY SOURCES

Pause at line 6. Is this article a **primary source** or a **secondary source**? What details in the first paragraph tell you?

____

____

____

____

____

IDENTIFY & ELABORATE

Re-read lines 11–18. Circle the **main idea** of the paragraph. Then, elaborate on the main idea by formulating questions about it.

____

____

____

____

____

____

VOCABULARY

probability (präb′ə·bil′ə·tē) *n.:* likelihood.

At the beginning of the World Series of 1947, I experienced a completely new emotion when the national anthem was played. This time, I thought, it is being played for me, as much as for anyone else. This is organized Major League baseball, and I am standing here with all the others; and everything that takes place includes me.

About a year later, I went to Atlanta, Georgia, to play in an exhibition game. On the field, for the first time in Atlanta, there were Negroes and whites. Other Negroes, besides me. And

10 I thought: What I have always believed has come to be.

And what is it that I have always believed? First, that imperfections are human. But that wherever human beings were given room to breathe and time to think, those imperfections would disappear, no matter how slowly. I do not believe that we have found or even approached perfection. That is not necessarily in the scheme of human events. Handicaps, stumbling blocks, prejudices—all of these are imperfect. Yet, they have to be reckoned with because they are in the scheme of human events.

Whatever obstacles I found made me fight all the harder.

20 But it would have been impossible for me to fight at all, except that I was sustained by the personal and deep-rooted belief that my fight had a chance. It had a chance because it took place in a free society. Not once was I forced to face and fight an immovable object. Not once was the situation so cast-iron rigid that I had no chance at all. Free minds and human hearts were at work all around me; and so there was the **probability** of improvement. I look at my children now, and know that I must still prepare them to meet obstacles and prejudices.

Baseball legend Jackie Robinson.
Allan Grant/Getty Images

But I can tell them, too, that they will never face some of
these prejudices because other people have gone before them.
And to myself I can say that, because progress is unalterable,
many of today's dogmas° will have vanished by the time they
grow into adults. I can say to my children: There is a chance for
you. No guarantee, but a chance.

And this chance has come to be, because there is nothing
static with free people. There is no Middle Ages logic so strong
that it can stop the human tide from flowing forward. I do not
believe that every person, in every walk of life, can succeed in

---

°   **dogmas** (dôg′məz) *n.:* beliefs

IDENTIFY CAUSE & EFFECT

Pause at line 34. According
to Robinson, why will his
children face less prejudice
than he did?

VOCABULARY

static (stat′ik) *adj.:* not
moving or changing.

In your own words, express the **main idea** of lines 35–43.

____

____

____

____

Re-read lines 44–53. Underline instances in which the author mentions "a free society." What do you think it means to live in a free society?

____

____

____

____

____

____

Look back through this article, and circle the words *believe* and *belief* everywhere they occur. What does the repetition of these words tell you about the objectivity or subjectivity of this source?

____

____

____

____

____

40 spite of any handicap. That would be perfection. But I do believe—and with every fiber in me—that what I was able to attain came to be because we put behind us (no matter how slowly) the dogmas of the past: to discover the truth of today; and perhaps find the greatness of tomorrow.

I believe in the human race. I believe in the warm heart. I believe in man's integrity. I believe in the goodness of a free society. And I believe that the society can remain good only as long as we are willing to fight for it—and to fight against whatever imperfections may exist.

50 My fight was against the barriers that kept Negroes out of baseball. This was the area where I found imperfection, and where I was best able to fight. And I fought because I knew it was not doomed to be a losing fight. It couldn't be a losing fight—not when it took place in a free society.

And in the largest sense, I believe that what I did was done for me—that it was my faith in God that sustained me in my fight. And that what was done for me must and will be done for others.

    Reading Informational Texts

Jackie Changed the Face of Sports

Larry Schwartz

It's not often that the essence of a man, especially a complicated man, can be summed up in one sentence. But then again, there haven't been many people like Jackie Robinson.

"A life is not important," he said, "except in the impact it has on other lives."

By that standard, few people—and no athlete—this century has impacted more lives. Robinson lit the torch and passed it on to several generations of African American athletes. While the Brooklyn Dodgers infielder didn't make a nation color blind, he at least made it more color friendly.

And he accomplished this feat by going against his natural instincts. He was an aggressive man, outraged at injustice, and quick to stand up for his rights. He had the guts to say no when ordered to the back of the bus in the army, and was court-martialed for his courage. His instinct wasn't to turn the other cheek, but to face problems head on. He was more **prone** to fighting back than holding back.

That's what Robinson had to do when Dodgers president Branch Rickey selected him to become the first African American to play in the majors this century. Rickey wanted a man who could restrain himself from responding to the ugliness of the racial hatred that was certain to come.

A shorthand version of their fateful conversation in August 1945:

Rickey: "I know you're a good ballplayer. What I don't know is whether you have the guts."

IDENTIFY & ELABORATE

Re-read lines 1–10, and consider the title of this article. What do you think the **main idea** of the article is? How is this idea connected to the main idea of the previous article?

VOCABULARY

prone (prōn) *adj.*: having a tendency.

IDENTIFY SOURCES

Pause at line 24. Note that the writer is recounting a conversation in which he was not involved. What does that fact tell you about whether this article is a **primary source** or a **secondary source**?

How does the mood of the exchange between Robinson and Rickey in lines 25–30 differ from the mood of the two men depicted in the photo?

____

____

____

____

____

Robinson: "Mr. Rickey, are you looking for a Negro who is afraid to fight back?"

30   Rickey, exploding: "Robinson, I'm looking for a ballplayer with guts enough not to fight back."

This unwritten pact between two men would change the course of a country. Baseball might only be a game, but in the area of black and white, it often is a leader. Robinson's debut for the Dodgers in 1947 came a year before President Harry Truman desegregated the military and seven years before the Supreme Court ruled segregation in public schools was unconstitutional.

Rickey was dead-on about the racism. As *Sports Illustrated*'s Bill Nack wrote: "Robinson was the target of racial **epithets** and

Jackie Robinson shakes hands with Dodgers president Branch Rickey after signing his contract.
Bettmann/CORBIS

flying cleats, of hate letters and death threats, of pitchers throw-
40   ing at his head and legs, and catchers spitting on his shoes."

Robinson learned how to exercise self-control—to answer
insults, violence and injustice with silence. A model of unselfish
team play, he earned the respect of his teammates and, eventually, the opposition.

The six-foot, 195-pound Robinson was the Rookie of the
Year and two years later he was MVP (Most Valuable Player).
His lifetime average was .311° and he was voted into the Baseball
Hall of Fame in his first year of eligibility.

Pigeon-toed and muscular, it was No. 42's aggressiveness
50   on the basepaths that thrilled fans. It wasn't so much his two
stolen-base titles or his 197 thefts. It was the way he was a disruptive force, dancing off the base, drawing every eye in the stadium,
making the pitcher crazy, **instilling** the Dodgers with the spirit
that would help them win six pennants in his ten seasons.

"Robinson could hit and bunt and steal and run," Roger
Kahn wrote in *The Boys of Summer*. "He had intimidation skills,
and he burned with a dark fire. He wanted passionately to win.
He bore the burden of a pioneer and the weight made him
stronger. If one can be certain of anything in baseball, it is that
60   we shall not look upon his like again."

★ ★ ★ ★ ★ ★ ★ ★

How should we remember this grandson of a slave and
son of a sharecropper? Maybe by what he told a white New
Orleans sportswriter: "We ask for nothing special. We ask
only to be permitted to live as you live, and as our nation's
Constitution provides."

With such simple and justifiable demands, it's no wonder
the man had such an impact on so many lives.

°   **lifetime average was .311:** ratio of base hits to number of times at
bat. Robinson made a base hit approximately one out of every three
times at bat.

Is the *Sports Illustrated* article referred to in lines 37–40 a **primary source** or a **secondary source**? Explain.

Pause at line 60. In *The Boys of Summer,* Roger Kahn details his travels with the Brooklyn Dodgers. Is the book a **primary source** or a **secondary source**? Explain.

epithets (ep′ə·thets′) *n.:* terms, often insulting, used to characterize a person or thing.

instilling (in·stil′ēŋ) *v.* used as *adj.:* gradually implanting an idea or belief.

Free Minds and Hearts at Work; Jackie Changed the Face of Sports

Reading skills
Identify and elaborate on main ideas.

Analysis, Evaluation, and Elaboration Grid The articles "Free Minds and Hearts at Work" and "Jackie Changed the Face of Sports" are both about Jackie Robinson's overcoming prejudice as the first African American Major League baseball player of the modern era. Fill in the chart below to help you analyze, evaluate, and elaborate on these sources. Use details from the texts.

- **Analyze:** What is the main idea of each article?
- **Evaluate:** Has the writer provided adequate support for his position?
- **Elaborate:** What information could you add?

	"Free Minds and Hearts at Work"	"Jackie Changed the Face of Sports"
ANALYZE		
EVALUATE		
ELABORATE		

Free Minds and Hearts at Work;
Jackie Changed the Face of Sports

VOCABULARY AND COMPREHENSION

A. Word Knowledge: What's the Difference?   Answer each question below by explaining the differences in meaning between the two words. They may be antonyms or synonyms with different connotations, or they may be different in other ways.

1. What's the difference between *epithets* and *descriptions*? _______________

____

2. What's the difference between *prone* and *disinclined*? _______________

____

3. What's the difference between *instilling* and *instructing*? _______________

____

4. What's the difference between *probability* and *chance*? _______________

____

5. What's the difference between *static* and *dynamic*? _______________

____

B. Reading Comprehension   Answer each question below.

1. What are Robinson's beliefs about imperfections? _______________

____

2. According to Robinson, what is required for a society to remain good?

____

____

3. What character trait was the Dodgers president, Branch Rickey, looking for in his first African American player? _______________

____

Word Box
probability
static
prone
epithets
instilling

SKILLS FOCUS

Vocabulary Skills
Clarify word meanings.

Before You Read

Be an Everyday Freedom Hero!

by the National Underground Railroad Freedom Center

Like most people, you've probably read your share of articles that give you advice or suggest that you do something. Many such articles focus on how you can improve yourself or the world around you. Why do you forget most of these articles, while a few stick with you? It is the power of an author's argument that makes an article convincing.

INFORMATIONAL FOCUS: ARGUMENT

A **claim** is the position a writer takes on an issue. A writer creates an **argument,** a series of persuasive details, to support a claim. The writer of the following article thinks people should take action against a problem that plagues society and presents evidence to defend this claim.

Arguments can consist of both logical and emotional appeals: They can appeal to both our hearts and our minds. Writers build **logical appeals** by presenting facts. Writers create **emotional appeals** through loaded words and through their **tone,** or attitude. If you find that a piece of writing relies mainly on emotional appeals, the writer is probably unable to support his or her argument with hard evidence.

Generalizations are broad statements about something or someone. Some can be supported, but others unfairly reflect bias or unsound thinking.
- As you read, consider and identify the writer's argument. What is the point he or she is making?
- Distinguish between logical and emotional appeals as you evaluate the writer's evidence.
- Identify generalizations, and decide whether or not they are justified.

READING SKILLS: PARAPHRASING

When you restate ideas from a text in your own words, you are **paraphrasing.** Paraphrasing can help you understand the ideas in a piece of writing. It is also a useful skill when you are writing research papers. A paraphrase should contain all of the information in the original. Here's an example:

Original Text	Paraphrase
Nazi Germany attacks other countries, triggering World War II.	Nazi Germany's attacks on other nations lead to World War II.

Reading Skills
Understand the elements of an author's argument. Paraphrase a text.

Vocabulary Skills
Use context clues to understand the meaning of words.

VOCABULARY DEVELOPMENT

PREVIEW SELECTION VOCABULARY

Preview these vocabulary words before you begin to read:

detains (dē·tānz′) *v.:* keeps in custody; confines.

> *If a country **detains** people who haven't committed a crime, citizens should demand that they be freed.*

boycott (boi′kät′) *n.:* organized refusal to buy, use, or deal with, usually as a form of protest.

> *African Americans' refusal to use the city buses in Montgomery, Alabama, was a famous and effective **boycott**.*

servitude (sʉr′və·to͞od′) *n.:* subjection to a master or owner.

> *Involuntary **servitude**, banned by the Thirteenth Amendment, is like a prison without bars.*

contemporary (kən·tem′pə·rer′ē) *adj.:* modern; of the current time.

> *A main cause of **contemporary** slavery is the persistent desire for cheap labor.*

statistics (stə·tis′tiks) *n.:* numerical data.

> *Slavery **statistics** are shocking: an estimated 27 million people are enslaved worldwide.*

CONTEXT CLUES: SOLVING WORD MYSTERIES

When you come across an unfamiliar word while reading, you may be able to use **context clues** to figure out what the word means. Context clues are words or phrases near the word that hint at its meaning. They may define or restate the word, provide examples of the word, or compare or contrast the word with another. Consider the italicized sentences above with this selection's vocabulary. They contain the types of context clues in the chart below.

Type	Definition	Restatement	Example	Comparison	Contrast
Vocabulary word	boycott	contemporary	statistics	servitude	detains
Context clue in sentence	"refusal to use"	"exists . . . today"	"27 million people"	"like a prison"	"be freed"

Be an Everyday Freedom Hero!

National Underground Railroad Freedom Center

BACKGROUND: Informational Text and Social Studies
Like a freedom conductor of the Underground Railroad who helped slaves to freedom, an "Everyday Freedom Hero" takes action when he or she sees injustice. It all starts simply, with one person stepping forward or speaking out to make things better. Here's a time line of some Everyday Freedom Heroes that shows how the power of one person can make a difference.

AUTHOR'S ARGUMENT

Re-read the background information above. Based on this information, what do you think the writer will argue in the text?

TEXT STRUCTURE

Is the time line at the beginning of this selection an example of an **argument** or of **evidence?** Explain.

____

____

____

____

____

____

____

"Be an Everyday Freedom Hero!" from *FreedomCenter.org.* Reproduced by permission of the **National Underground Railroad Freedom Center.**

Time Line

1830 Forced from his South Carolina home because of his anti-slavery beliefs, Rev. James Gilliland relocates to Ohio, where he forms his own anti-slavery church.

1849 Runaway slave Harriet Tubman becomes a Freedom Conductor for the Underground Railroad, a secret network by which runaway slaves are led to freedom. She risks her life numerous times by venturing into slave states to guide slaves to freedom.

10

1920 William DeHart Hubbard is blocked from playing on his high school football team because he's black. His teammates refuse to play until that rule is overturned. Hubbard goes on to become the first African American to win an individual Olympic medal.

1939 Nazi Germany attacks other countries in Europe, triggering World War II. German soldiers round up Jews and other "undesirables" in a program that results in the murder of more than 9 million people. In Poland, Dr. Jan Zabinski risks his life to hide dozens of Jews.

| 1942 | The U.S. **detains** more than 100,000 Japanese Americans in camps for fear that they will aid Japan in its war against the U.S. Minoru Yasui, a Japanese American lawyer, challenges the order in court. The U.S. apologizes to Japanese Americans thirty-six years later. |

20

| 1955 | In Montgomery, Alabama, Rosa Parks is arrested for not giving her seat on a bus to a white man. Her act leads to a bus **boycott** that puts the Civil Rights Movement into high gear. |

| 1965 | Several years after his retirement from baseball, Jackie Robinson helps to start the first black-run bank, Freedom National Bank, in New York City. |

30

| 1975 | When he is nine, Arn Chorn-Pond's entire family is murdered in Cambodia after rebels overrun the country. Chorn-Pond escapes in 1979. He becomes an accomplished flutist and now regularly returns to his native land to help revive its culture. |

| 1995 | Inspired by an article about child slavery, twelve-year-old Canadian Craig Kielburger creates an organization called Kids Can Save the Children. To date, the organization has sent millions of dollars' worth of medical supplies to help poor, homeless, and enslaved children around the world. |

40

| 2002 | In a peaceful demonstration, Laquetta Shepard stands in the middle of a rally of the racist organization Ku Klux Klan. Because of her courageous stand, the group cuts its meeting short. |

Listen Up!

Think there's nothing to stand up for? Sometimes it's easy to recognize injustice and sometimes it's not. Being a Freedom Hero means keeping your eyes and ears open—and not looking
50 the other way. There are plenty of problems in the world that Everyday Freedom Heroes can take action against: hunger, poverty, homelessness, illiteracy, slavery.

You read right: slavery. Sure, slavery in the U.S. was officially outlawed in 1865 following the end of the Civil War as lawmakers added the Thirteenth Amendment to the U.S. Constitution. It reads: "Neither slavery nor involuntary **servitude,** except as a punishment for crime . . . shall exist within the United States. . . ." But slavery wasn't erased from the face of the earth with that amendment. Experts figure there are at least 27 million slaves
60 in the world _today_—many of them young kids.

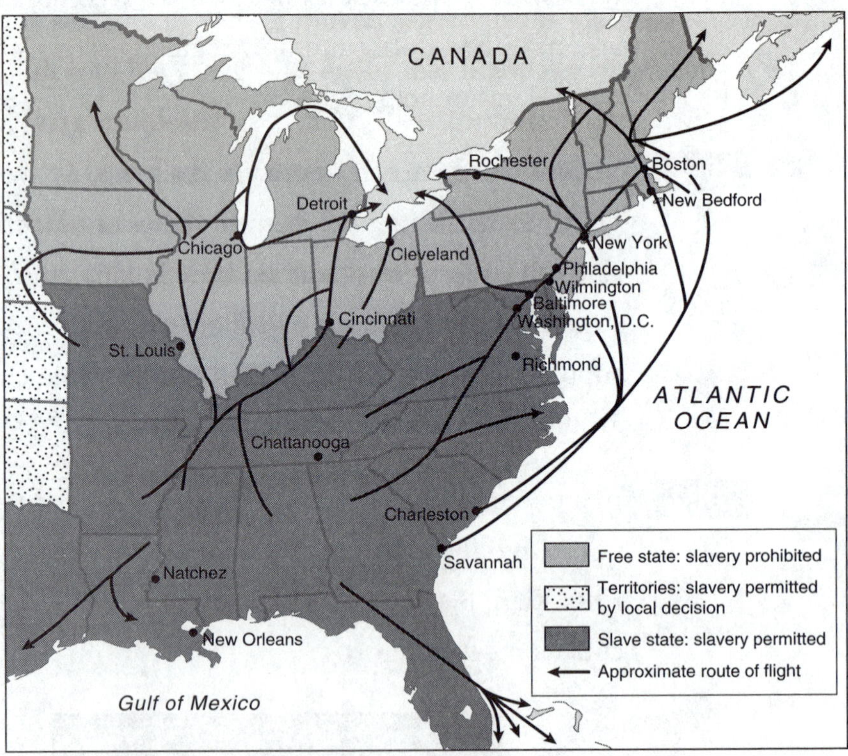

This map shows the routes that enslaved African Americans followed to escape slavery.

Why Does Slavery Still Exist?

The answer is spelled M-O-N-E-Y. Most **contemporary** slavery exists because of poverty and greed. In such situations, it's easy for poor kids to get thrown into slavery. And in most cases, owners prefer their slaves to be kids because they're easier to control. But back to the money . . . Slave labor is cheap—no pay, no health care, nothing—well, maybe you get a blanket and a bowl of beans, if you're lucky. And if it costs less to make some-thing, sellers can put more money in their pockets and buyers will save more money because they can buy stuff more cheaply.

Check This Out

In Haiti some 300,000 kids—called *restavecs*—toil from sunrise to sunset in other people's homes in exchange for food.

In central Asia, gangs kidnap young boys and sell them in the United Arab Emirates. While there, these slaves are trained as camel jockeys—a very dangerous job.

In West Africa, thousands of kids are tricked or sold into slavery to harvest cocoa beans. Investigators have learned that some of the chocolate we eat is produced with slave labor.

In India and Pakistan, many poor families sell their chil-dren into slavery to pay off debts. Hundreds of thousands of these kids are then forced to work long hours under brutal con-ditions as carpet weavers, toy makers, and other laborers.

In Africa, Asia, and South America, tens of thousands of kids are forced into military units to fight, kill, and die on the front lines.

<table>
<tr><td colspan="1" style="background:black;color:white">Terms of Freedom</td></tr>
</table>

slavery: a system in which people own other people and can control everything they do.

"unfreedom": a situation in which people's freedom has been lost or taken away by injustice.

____

____

____

____

____

____

____

____

____

____

____

____

____

____

____

____

____

____

Take Action

- Educate others. Write an article or letter to the editor about contemporary slavery for your school Web site, school newspaper, or local newspaper. Use facts and **statistics** to let people know that slavery is still wrecking lives. What can speaking up do to stop an injustice? Did you know that Craig Kielburger was inspired after reading an article about the death of an enslaved twelve-year-old boy?

- Ask your teachers about tutoring others. Have you ever struggled with a school subject? Feels lousy, doesn't it? Consider helping other students in a subject you're good at. How can helping others help build friendships and community?

90

100

Be an Everyday Freedom Hero!

Argument Evaluation Chart   The writers of "Be an Everyday Freedom Hero!" argue that people should take action against slavery, which still exists today. Evaluating an argument involves looking at the details that support the writer's claim. To organize your ideas, complete this chart using examples from the text.

Claim	
Logical appeals	
Emotional appeals	
Generalizations	
Loaded words	
My evaluation	

Skills Review

Be an Everyday Freedom Hero!

VOCABULARY AND COMPREHENSION

<table>
<tr><td>

Word Box

detains

boycott

statistics

servitude

contemporary

</td></tr>
</table>

A. Context Clues   Complete the paragraph below by writing the correct words from the Word Box in the blanks. Not all of the words will be used.

I was shocked by the fact that slavery exists in

(1) _________________________ times. The (2) _________________________ cited

by the writer show that people, many of them children, are being held in

(3) _________________________. I am going to try to raise people's awareness

of this issue by taking part in a (4) _________________________ of any com-

panies that engage in these illegal practices.

B. Reading Comprehension   Answer each question below.

1. Why were 100,000 Japanese Americans detained in camps in 1945?

   ____

   ____

2. What did Jackie Robinson help establish after his retirement from baseball?

   ____

   ____

3. Why does slavery still exist in the world today?

   ____

   ____

4. According to the article, what actions can you take to raise awareness about slavery?

   ____

   ____

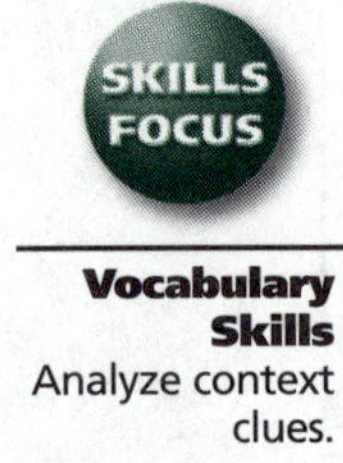

SKILLS FOCUS

Vocabulary Skills
Analyze context clues.

Consumer, Workplace, and Public Documents

Academic Vocabulary

These are the terms you should know as you read
and analyze the selections that follow.

Consumer documents Documents relating to the sale, purchase, and use of products. Some consumer documents, such as warranties, protect the rights of the purchaser and the seller. Other consumer documents include advertisements, contracts, instruction manuals, and product information.

Public documents Documents that inform the public. Public documents are created by governmental, social, religious, or news-gathering organizations. They include safety information, government regulations, schedules of events, explanations of services, and newspaper items.

Workplace documents Job-related documents used in offices, factories, and other work sites to communicate information. These include business letters, job applications, contracts, instruction manuals, memorandums, and safety information.

Technical documents Documents used to explain or establish procedures for using technology, such as mechanical, electronic, or digital products or systems. Technical documents include how-to instructions, installation instructions, and instructions on carrying out scientific procedures.

Functional documents Documents prepared for a specific function, such as consumer, public, workplace, and technical documents.

Before You Read

Equal Employment Opportunity Is the Law

Suppose you are applying for a job you've always wanted. How do employees of a company know that the company they work for does not discriminate? One way is to be sure is if the company displays the following poster from the U.S. Equal Employment Opportunity Commission. By hanging this poster in a visible area, a company is promising to give all employees and applicants a fair deal.

INFORMATIONAL FOCUS: WORKPLACE DOCUMENTS

The purpose of most **workplace documents** is to present accurate information as briefly and clearly as possible. The excerpts of the document you will read next fulfill that purpose.

- Workplace documents are often divided into sections, each with its own header. Placing each main idea in its own section makes it easy for the reader to locate information. The separation also highlights major points so the reader is sure to notice them all.
- Workplace documents are designed to be effective. They are formatted to focus the reader's attention on key words, sections, and ideas. Formatting elements include bold and italic type, and the use of line spacing and margin widths. Though the document you are about to read does not include them, graphic elements such as illustrations and photos are frequently used in workplace documents.

TERMS TO KNOW

Boldface: dark, heavy type.

Format: the design of the document.

Header: a label or heading that introduces a document or part of a document.

Title: a label or heading, usually centered, that clearly states the purpose of an entire document.

Numbers: Numerical identification of each major section.

Reading Skills
Understand the purpose and structure of workplace documents.

Equal Employment Opportunity Is the Law

BACKGROUND: Informational Text and Social Studies

Congress established the U.S. Equal Employment Opportunity Commission (EEOC) to enforce Title VII of the Civil Rights Act of 1964. With headquarters in Washington, D.C., and fifty field offices nationwide, the EEOC is the federal government's premier civil rights agency. Every employer covered by the nondiscrimination and EEO laws is required to post on its premises the poster "Equal Employment Opportunity Is the Law." The notice must be placed where it can readily be seen by employees and applicants for employment. It provides information concerning the laws and procedures for filing complaints of violations of the laws. The EEOC's poster is available in English, Arabic, Chinese, and Spanish.

Equal Employment Opportunity is

THE LAW

1 — Employers Holding Federal Contracts or Subcontracts

Applicants to and employees of companies with a Federal government contract or subcontract are protected under the following Federal authorities:

RACE, COLOR, RELIGION, SEX, NATIONAL ORIGIN

Executive Order 11246, as amended, prohibits job discrimination on the basis of race, color, religion, sex or national origin, and requires affirmative action to ensure equality of opportunity in all aspects of employment.

INDIVIDUALS WITH DISABILITIES

Section 503 of the Rehabilitation Act of 1973, as amended, prohibits job discrimination because of disability and requires affirmative action to employ and advance in employment qualified individuals with disabilities who, with reasonable accommodation, can perform the essential functions of a job.

VIETNAM ERA, SPECIAL DISABLED, RECENTLY SEPARATED, AND OTHER PROTECTED VETERANS

38 U.S.C. 4212 of the Vietnam Era Veterans' Readjustment Assistance Act of 1974, as amended, prohibits job discrimination and requires affirmative action to employ and advance in employment qualified Vietnam era veterans, qualified special disabled veterans, recently separated veterans, and other protected veterans.

Any person who believes a contractor has violated its nondiscrimination or affirmative action obligations under the authorities above should contact immediately:

The Office of Federal Contract Compliance Programs (OFCCP), Employment Standards Administration, U.S. Department of Labor, 200 Constitution Avenue, N.W., Washington, D.C. 20210 or call (202) 693-0101, or an OFCCP regional or district office, listed in most telephone directories under U.S. Government, Department of Labor.

2 — Private Employment, State and Local Governments, Educational Institutions

Applicants to and employees of most private employers, state and local governments, educational institutions, employment agencies and labor organizations are protected under the following Federal laws:

RACE, COLOR, RELIGION, SEX, NATIONAL ORIGIN

Title VII of the Civil Rights Act of 1964, as amended, prohibits discrimination in hiring, promotion, discharge, pay, fringe benefits, job training, classification, referral, and other aspects of employment, on the basis of race, color, religion, sex or national origin.

DISABILITY

The Americans with Disabilities Act of 1990, as amended, protects qualified applicants and employees with disabilities from discrimination in hiring, promotion, discharge, pay, job training, fringe benefits, classification, referral, and other aspects of employment on the basis of disability. The law also requires that covered entities provide qualified applicants and employees with disabilities with reasonable accommodations that do not impose undue hardship.

AGE

The Age Discrimination in Employment Act of 1967, as amended, protects applicants and employees 40 years of age or older from discrimination on the basis of age in hiring, promotion, discharge, compensation, terms, conditions or privileges of employment.

SEX (WAGES)

In addition to sex discrimination prohibited by Title VII of the Civil Rights Act of 1964, as amended (see above), the Equal Pay Act of 1963, as amended, prohibits sex discrimination in payment of wages to women and men performing substantially equal work in the same establishment.

3

Retaliation against a person who files a charge of discrimination, participates in an investigation, or opposes an unlawful employment practice is prohibited by all of these Federal laws.

If you believe that you have been discriminated against under any of the above laws, you should contact immediately:

The U.S. Equal Employment Opportunity Commission (EEOC), 1801 L Street, N.W., Washington, D.C. 20507 or an EEOC field office by calling toll free (800) 669-4000. For individuals with hearing impairments, EEOC's toll free TDD number is (800) 669-6820.

4 — Programs or Activities Receiving Federal Financial Assistance

RACE, COLOR, RELIGION, NATIONAL ORIGIN, SEX

In addition to the protection of Title VII of the Civil Rights Act of 1964, as amended, Title VI of the Civil Rights Act prohibits discrimination on the basis of race, color or national origin in programs or activities receiving Federal financial assistance. Employment discrimination is covered by Title VI if the primary objective of the financial assistance is provision of employment, or where employment discrimination causes or may cause discrimination in providing services under such programs. Title IX of the Education Amendments of 1972 prohibits employment discrimination on the basis of sex in educational programs or activities which receive Federal assistance.

INDIVIDUALS WITH DISABILITIES

Sections 501, 504 and 505 of the Rehabilitation Act of 1973, as amended, prohibits employment discrimination on the basis of disability in any program or activity which receives Federal financial assistance in the federal government. Discrimination is prohibited in all aspects of employment against persons with disabilities who, with reasonable accommodation, can perform the essential functions of a job.

If you believe you have been discriminated against in a program of any institution which receives Federal assistance, you should contact immediately the Federal agency providing such assistance.

TEXT FEATURES

Circle the three main section headers of the document. How are they connected to the title of the document?

TEXT FEATURES

The tinted and numbered sections of the document are presented in larger print on pages 336–337.

1 Employers Holding Federal Contracts or Subcontracts

Applicants to and employees of companies with a Federal government contract or subcontract are protected under the following Federal authorities:

Race, Color, Religion, Sex, National Origin

Executive Order 11246, as amended, prohibits job discrimination on the basis of race, color, religion, sex or national origin, and requires affirmative action to ensure equality of opportunity in all aspects of employment.

10   **2 Private Employment, State and Local Governments, Educational Institutions**

Applicants to and employees of most private employers, state and local governments, educational institutions, employment agencies and labor organizations are protected under the following Federal laws:

Race, Color, Religion, Sex, National Origin

Title VII of the Civil Rights Act of 1964, as amended, prohibits discrimination in hiring, promotion, discharge, pay, fringe benefits, job training, classification, referral, and

20   other aspects of employment, on the basis of race, color, religion, sex or national origin.

3 Retaliation° against a person who files a charge of discrimination, participates in an investigation, or opposes an unlawful employment practice is prohibited by all of these Federal laws.

If you believe that you have been discriminated against under any of the above laws, you should contact immediately:

The U.S. Equal Employment Opportunity Commission (EEOC), 1801 L Street, N.W., Washington, D.C. 20507 or an EEOC field office by calling toll free (800) 669-4000.

---

4 **Programs or Activities Receiving Federal Financial Assistance**

Race, Color, Religion, Sex, National Origin

In addition to the protection of Title VII of the Civil Rights Act of 1964, as amended, Title VI of the Civil Rights Act prohibits discrimination on the basis of race, color or national origin in programs or activities receiving Federal financial assistance. Employment discrimination is covered by Title VI if the primary objective of the financial assistance is provision of employment, or where employment discrimination causes or may cause discrimination in providing services under such programs. Title IX of the Education Amendments of 1972 prohibits employment discrimination on the basis of sex in educational programs or activities which receive Federal assistance.

° **retaliation** (ri·tal'·ē·ā'·shun') *n:* act of taking revenge.

Equal Employment Opportunity Is the Law

Workplace Documents Organizer   Sometimes workplace documents can seem complicated. Most well-written workplace documents, however, are formatted and structured to make accessing the information predictable and easy. Look at the EEOC poster again, paying close attention to the text features circled below. Then, fill in an example of each. Finally, write an explanation of the feature's importance.

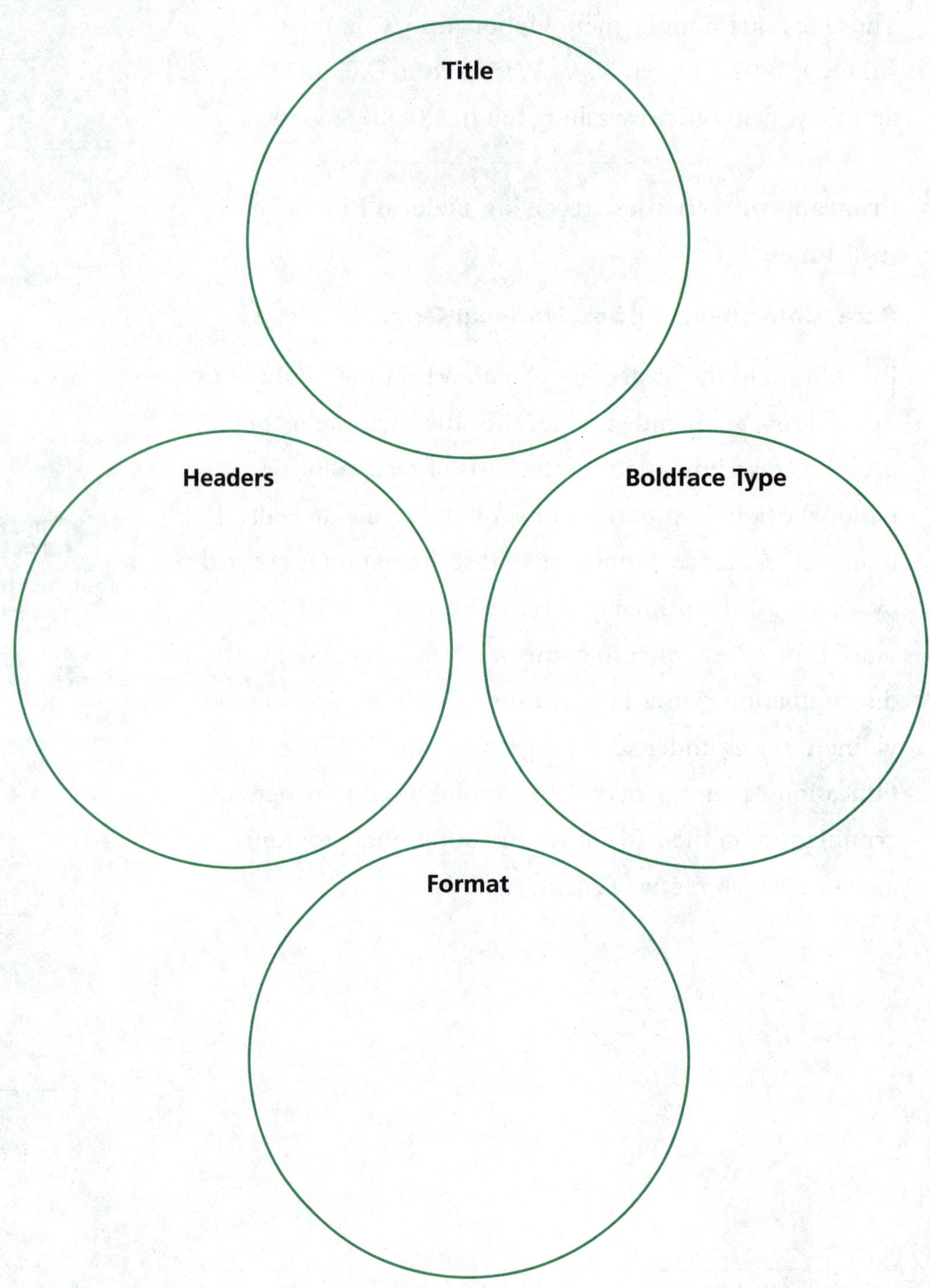

Equal Employment Opportunity Is the Law

READING COMPREHENSION

Answer each question below.

1. What is the title of the poster? What do the numbers indicate?

   ____

   ____

   ____

2. What feature is repeated throughout the poster?

   ____

   ____

   ____

3. According to the poster, what does affirmative action guarantee?

   ____

   ____

   ____

4. What is the key information in Section 2?

   ____

   ____

   ____

5. What should employees do if they feel their employers are retaliating against them?

   ____

   ____

   ____

Documenting Invention
by Alison Oswald

Victor Ochoa's Biographical Sketch

Imagine you invented something and never received the credit you deserved for your invention. The following series of documents will tell you about the Modern INventors Documentation program, a program launched to keep track of scientific advancement. In the selection that follows, you will read directions on how to contribute to this program. The family of Victor Ochoa recently used these directions to ensure that he receives credit for his achievements. You will also find interesting biographical information on Ochoa in the pages to follow.

INFORMATIONAL FOCUS: TECHNICAL DOCUMENT

As you read the documents that follow, look for these graphic features, which will convey important information:

- Drawings and captions that illustrate the text.
- Boldface headers that identify procedures.
- A numbered list that presents directions in a step-by-step sequence.
- A bulleted list that lists items in a point-by-point sequence.

TERMS TO KNOW

Boldface: dark, heavy type.

Bullets: dots, diamonds, squares, or other shapes used to introduce lists in a point-by-point sequence.

Caption: text that labels, explains, or describes an illustration, diagram, or photograph.

Format: the design of the document.

Graphic: any visual device used to illustrate, demonstrate, or highlight the text.

Header: a label or heading that begins a document or a section of it.

Point-by-point sequence: a sequence that states each point in no particular order.

Step-by-step sequence: a sequence that tells what to do first, second, third, and so on.

SKILLS FOCUS

Reading Skills
Understand elements of technical documents.

Documenting Invention

Alison Oswald, Lemelson Center Archivist

BACKGROUND: Informational Text and Social Studies

To ensure that the rich history of invention is preserved for the future, the Lemelson Center and the National Museum of American History (NMAH) Archives Center launched the Modern INventors Documentation (MIND) program in 1997.

A brochure helps provide information for inventors who wish to donate their records. It outlines the donation process, giving advice on finding an appraiser[1] and an appropriate repository and, for those who are not yet ready to donate their collections, on basic preservation techniques. This information recently guided the family of a Mexican American inventor, Victor L. Ochoa, on the donation of his papers.

MIND
Modern Inventors Documentation Program

WHAT YOU CAN DO

The history of invention is in your hands. Whether you are an independent inventor or working in a corporate or academic laboratory, you can help save the records of your life's work. The papers, artifacts, and electronic media that you have generated attest to the creative spirit of American invention. By making sure these materials are preserved, the achievements of individuals like you, who have made significant contributions to American life, will be recognized by many groups.

10

---

1. **appraiser** (ə·prāz′·ər) *n.:* one who estimates the value of things.

> **IDENTIFY**
>
> What information does the **header** in line 4 highlight?

Why are the questions on this page numbered? Why do the items have box-shaped bullets?

THINKING ABOUT YOUR HISTORICAL RESOURCES

To assist inventors and their families in preserving the historical resources of invention, this checklist may be used as preparation for more detailed discussions with an archival repository. We urge you to act now while the materials are still intact.

1. What types of materials do you have?
   - ❏ Artifacts/Objects—models, parts of inventions, prototypes,[2] tools
   - ❏ Company Records
   - ❏ Computer Disks
   - ❏ Correspondence—business, legal, personal
   - ❏ Course Notes
   - ❏ Diaries
   - ❏ Drawings
   - ❏ Financial Records
   - ❏ Grant Applications
   - ❏ Instructional Materials
   - ❏ Laboratory Notebooks
   - ❏ Logbooks
   - ❏ Patents/Patent Applications
   - ❏ Photographs
   - ❏ Publications—catalogs, reports
   - ❏ Sound Recordings
   - ❏ Videotapes/Films
2. Are your materials in good physical condition?
3. Are your materials organized?
4. Do you have an inventory list?
5. What is the approximate time span of the materials?
6. What is the approximate size of your collection?
7. Where and how are the materials stored?

---

2. **prototypes** (prōt′ə·tīps′) *n.:* original models.

50

MODERN INVENTORS DOCUMENTATION PROGRAM

An Inventor's Guide to the Preservation, Protection, and Donation of Personal Papers

Send for information on the following topics:

❑ Understanding the donation process

❑ Artifacts

❑ Preservation of materials

❑ Locating an appropriate repository

❑ Locating an appraiser

❑ Financial and tax implications

❑ Copyright/intellectual property rights

Name _______________________________________

Address ____________________________________

City ____

State/Zip ___________________________________

TEXT FEATURES

What does the information in **boldface** type tell you about the information to follow?

____

____

____

____

____

____

____

TEXT FEATURES

Suppose you have an item related to an invention, but you're not sure how much it is worth. What box would you check off if you wanted to request more information about pricing? Explain.

____

____

____

____

____

____

____

Do you think this biographical sketch should have come before the directions for documenting invention or is the sequence of the documents adequate as it is? Explain.

____

____

____

____

____

____

____

____

____

____

Pause at line 9. What do you learn about Victor Ochoa in the opening lines of the Web page?

____

____

____

____

____

____

____

____

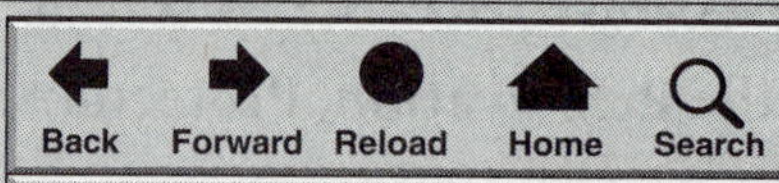

VICTOR OCHOA'S BIOGRAPHICAL SKETCH

Ochoa was born around 1850 in Ojinaga, Mexico, of Spanish and Scotch ancestry. As a boy he came to the United States and lived in Texas and the Southwest. Angry about injustices in Mexico, he published a newspaper and pamphlets in El Paso, urging a free Mexican government. He roused fellow Texas Mexicans by delivering speeches about fair labor practices, such as hiring local workers and paying equal wages.

10   Ochoa was highly opposed to the dictatorship of Mexico's president, Porfirio Díaz, and organized a band of several hundred Mexican rebels to overthrow him. Some historians consider Victor Ochoa to be the originator of the Mexican Revolution.

    In retaliation, the Díaz government offered $50,000 in gold as reward for Ochoa, dead or alive. He avoided bounty hunters but finally gave himself up to the Texas Rangers. He was charged with forming an army in the United States in order to invade

20   another country, was tried, and was sent to the federal prison in Brooklyn, New York. His friend

Theodore Roosevelt° worked to reduce his sentence and, finally, had it suspended. Because of the $50,000 bounty still on his head, it is said that Ochoa spread the rumor that he had died in an asylum.

Ochoa continued to live in the Northeast, manufacturing fountain pens for a living. He invented a number of important products, such as an adjustable wrench, a reversible motor, and the electric brake for streetcars. A windmill he invented cost one fifth that of ordinary windmills and was able to create and store electricity. His best-known invention is the Ochoaplane: a remarkable collapsible airship whose shape was based on the shape of the wings of birds.

Throughout his life Ochoa supported Mexico's struggle for democracy and its revolution, which lasted until 1920. He moved back to Mexico in 1936, and it is believed he died there in 1945.

° **Theodore Roosevelt** (1858–1919): U.S. president from 1901 to 1909; during the time Ochoa was in prison, Roosevelt was a New York City police commissioner, U.S. assistant secretary of the navy, and an officer in the Spanish-American War.

IDENTIFY

Underline Ochoa's inventions mentioned in lines 29–33. How is Ochoa's windmill different from conventional windmills?

IDENTIFY

What information is given in the footnote at the bottom of the page?

TEXT FEATURES

Illustrations often highlight important details from a text. How does this illustration help increase your understanding of the text?

____

____

____

____

____

EVALUATE

Re-read lines 7–16. Is the information in this paragraph likely to be of interest to the people who run the MIND program? Why or why not?

____

____

____

____

____

____

____

____

____

____

____

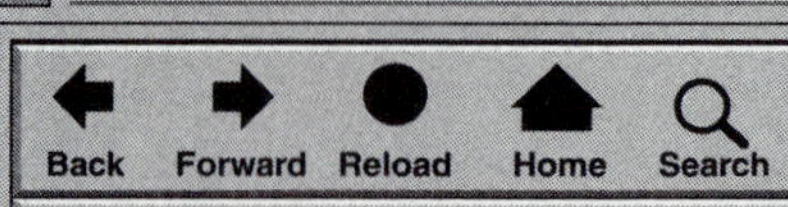

THE OCHOAPLANE

Victor Ochoa worked on this invention for more than twenty years and succeeded in that time in putting together several machines that flew successfully for short distances. The first was an amazingly accurate reproduction of a bird with six wings. With this he believed he had solved the problem of flight.

The Ochoaplane consists of a canvas-covered steel framework that could be folded up. The whole arrangement is mounted on two bicycles whose wheels form the groundwork. Between the bicycle frames, Ochoa placed a seat for the operator, with a six-horsepower motor mounted below it. More than four times as wide as it is long, the plane measures about twenty-six feet wide and six feet from front to back, with a rear rudder similar in shape to a bird's tail. The whole machine weighs about 250 pounds.

10

Documenting Invention; Victor Ochoa's Biographical Sketch

Key Information Chart   Technical documents can cover a wide array of topics, from how to set up your computer to how to vote. When you read informational documents, it's important to isolate the key information in the text. Fill out the chart below with five pieces of key information you found in "Documenting Invention" and "Victor Ochoa's Biographical Sketch." Then, describe where in the document you found that information; for example, was it under a subhead, in a chart, or on a list?

Reading Skills
Analyze elements of technical documents.

Key Information	Where Information Is Located

Documenting Invention;
Victor Ochoa's Biographical Sketch

READING COMPREHENSION

Answer the following questions.

1. What is the purpose of the Modern INventors Documentation Program brochure?

2. What is the purpose of the checklist in the brochure?

3. What is the purpose of the application at the end of the directions?

4. Why did Victor Ochoa publish a newspaper?

5. Describe the way the Ochoaplane was assembled.

Before You Read

from Recycling Guide for Native American Nations; U.S. Recycling Symbols

We've all experienced the frustration that comes from trying to follow procedures that are poorly written. Unclear writing can lead to confusion. The information about recycling in the documents that follow is meant to be easily grasped and understood. Does it seem clear and logical to you?

INFORMATIONAL FOCUS: FUNCTIONAL DOCUMENTS

The following functional documents contain information about recycling, including tips for planning a recycling program and the origin of the recycling symbol.

- To make the information clear and accessible, a variety of text features are used, such as boldface headers, different kinds of type, and bulleted or numbered lists.
- Information is presented in the logical sequence most appropriate for understanding, such as **step-by-step** or **point-by-point sequence.**
- Packaging **symbols** related to recycling are shown and explained.

TERMS TO KNOW

Boldface: dark, heavy type.

Bullets: dots, diamonds, squares, or other shapes used to introduce lists in a point-by-point sequence.

Logical sequence: a sequence that makes sense.

Packaging symbols: standardized symbols used to indicate something about a product or its packaging.

Point-by-point sequence: a sequence that states each point in no particular order.

Step-by-step sequence: a sequence that tells what to do first, second, third, and so on.

**Reading
Skills**
Understand elements of functional documents.

Underline the portion of the title that reveals this document's audience. Then, read on, and decide if the document contains information that could be useful to others.

IDENTIFY

What is the purpose of the "ancient story of recycling" told in lines 1–7?

EVALUATE

Underline the definition of *recycling* in lines 13–15. Is it **logical** to include this information here? Why or why not?

Environmental Protection Agency

from
Recycling Guide for Native American Nations

A Pueblo jar.
© Museum of Fine Arts, Houston, Texas, USA, Gift of Miss Ima Hogg/
The Bridgeman Art Library

This Acoma Pueblo pot tells an ancient story of recycling. Pueblo Indian women crafted clay pots that lasted for years of use. When the pots eventually broke, they were not thrown into a dump. The broken pots were crushed down to a fine clay powder. The powder was then soaked to soften it to a workable clay consistency. This recovered clay was used to make strong and beautiful new pots.

Today, we use many materials once, and then consider them waste. Like broken pots, these materials are actually precious resources. We are all learning that we cannot afford to continue throwing away resources in our garbage cans. Our task now is to develop again the age-old art of recycling.

Recycling is defined as the collecting, manufacturing, and selling/buying of new products made from what once

10

was thought of as waste. The recycling symbol of chasing arrows represents the three components necessary to make a difference through recycling: (1) collection, (2) manufacture, and (3) purchase. Everyone has a vital role to play.

SETTING UP A RECYCLING PROGRAM

20 Before setting up a recycling program, a careful planning process should address these questions:

- What type of program best suits the community?
- What is the quantity and composition of recyclables in the community's waste stream?
- What will the program cost, and how can it be funded?
- Where can the collected recyclables be taken?
- Who will staff the recycling program?
- How can participation be encouraged?
30 - What expertise can other recycling programs share?

EDUCATING THE COMMUNITY

Instilling new habits takes time. The success of a recycling program will depend on early community involvement, followed by continuing educational efforts. Start by determining residents' interest in recycling and their concerns about how the recycling program will work. Be responsive to their input and provide clear information. Make the recycling program 40 a source of community pride and involvement.

One of the best ways to ensure strong participation in the program is to introduce recycling to schools first. When children learn about recycling at school, they serve as recycling ambassadors, sharing what they have learned with their families and others in the community.

Re-read lines 7–9. What led to the contest in which the recycling symbol was created?

____

____

____

____

Are the plastics listed in a **logical sequence**? Why or why not?

____

____

____

____

____

____

What **packaging symbol** should you avoid if possible when buying products in plastic containers? Why?

____

____

____

U.S. Recycling Symbols

Origin of the Recycling Symbol

The symbol represents a Möbius loop[1] consisting of three chasing arrows in the shape of a triangle. The original recycling symbol was designed in 1970 by Gary Anderson, a senior at the University of Southern California at Los Angeles. It was submitted as part of a nationwide contest for high school and college students. The contest was a result of continuing growth of consumer awareness and environmentalism and a response to the first Earth Day.

10

Recycling Symbols for Plastic Packaging

Plastic bottles, containers, and packaging typically have a symbol with a number and usually, but not always, an acronym[2] below it. The triangle indicates the type of plastic resin[3] that the item is made from. The following symbols list the chemical name of the resin and the types of products it is used for:

Polyethylene Terephthalate
Water bottles, peanut butter containers, juice bottles

High Density Polyethylene
Milk containers, trash bags, cereal box liners

20

Polyvinyl Chloride
Window cleaner and detergent bottles, cooking oil bottles

Low Density Polyethylene
Squeezable bottles, bread bags, carpet

Polypropylene
Yogurt containers, straws, medicine bottles

Polystyrene
Styrofoam, cutlery, compact disc jackets

30

Other
All other types of plastic (rarely recycled)

---

1. **Möbius** (mā′bē·əs) **loop**: discovered in 1858 by the German mathematician August Ferdinand Möbius (1790–1868); one-sided strip made from a rectangle by holding one end fixed and twisting the other end 180 degrees, then connecting it to the fixed end.
2. **acronym** *n.:* word that is made from the first letter of each of a group of words.
3. **resin** *n.:* chemical substance used to make plastics.

from Recycling Guide for Native American Nations; U.S. Recycling Symbols

Sequence Chart   Functional documents should contain information in a logical sequence. When information is presented in the most appropriate order, it is easiest to understand and use. The chart below contains pieces of information from the beginning and the end of the documents you read. Place information in the empty boxes in a logical order to get from the first point to the last point.

SKILLS FOCUS

Reading skills
Understand elements of functional documents.

	from Recycling Guide for Native American Nations	U.S. Recycling Symbols
1.	In ancient times the Acoma Pueblo people made new pots from the pieces of broken ones.	The recycling symbol is made up of three arrows that together form a triangle.
2.		
3.		
4.		
5.	Community education is crucial to the success of your recycling program.	Recycling symbols represent the name of the resin and the types of products it is used for.

Skills Review

from Recycling Guide for Native American Nations; U.S. Recycling Symbols

READING COMPREHENSION

Answer each question below.

1. What did Pueblo Indian women do with broken clay pots?

2. What does the recycling symbol (chasing arrows) represent?

3. According to the document, where should a new recycling program be introduced first? Why?

4. What examples of polyethylene terephthalate containers does the document give?

5. Describe the recycling symbol for polypropylene plastic containers.

Works Cited List: Recycling

Recycling is an important topic. To find out more about recycling, including the recycling habits of Native Americans, you might want to do some research on the Internet. If you prepare a report on your research, you'll need to include a bibliography or Works Cited list.

INFORMATIONAL FOCUS: DOCUMENTATION

- The following *Works Cited* list is a listing of Internet resources on the topic of recycling.
- The citations are listed in alphabetical order by author and title, following the style of the Modern Language Association.
- The electronic address (URL) is listed with each citation.
- The date the Web site was accessed comes right before the URL.

TERMS TO KNOW

Bibliography: a list of sources of information on a subject, also called *Works Cited.*

Citation: an entry on a list of sources on a subject.

Source: a book, document, or person that provides information.

URL: uniform resource locator, a site's Internet address.

Reading Skills
Understand how to cite sources in a *Works Cited* list.

Order in Which Information Is Presented in an Internet Citation

1. Author's Last Name [,] Author's First Name and Middle Initial (if given) [,] abbreviation such as *Ed.* (if appropriate) [.]

2. ["] Title of Work Found in Online Scholarly Project, on Database, or in Periodical ["] or ["] Title of Posting to Discussion List or Forum (taken from the subject line) [.] ["] Followed by the description Online posting [.]

3. <u>Title of Book</u> (underlined) [.]

4. The abbreviation *Ed.* followed by Name of editor (if relevant and not cited earlier, as in *Ed. Susan Smith*) [.]

5. Publication information for any print version of the source: City of Publication [:] Name of Publisher [,] year of publication [.]

6. <u>Title of Scholarly Project, Database, Magazine, Professional Site, or Personal Site</u> (underlined) [.]

7. Name of Editor of Scholarly Project or Database (if available) [.]

8. Volume number, issue number, or other identifying number of the source (if available) [.]

9. Date of electronic publication, posting, or latest update (often found at the bottom of the site's home page) [.]

10. Name of Subscription Service [,] and, if a library, Name of Library [,] Name of City [,] and Abbreviation of State in which library is located [.]

11. For a posting to a discussion list or forum, Name of List or Forum[.]

12. If sections are numbered, number range or total number of pages, paragraphs, or other sections (if information is available) [.]

13. Name of Institution or Organization sponsoring or associated with the Web site [.]

14. Date on which source was accessed [.]

15. [<] Electronic address (URL) of source [>] or, if a subscription service, [<] URL of service's main page (if known) [>] and [Keyword: Keyword Assigned by Service] or [Path: sequence of topics followed to reach page cited, as in the First Topic [;] Second Topic [;] Third Topic [;] and so on, ending with the page you are citing] [.]

WORKS CITED

American Forest and Paper Association. A Guide to Recycling at Work. Recycling: It Starts with You. Washington: Amer. Forest and Paper Assoc. 23 Feb. 2006 <http://www.paperrecycles.org/news/print_materials/work_guide.pdf>.

Hecker, Gavin. "Curbside Recycling: A Step Toward Sustainability." Green Design Etc.: A Starting Point for Ideas about Green and Sustainable Design. Nov. 2005. 12 Mar. 2006 <http://www.greendesignetc.net/Flows_05_(pdf)/Gavin_Hecker_Curbside_Recycling(paper).pdf>.

National Recycling Coalition. "Native American Tribes Connect Composting with Cultural Values and Traditions." Congress Daily. 30 Aug. 2005: 1. 6 Mar. 2006 <http://www.nrc-recycle.org/congress/mn05/MNTuesdayDaily.pdf>.

Rural Community Assistance Partnership. Who We Are. 14 Feb. 2006 <http://www.rcap.org/who_we_are/about_rcap.html>.

United States. Environmental Protection Agency. "Learning to Protect Mother Earth." EPA Native American Network: A RCRA Information Exchange 3 (Summer/Fall 1991): 5-6. 19 Mar. 2006 <http://www.p2pays.org/ref/12/11667.pdf>.

—. —. Recycling Guide for Native American Nations. Washington: EPA, 1995. 16 Feb. 2006 <http://www.epa.gov/tribalmsw/pdftxt/ntverecy.pdf>.

Skills Review

Works Cited List: Recycling

READING COMPREHENSION

Answer the questions below.

1. In what order are citations listed in a *Works Cited* List?

2. Where does the date an article was accessed go in a citation?

3. What kind of document is "Native American Tribes Connect Composting with Cultural Values and Traditions"? Explain.

4. In the final entry, why is "Recycling Guide for Native Americans" underlined?

SKILLS FOCUS

Reading Skills
Analyze the structure and format of a *Works Cited* list.

All-American Girl 103
Alvarez, Julia 103, *104*

Bambara, Toni Cade 34, *43*
Barbara Johns: Carrying on the Speaking . . 274
Be an Everyday Freedom Hero! 326
Bruchac, Joseph 211, *212*

Cebulska, Marcia 282, *287*
Childress, Alice 184, *186*
Cisneros, Sandra 128, *135*
Codes of Conduct 191
Cofer, Judith Ortiz 48, *59,* 215
Colón, Jesús 108, *113*

De Lange, Flo Ota 274
Dixon, Dianne E. 66, *78*
Documenting Invention 341
Dream Deferred 172

Ellis Island 211
Equal Employment Opportunity
    Is the Law 335
Erdoes, Richard 249, *257*

Free Minds and Hearts at Work 316

Goss, Clay 158, *161*

Habit of Movement, The 215
Homecoming 302
Hughes, Langston *173*
Hunger of Memory, *from* 94
Hurdles 139

Interview with Mae 294
Ishi Apparently Wasn't the
    Last Yahi 306

Jackie Changed the Face of Sports 319
Jemison, Mae 294
"jump mama" 176

Kass, Pnina 83, *87*
Keeter, Nicole 120, *123*
Kell, Gretchen 306
Kipling and I 108
Kim, Derek Kirk 139, *141*
Komunyakaa, Yusef 167, *169*

Lamkin, Kurtis 176, *178*
Lesson, The 66
Lewis, John 148, *153*

March 158
Marshall, Joseph M., III 234, *244*
Memory Stone, The 220
Mihesuah, Devon A. 6, *11*
Minatoya, Lydia 199, *205*
Mr. Shaabi 83
Music Lady 16
My Delicate Heart Condition 34
My Horse 6

New Girl, The 120
Now Let Me Fly, *from* 282

One Who Watches, The 48
Orpheus and Eurydice 262
Ortiz, Alfonso 249, *257*
Oswald, Alison 341

Pocketbook Game, The 184

Recycling Guide for Native
    American Nations, *from* 350
Repatriation of Ishi, the Last
    Yahi Indian, The 310
Robinson, Jackie 316
Rodriguez, Richard 94, *99,* 302
Russell, William F. 262, *267*

Schwartz, Larry 319
Sears, Vickie 16, *21*
Slam, Dunk, & Hook 167
Spirit Wife, The 249
Story of the Eagle, The 234
Su, Adrienne 191, *194*

Three Wise Guys 128
Trees 25
Tseng, Jennifer 25, *28*

Victor Ochoa's Biographical Sketch 344

Walking with the Wind, Prologue *from* . . . 148
Works Cited List: Recycling 357

Yee, Paul 220, *227*

Vocabulary Development

Pronunciation guides, in parentheses, are provided for the vocabulary words in this book. The following key will help you use those pronunciation guides.

As a practice in using a pronunciation guide, sound out the words used as examples in the list that follows. See if you can hear the way the same vowel might be sounded in different words. For example, say "at" and "ate" aloud. Can you hear the difference in the way "a" sounds?

The symbol ə is called a **schwa**. A schwa is used by many dictionaries to indicate a sort of weak sound like the "a" in *ago*. Some people say that the schwa sounds like "eh." A vowel sounded like a schwa is never accented.

The vocabulary words in this book are also provided with a part-of-speech label. The parts of speech are *n.* (noun), *v.* (verb), *pro.* (pronoun), *adj.* (adjective), *adv.* (adverb), *prep.* (preposition), *conj.* (conjunction), and *interj.* (interjection).

To learn more about the vocabulary words, consult your dictionary. You will find that many of the words defined here have several other meanings.

---

at, āte, cär; ten, ēve; is, īce; gō, hôrn, look, to͞ol; oil, out; up, fʉr, ə *for unstressed vowels, as* a *in* ago, u *in* focus; ' *as in* Latin (lat'ʼn); chin; she; zh *as in* azure (azh'ər); thin, *the*; ŋ *as in* ring (riŋ)
